D0517356

ON FLIRTATION

ON FLIRTATION

ADAM PHILLIPS

HARVARD UNIVERSITY PRESS
Cambridge, Massachusetts

LIBRARY OF CONGRESS CATALOGING-IN-PUBLICATION DATA

Phillips, Adam.
On flirtation / Adam Phillips.
p.   cm.
Includes bibliographical references and index.
ISBN 0-674-63437-3
1. Psychoanalysis.   2. Psychoanalysis and literature.   I. Title.
BF173.P57   1994
150.19′5—dc.20   94-18821
CIP

For Kate and Geoffrey Weaver

*No truth is so sublime but it may be trivial tomorrow
in the light of new thoughts.*
Emerson, 'Circles'

*Experiment escorts us last –
His pungent company
Will not allow an Axiom
An Opportunity*
Emily Dickinson

Nothing will fit if we assume a place for it.
Robert Creeley, *The New Writing in the USA*

Who can say we are wrong to fail the circuit of guesses –
Alvin Feinman, 'Relic (2)'

Contents

CONTENTS

Preface

It can be easy for the psychoanalyst and his or her 'patient' – not to mention the readers of psychoanalysis – to forget that they are there for pleasure (even if pleasure is sometimes a complicated and various thing). So R. D. Laing's comment, appreciatively quoted by Nina Coltart in her book reviewed here (see chapter 13), can stand as a coda to this book, and to the kind of psychoanalysis that I have confidence in:

Let us try to celebrate and enjoy ourselves – I am really only interested in trying to entice people with all the skills at my disposal to live in that sort of way if they possibly can.

Despite the work of Winnicott, Lacan and Bion, amusement is always secondary to instruction in psychoanalytic writing, but there is no good reason for this. Freud showed us – if we needed showing – that it is not more truthful to be serious. Psychoanalysis with a light touch, so to speak, need not be a contradiction in terms.

For me, psychoanalysis has always been of a piece with the various languages of literature – a kind of practical poetry – taking its life, as theory and practice, from a larger world of words. Indeed, one of the pleasures of child psychotherapy is that it is, as it were, psychoanalysis for a non-psychoanalytic audience. Psychoanalysis, as some of the essays here suggest, has been stifled by keeping itself to itself, by being over-committed to its own language and audience. And by the same token psychoanalytic writing has become a way of making or joining clubs. This book is about the virtues – in psychoanalysis, and not only there – of being uncommitted, that Freud referred to with his notion of free-floating attention. With his description of the unconscious – and particularly of the dream-work – Freud radically revised our sense of ourselves as creatures of conviction (you can no more believe in the unconscious than you can quote from it). Free association itself is the psychic act of relinquishing, as far as is possible, one's slavish devotion to internal censors. It is one of the advantages of flirtation that it can protect us from idolatry – and its opposite – while acknowledging the draw of such grand absolutes. Flirting, in other words, is an often unconscious form of scepticism. States of conviction conceal the sense in which we are continually making our minds up.

In any shift of allegiances, in any transition, there may have to be some flirtation. But flirtation in itself, as a relationship to people and ideas, has always had a bad press. Psychoanalysis, however, has been able to give us good descriptions of what we are doing when we regard something as trivial; the ironic sense in which we dispense with things according to their value. Michael Wood wrote recently of Genet, in the *London Review of Books*, that 'unlike many other literary players in the world of politics, Genet remembered the irremediable; or better, it dogged him and he flirted with it, and so got to know it better than those who marry it or forget it or bury it in easier dreams of liberation'. This expresses eloquently the kinds of relationship – the uses of flirtation – explored in this book. Each of the writers discussed in section 3 are provoked by these questions of commitment. Flirtation keeps things in play, and by doing so lets us get to know them in different ways. It allows us the fascination of what is unconvincing. By making a game of uncertainty, of the need to be convinced, it always plays with, or rather flirts with, the idea of surprise. In the terms of this book flirtation is among other things a way of acknowledging the contingency of our lives – their sheer unpredictability, how accident-prone we are – without at the same time turning this unpredictability itself into a new kind of masterplot. Flirtation confirms the connection between excitement and uncertainty, and how we make uncertainty possible by making it exciting. Philosophers often make us doubt that scepticism is erotic.

Apart from chapter 5, 'Besides Good and Evil', all of these lectures and essays were written originally for non-psychoanalytic audiences; and I have kept them to their occasions, which can be found in the Acknowledgements. This may only be obtrusive, if at all, in the lecture 'On Success', which was written for an audience of student counsellors. All writing, like all flirting, is occasional (though some writing may depend upon concealing its occasions). The few repetitions in the book, of quotations and phrases, indicate preoccupations and so have been left as such.

I have been fortunate in having the following people as the immediate audience for the pieces that I have written: Lisa Appignanesi, Jane Brodie, Alex Coren, John Forrester, Glenda Fredman, Paul Van Heeswyk, Mary Mackintosh, Morian Roberts, Fiona Shaw, Sarah Spankie, Geoffrey Weaver, Kate Weaver, and Peter Wilson. The enthusiasm and interest of Frank Kermode, Dick Poirier, Suzanne Hyman, Michel Gribinski, and J.-B. Pontalis have sustained my writing of psychoanalysis; and Ed Corrigan, who has a way of making things possible, has sustained my talking about it in America. The conversation, and writing, of Christopher Bollas, Michael Eigen and Harold Boris have kept my mind changing on the subject. Andrew Motion, by seeing there might be a book on this subject, made it possible; Julian Loose, my editor at Faber, has been consistently full of improving suggestions.

I am also grateful to my colleague Peter Reder, who has always promoted and sustained as far as possible in our department at Wolverton Gardens a professional ethos committed to writing and research; that is a rare thing now, and it makes a good deal of difference.

Hugh Haughton and Jacqueline Rose brought out the best in this book; I have gained a lot from the quality of their attention.

Acknowledgements

In Part I, 'The Uses of the Past', chapter 3 was published in 'A Symposium on Love' in *The Threepenny Review*, (San Francisco, Summer 1993); chapter 6 was given as a lecture at the University of London Institute of Romance Studies Conference on 'The Autobiographical Impulse'; chapter 1 was published first in *Raritan* (Fall 1993), *Nouvelle Revue de Psychanalyse* (Spring 1994) and *Winnicott Studies* (1993). Chapter 2 was given as a lecture in the King's College, Cambridge, interdisciplinary seminar on 'Memory' (1993); chapter 4, as a lecture to the Oxford University Student Counselling Conference (1993); chapter 5 was published in *Winnicott Studies* (1990). In Part II, 'Psychoanalysis Reviewed', chapters 7, 8, 9, 10, 11, 13, 14 and 15 were published in the *London Review of Books* (1987–93); chapter 10 also in *Nouvelle Revue de Psychanalyse* (Spring 1994); chapter 12 was published in *The New Republic*. In Part III, 'Writing Outside', chapters 16 and 18 were published in the *London Review of Books* (1990); chapter 17 was given as a lecture to YAKAR, in London (1991); chapter 19 was published in *John Clare in Context*, ed. Hugh Haughton, Adam Phillips and Geoffrey Summerfield (Cambridge, Cambridge University Press, 1994). Some of the essays have been slightly revised. I am very grateful to the editors of the above journals – Wendy Lesser, Michel Gribinski, J.-B. Pontalis, Suzanne Hyman, Dick Poirier, Mary-Kay Wilmers – and to those people who have invited me to speak.

On Flirtation: An Introduction

*. . . hurrying in pursuit of their schedules, loitering
in flirty talk . . .*

Christopher Isherwood, *A Single Man*

I

The fact that people tend to flirt only with serious things – madness, disaster, other people – and the fact that flirting is a pleasure, makes it a relationship, a way of doing things, worth considering. But our preference for progress narratives can make flirtation acceptable only as a means to a predictable end; flirting is fine, but to be a flirt is not (it is one of the many curious and telling things about flirtation that, despite the impossibility of flirting by yourself, flirts are traditionally considered to be women). Flirts are dangerous because they have a different way of believing in the Real Thing. And by 'believing in' I mean 'behaving as if' it exists. Critics of flirtation tend to assume that there is a self which is not, by definition, elusive.

Exploiting the ambiguity of promises – the difference, say, between someone being promising and someone making a promise – flirtation has always been the saboteur of a cherished vocabulary of commitment. In so far as we value reliability and the relatively predictable, it is inevitable that flirtation – the (consciously or unconsciously) calculated production of uncertainty – will be experienced at best as superficial and at worst as cruel. Flirtation as sado-masochism with a light touch is a modest exposé of excitement as inextricable from tantalization; of desire as desire for a certain kind of torture, an enlivening torture, so to speak (in the original myth, Tantalus is named after his punishment; like Sisyphus, the other anti-hero of flirtation, he is taught the rigours of incompletion). The generosity of flirtation is in its implicit wish to sustain the life of

xvii

desire; and often by blurring, or putting into question, the boundary between sex and sexualization. Flirting creates the uncertainty it is also trying to control; and so can make us wonder which ways of knowing, or being known, sustain our interest, our excitement, in other people. What can be dismaying about flirtation – or exhilarating, depending on one's point of view – is what it might then reveal about the nature of people's interest in each other; an area that psychoanalysis has often been too quick to pathologize (or standardize). Wherever psychoanalysts pathologize, they are describing a counter–culture, even if it is one of suffering and cruelty.

The fact that children make and need attachment objects has been used in much psychoanalytic theory as a guide, or blueprint, for adult sexual relations. But this model brings with it the idea that the value or quality of a relationship is measured by its duration and fidelity. 'Good' relationships become those in which people can tolerate a lot of frustration, as children, indeed, have to do (people who are good at waiting may just have nothing better to do). In psychoanalytic stories it is as though the adult is always succumbing to the child within. But it is one of the advantages of growing up that one can extend the repertoire of possible relationships: one's initiative has more scope, because adults are also very different from children. There is only one mother and father in the world, but there are a lot of men and women. It was this that Oedipus was unable, or unwilling, to believe (psychoanalysis is about why we resist this radical shift of perspective). He couldn't find or, rather, desire anyone other than his parents. Oedipus, in other words, interpreted his own myth too literally. In some contexts, of course, such literal interpretations are called Destinies or a commitment to Truth.

To be committed to something – a person, an ideology, a vocabulary, a way of going about things – one has first to be committed, perhaps unconsciously, to commitment itself. The question need not be: should we dispense with our capacity for commitment? But, what does commitment leave out of the picture that we might want? If our descriptions of sexuality are tyrannized by various stories of committed purpose – sex as reproduction, sex as heterosexual intercourse, sex as intimacy – flirtation puts in disarray our sense of an ending. In flirtation you never know whether the beginning of the story – the story of the relationship – will be the end; flirtation, that is to say, exploits the idea of surprise. From a sadistic point of view it is as though the known and wished-for end is being refused, deferred or even denied. But from a pragmatic point of view one could say that a space is being created in which aims or ends can be worked out; the assumed wish for the more or less obvious sexual combinations, or commitments, may be a way of pre-empting the elaboration of, making time for, less familiar possibilities. Flirtation, if it can be sustained, is a way of cultivating wishes, of playing for time. Deferral can make room.

II

In 1915, soon after the outbreak of the First World War, Freud wrote two essays entitled 'Thoughts for the Times on War and Death' in which he tried to understand the 'mental distress' caused by the catastrophe. The sense of disillusionment brought about by the war – 'no event has ever destroyed so much that is precious in the common possessions of humanity' – is, he intimates, like a second Fall. 'I attribute our present sense of estrangement in this once lovely and congenial world,' he begins the second essay, which was presented to the Jewish B'nai B'rith club in Vienna, 'to the disturbance that has taken place in the attitude we have hitherto adopted toward death.' It is unusually pastoral of Freud to describe the world as lovely and congenial. Paradise is not a psychoanalytic concept; and there was certainly very little in psychoanalytic theory suggestive of such delights (within two years of the war, in *Beyond the Pleasure Principle*, Freud was to introduce the daunting idea of a death *instinct*). His version of paradise lost here involved him in a parodic version of the Fortunate Fall. In Milton, Adam and Eve garden before the Fall; in Freud, as we shall see, they flirt. Surprisingly, it is thoughts of war and death that bring flirtation to his mind.

Before the war, in Freud's view, there had been a disturbing contradiction in people's attitude towards death. On the one hand everyone acknowledged that death was 'natural, undeniable and unavoidable'; and yet, as he says, we 'behave as if it was otherwise', putting death 'on one side' (in one sense, where it has always been) and living as though it is nothing to do with us, so to speak. Since, after all, it is death that expels us it is as though, by a piece of mimic (or mock-) mastery, *we* have expelled *it*. In this fool's paradise or, as Freud puts it, 'in the unconscious every one of us is convinced of his own immortality'. Every man, Borges wrote, runs the risk of being the first immortal; every man, in Freud's view, runs the risk of being the first mortal. We are all the same age – very young – in our relationship with death.

'The civilised adult,' Freud writes, unlike most children 'can hardly even entertain the thought of another person's death without seeming to himself hard-hearted and wicked.' Death is the catastrophic knowledge, the truly forbidden thing, that everyone has to be protected from because no one can be. And yet, as Freud shows, this protection racket – like all protection rackets, and particularly the ones arranged with oneself – leaves us radically unprotected. 'The complement to this cultural and conventional attitude toward death is provided by our complete collapse when death has struck down someone whom we love . . . our hopes, our desires and our pleasures lie in the grave with him, we will not be consoled, we will not fill the lost one's place.' There is heartfelt insistence in this. Death confronts us with the fact that, despite the capacity for substitution that development, in psychoanalytic terms, depends upon, there are no substitutes (or, as Freud intimates, we may need to refuse the possibility that there are). His 'once lovely and congenial world' must, then, have been a world without death. But it is the paradox of nostalgia that it always tries to recapture a world without loss.

A world without loss, however, is a world without morality. Life is only of value, Freud asserts in this essay, because, or when, we can risk it. It is worth having – and Freud here inserts the notion of choice – because we can live in a way that endangers it. In war, for example, or love:

Life is impoverished, it loses in interest, when the highest stake in the game of living, life itself, may not be risked. It becomes as shallow and empty as, let us say, an American flirtation, in which it is understood from the first that nothing is to happen, as contrasted with a continental love-affair in which both partners must constantly bear its serious consequences in mind.

Freud's attitude to America was consistently, and insistently, disparaging ('I don't hate America,' he wrote famously, 'I regret it!') – second only, perhaps, to his prejudice against religions. America seems to have represented for him both passionless conformism ('sexual morality as defined by society, in the most extreme form that of America, strikes me as very contemptible. I stand for an infinitely freer sexual life') and impoverished materialistic ideals (in America, he wrote to Ernest Jones, 'success means money. Can an American live in opposition to the public opinion, as we are prepared to do?'). Repeating a conventional opposition between the Depth of Europe (more history and high culture) and the Superficiality of America ('they have no private resources apart from their profession,' Freud wrote revealingly to Jones, 'no hobby, games, love or other interests of a cultured person'), he turns to the New World for an example of the shallow and empty life; and – strangely in this context – to flirtation, in contrast to the real thing, a continental love affair (interestingly, in *Daisy Miller* (1879) Henry James had used the idea of flirtation to dramatize and ironize, a similar preoccupation; flirtation confusing the relationship between innocence and experience, between the Old World and the New World). In an American flirtation – Freud uses the term collusively as though 'we' all know exactly what he means – like Adam and Eve before the Fall, nothing is to happen. No real choices are being made. As the German sociologist Georg Simmel wrote in his remarkable contemporary essay 'Flirtation', 'Every conclusive decision brings flirtation to an end.' Perhaps for people who can't make choices, death is the exemplary decision. In flirtation one does not take risks, one only sustains their possibility.

For Freud this 'empty' American alternative is an act of trivialization; it represents a failure of commitment or seriousness in the stakes of life. But it is always of interest in psychoanalytic theory (and practice) where the psychoanalysing stops; the points in the story where it is assumed – or rather, wished – that no further interpretation needs to take place, or where it seems irrelevant to bother; the points, that is, where the 'god-terms' – like 'Oedipal' or 'desire', or 'dependence', for example – creep back in. What Freud does not analyse here but asserts – and it is usually in these moments in his writing that we imagine we get to know him – is the essential value of risk, and of the continental love affair with its serious consequences (flirtation, of course, stops when you take it seriously). But every statement of preference is implicated in a wider context of values. The comparison Freud uses to illustrate what he thinks of as 'the highest stake in the game of living' brings a world with it (call it: that world organized around the heroism of passion). Freud assumes that flirtation tells us nothing about the nature of passion; what he is actually telling us is what his story of passion needs to exclude. Psychoanalysis has always shown us the ironic sense in which definitions are sustained by their exclusions.

Flirtation, as the 'easy' or much maligned double of things done properly, might simply describe a different kind of relation, another way of going about things. Assuming a hierarchy, as Freud does here, can be a way of pre-empting interest in the diminished thing. In our erotic life – and not only there, of course – hierarchies and putative oppositions can be used to constrain the possibilities of difference, compelling us to make moral and erotic choices before we have been able to find out what there is to choose from (and whether the repertoire itself is sufficient). Flirting may not be a poor way of doing something better, but a different way of doing something else.

The contrast in Freud's example works because flirtation, as a relationship – a form of exchange between people – is only available in its malign or trivial aspects. But it may be important that aspects of a thing – a person, an idea, a relationship – are not used to blank each other out. Apparent opposites can be ingredients of each other; flirtations and continental love affairs may be more compatible than Freud wants us, or himself, to think. In fact psychoanalysis can be a good way of finding out how complicated we can allow ourselves to be (in this sense, psychoanalysis is only in its beginnings). For

Freud, who did so much to incite our moral curiosity – and to do interesting justice to the complexity of our erotic lives – flirtation was the relationship for those who were too fearful of death, those who must agree to make nothing happen. But like the continental lovers, of course, they cannot agree not to die. Defiance can be a form of acknowledgement. Freud's very misgivings suggest a different reading; flirtation keeps the consequences going. By keeping the future open, it acknowledges something about the future.

III

When Philip Larkin writes of Sylvia Plath's *Collected Poems* – one of his three 1981 Books of the Year in the *Observer* – that it 'enabled the reader to chart her long flirtation with instability in language', he makes us wonder, as flirtation does, where the instability is (and how she kept it up). And, of course, what kind of praise, what kind of recommendation, this is. What would it have been for her not to flirt with 'instability in language'? What else might she have done with it?

The word in a text, like the performance itself, creates an atmosphere of uncertainty. Disfiguring the difference between innocence and experience, intent and opportunity, flirtation does not make a virtue of instability, but a pleasure. It eroticizes the contingency of our lives by turning doubt – or ambiguity – into suspense. It prevents waiting from becoming a useless passion. So it's not surprising that flirtation – the art of making ambivalence into a game, the ironic art of making it a pleasure (or at least an excitement) – begins in childhood. Flirting is, in a sense, *all* children can do sexually with their parents, assuming the parents maintain the Oedipal prohibition. And by doing this they nurture the child's sense of possible and future selves. But the child's uncertainty, in fantasy, about what might happen must be met by the parents' definition of what will happen. The child finds limits by provoking them. Most of the rules of childhood are made by being broken; the incest taboo – at least in theory – is made by being broken *only in fantasy*. Teasing is the child's cure for scepticism: a way of discovering the incest taboo by trying to sabotage it. (Ideally, in this sense, an adult is always a child who has failed.) Flirtation is the game of taking chances, of plotting illicit possibilities.

The flirtation of childhood – the often delightful attempts by children to seduce and rival the parents of both sexes – produces in the child, providing it can be enjoyed but ultimately withstood, a mixture of pleasure, frustration and relief. If, as Freud said, one of the child's strongest wishes is to be big like the grown-ups, he or she will find, as they get bigger, that this is the mixture they cannot shake off; the mixture on which their development depends, as much as it depends upon their trying to find ways round it. In the Oedipal flirtations of childhood, that are a blueprint for the future, one person, the adult, is certain that nothing will happen, and one person, the child, urgently wants something to happen but can't be sure what it is (and is not yet equipped to deal with it). The two adolescents or adults, who will be able to flirt with each other on equal terms, will both be bringing this bemusing childhood experience to the encounter. From the child's point of view – and it is a scene which will haunt him or her through life – one person knows and is certain, and one person wants but doesn't know what to do (is working out what to do). This inevitably unstable relationship then becomes internalized as one of the primary relationships one has with oneself. Adults flirt with their own (spurious) authority. Doubts flirt with convictions. Scepticism is always a provocation, though the person being provoked may be difficult to imagine (to remember or reconstruct).

Flirtation is an early version of the experimental life, of irreverence as curiosity. And yet it reveals an essential perplexity at the heart of the Oedipal dilemma: does flirtation merely enforce the rules it claims to disavow? Is it an area of (erotic) freedom that simply confirms the trap, a competence for the disempowered? Something, in that curious phrase, 'to grow out of'? Is flirtation, in other words, just a refusal to acknowledge that the repertoire of possible relationships is foreclosed, that three (or more) into two won't go? 'If only,' Bob Perelman wrote in his poem 'Anti-Oedipus', 'the plot would leave people alone.'

Flirtation, though, is more than a trivial nostalgia for a world before the war. Like all transitional performances it is an attempt to re-open, to rework, the plot; to find somewhere else, in the philosopher William James's words, 'to go from'. Oedipus, after all, had never had the opportunity to see *Oedipus Rex*; and Freud himself found a new place in our lives for the story, as, again, did Melanie Klein. (So we might wonder what the impact is on our lives – and on the myth itself – of our 'knowing' about the Oedipus complex, how we act accordingly.) From a psychoanalytic point of view the Oedipus myth is a story about the origins of virtue. But it is one of the virtues of the Oedipal plot that it makes us want to out-plot it (the ways we try and get round our Oedipus complex *is* our Oedipus complex). And it is one of the virtues of flirtation that it avoids making a necessity of virtue. By unsettling preferences and priorities flirtation can add other stories to the repertoire by making room for them. But flirtation is notoriously difficult to sustain: at least, between two people (though one can, of course, endlessly flirt with oneself).

'Only in the realm of fiction,' Freud writes in 'Thoughts for the Times on War and Death', perhaps with some relief, '[do] we find the plurality of lives which we need.' It is worth considering the plurality of lives we want, and our assumptions – our unconscious beliefs – about the only places they can be found.

When the American poet James Merrill said of his extraordinary poem 'The Thousand and Second Night', 'I don't know what the main subject is – the poem is flirtatious in that sense', he also said something unambiguous about flirtation. There is always another story, one we haven't necessarily bargained for.

I
THE USES OF THE PAST

1

Contingency for Beginners

I

If one considers chance to be unworthy of determining our fate,
it is simply a relapse into the pious view of the Universe which
Leonardo himself was on the way to overcoming when he wrote
that the sun does not move.

Freud, *Leonardo da Vinci, and a Memory of His Childhood*

A fifty-five-year-old woman, whose coming to see me was prompted by the death of her mother, began, after about a year of treatment, to pick up a theme that she described as 'something she had never been able to unpuzzle'. I wasn't sure whether 'unpuzzle' meant talking the puzzle out of something – stopping it from being an enigma – or just taking the puzzle apart like a jigsaw so one could redo it. When I asked her about this we realized that there was an instructive uncertainty in her as to whether she was inviting me to help her keep the puzzle, albeit in different terms, or help her get rid of it. And this related to one of her dilemmas about mourning her mother; do you keep someone by getting rid of them, or do you get rid of them by keeping them?

The puzzle that she was constantly preoccupied by – and which was clearly linked to the death of her mother – was that whenever she had fallen in love with a man, or even made an enthusiastic friendship, she was haunted, indeed obsessed, by the other person, but he (and occasionally she), though usually keen on her, did not seem quite so distracted. She described herself as someone who 'always took her chances', and she was clearly someone people were much attracted to. But in these relationships it was as though the continuity of her life was ruptured, whereas the continuity of the other person's life was simply enriched. She described this predicament often as 'just her luck', and I was struck by the paradox of her

3

having so often personalized her luck (one can often reconstruct very interesting bits of people's histories from their accounts of their luck); but of course her 'puzzle' seemed a dismayingly common, indeed banal, one. She had discussed this inequity in her relationships – which had begun, she knew, with her mother – with various friends and lovers over the years, and there had always seemed to be a kind of consensus that this was one of the differences between the sexes, and therefore one had to learn to manage this piece of alleged reality as a piece of biological bad luck. However, she had never been fully convinced by all this 'truth' and its relevance to her particular life, and so she had evolved a double-life attitude to it all: one part of her acknowledged the dispiriting sense of the conventional view, which at least simulated a solidarity with fellow-sufferers, but another part of her was keeping her ears open for a better story. The death of her mother had given renewed urgency to the question of her relationship to her own luck.

Since the asymmetry of the psychoanalytic situation – and of the mourning process – is one of its defining characteristics, we could obviously discuss her puzzle in terms of the transference, and this could be linked to the bewildering dissymmetries of the child's relationship with the parents, and the survivor's relations with the dead. But because this puzzle was such a crucial issue for her – it had become, as she put it, 'like a favourite walk' – she was very skilled at tolerating all the false leads and bits of folklore people could come up with when they talked about it with her. I suggested to her that she would recognize – register in some way through a stirring of curiosity – what was of interest to her, and she should let herself be ruthless with my contributions if they seemed irrelevant. Her evident relief at this showed me how much Wisdom she had had to endure in the past.

I should add by way of a parenthesis here that I think of these very idiosyncratic recurring personal preoccupations like this woman's puzzle – that often seem banal – as being (or being like) interpretations of a dream that a person has forgotten. So these insistent and consciously formulated issues put the patient and the analyst in the paradoxical position of having to reconstruct a dream from an interpretation. Or to put it another way, for people with these organized life-questions the aim of the analysis is not insight so much as reconstruction of the material out of which interpretation by the patient can be remade. It may be worth wondering why the idea of reconstructing dreams is so much more unthinkable than the idea of reconstructing personal histories. Even though we make our dreams, we think of them as beyond our own devices. We cannot – and this is integral to my subject – arrange to have dreams, or to have a dream again. (Nor, of course, can we arrange to have our histories again; we can only arrange to reconstruct them.) Analysis may be more of a search for dreams than of a search for insight. The fact that we may be able to interpret dreams does not make them any less contingent than the day residues they use (dreams are accidents of desire).

As we worked on this puzzle over several months, my patient stopped remembering her dreams (previously it had been 'her luck' that she could always remember what she dreamed). Our conversations ranged from a version of common sense (people metabolize emotional experience in different ways) to the more distinctively psychoanalytic (that through projective identification there was a division of emotional labour in her relationships: she would be obsessed, they would be relatively uninterrupted). She was unable to hold inside her a more ruthless, taking-it-and-leaving-it relationship to a love object, so she gave that bit to her partner; she was then swamped and sustained by the illusion of her partner's permanent presence within her. We talked of the pleasures of being swamped, and the terrors of not being dependent on someone one loves. Some of this fitted with and evoked some of her sense of her childhood, but none of it was enlivening enough to make her really thoughtful, or to make her fall back inside herself. Meanwhile I was aware of experiencing something in the counter-transference that began to be pertinent: a growing sense that I was always getting it a bit wrong, as though there was some rule I didn't know about. I was being left with a conversation in my mind between an abject person and a thoroughly and impatiently competent one. At one point I said to myself in one of these internal conversations, 'I can't keep my side of this bargain!'

The first thing that really redeemed her curiosity was something that gradually began to occur to me quite late in the treatment, although it seems in retrospect, as it always does, that she had repeatedly been giving us both clues, not the least of which was several sessions spent talking about marriage certificates and death certificates. I suggested to her that when she was interested in someone, or fell in love, she instantly drew up from the past a secret contract with the person about the nature of the emotional experience they were going to have. Although she herself was unaware of the contract, she was compelled to abide by it. So if she was not obsessed and haunted – which was her side of the furtive agreement, derived from earlier contracts in childhood – she would not only be letting herself down but letting her partner down as well. Thus she was, in a sense, tyrannized by her own integrity. The irony of the situation, if irony is the right word, was that neither of them had ever consciously seen the contract. Immediately alive to the complications, the potential for farce in these kinds of pact, she said, 'It's like a peace treaty signed in secret by only one side.' We went on to discuss the kinds of war she was always unconsciously wanting her relationships to be.

Of course it is not news, from a psychoanalytic or a family-therapy point of view, that people engage in unconscious contracts with each other, though the extent of these contracts – the small print, as it were – should never cease to amaze us (not to mention those even more hidden and binding contracts we enter into with ourselves). Given the number of contracts we enter into without apprising ourselves or other people that we are doing so, it is not surprising that our more official social contracts – rule-bound games, legal arrangements, socially sanctioned rituals – as attempts to organize or put a frame around our luck, can be so reassuring. The psychoanalytic contract for treatment is unusual because at its most radical it disfigures (or even dismantles) the possibility of contract. It provides a transition between the world of contract and whatever it is that the world of contract tries to exclude. In fact, the psychoanalytic contract is kept in order to show, but not to enact, what it is that contracts, indeed all agreements and connections, are always vulnerable to – that is, the unconscious and the unknowable future. People can never know in any situation exactly what they are agreeing to because the agreement includes at the very least the unconscious history and desire of the participants and, in that bizarre phrase, whatever the future holds. So Don Juan is the anti-hero of my paper, for he is the parodist of contract who pretends to master contingency by identifying with it. It is surprisingly difficult, as the Jewish proverb suggests, to make time for time. No one can be exempted from chance. Even though our wishes try to convince us otherwise, the future is not available to be repressed. It is not only the home of wishes but also the resort of accidents. We can only think of our lives as a progress narrative through time – in terms of development – because we happen by accident to have heard of the idea of development.

The wars that my patient had unconsciously been wanting to turn her relationships into represented a wish for more abrasive forms of contact, more action. War was a way of getting uncertainty back into the picture. Indeed, what was especially striking about her particular kind of unconscious contract was not only her difficulty in acknowledging the separateness of her partner, and her pervasive assumption, derived from a grievance with her mother, that the partner's emotional experience should be symmetrical with hers; it was also the way in which the unconscious contract was used (as Claude Lévi-Strauss said of dreams) as a machine for the suppression of time. My patient's unconscious contract, much like a pornographic image, was an attempt to seclude herself and her partner from luck – the good and the bad luck, the accidents and chances we are negotiating and using all the time. The contract was like an emotional spell cast over the relationship at the beginning to exempt her from contingency, to pre-empt the inevitable uncertainties of evolving time. I began, in other words, to find it useful to listen for clues about her relationship to time. In fact, I began to think of the transference as a re-creation, or repetition, of three early relationships that were distinct and overlapping: the relationship to the mother, the relationship to the father, and the relationship to time. The unconscious contract was an attempt to encapsulate time, to seal it off and isolate it like a part-object.

It was by analysing her transference to time – which meant her finding out what kind of parent it was for her, and her allowing herself to experience it as no kind of parent, just the matrix of chance – that my patient began to find in herself more flexible forms of exchange with other people, a repertoire rather than a fate.

My conversations with this woman left me preoccupied with a range of rather obvious, and clinically pertinent, questions. What kind of love affair is a person having with time, and what kind of object is it for them? Is it, for example, something that needs filling or something that tends to get wasted? Is there never enough or does a lot of it have to be killed? What makes us feel there is plenty of it or that it is running out? If we spend so much time planning to use it, what is the risk of leaving things to chance? Entrusting oneself to a person is quite different from entrusting oneself to time.

In his novel *Foe*, the South African writer J. M. Coetzee describes it like this:

In a world of chance is there a better and a worse? We yield to a stranger's embrace or give ourselves to the waves; for the blink of an eyelid our vigilance relaxes; we are asleep; and when we awake we have lost the direction of our lives. What are these blinks of an eyelid, against which the only defence is an eternal and inhuman wakefulness? Might they not be the cracks and chinks through which another voice, other voices, speak in our lives? By what right do we close our ears to them?

Perhaps it is not surprising that a novelist who grows up and writes under a totalitarian regime is alert to the voices of chance, the voices that cannot be coerced.

I want to suggest that in developmental terms the recognition of contingency, of what Coetzee calls 'other voices' – recognition of one's life turning on a series of accidents in time, of events beyond one's power – is every bit as problematic as and different from recognition of the object, and less amenable to psychoanalytic description. In fact, I want to offer here for consideration the hypothesis that the preoccupation in developmental theory with recognition of the object can be a defence against the full acknow-ledgement of contingency. It is one thing to recognize the object – another person – as separate and to make him or her available for

8

use, and quite another to live in time and make accidents available for use. If it has been useful in psychoanalysis to think that there is an instinct-driven self, we may need to add to this a self immersed in its contingency. We talk, in the bizarre language of property relations, of owning our instincts as personal intentions, but we talk rarely, if at all, of the more paradoxical idea of owning the contingency of our lives. Another way of saying this is to wonder why it is so difficult for us to believe – to live confidently as if – our lives are subject to accident.

The *OED* defines the once philosophically fashionable word 'contingency' as, 'liable to happen or not . . . happening or coming by chance . . . subject to accidents'. Given the obvious contingency of much of our lives – we do not in any meaningful sense intend or choose our birth, our parents, our bodies, our language, our culture, our thoughts, our dreams, our desires, our death, and so on – it might be worth considering, from a psychoanalytic point of view, not only our relationships to ourselves and our relationships to objects, but (as the third of the pair, so to speak) our relationship to accidents.

Psychoanalysis began, after all, with links being made by Freud between instinctual life and the 'accident' of trauma, with remarkable descriptions of lives being lived with unchosen desires in unchosen families and unchosen wars. But in Freud's work a whole range of accidents began to be redescribed as unconscious intentions; in psychoanalytic theory bodies were bled of their contingency. Indeed one of Freud's most popular and immediately appealing ideas was the parapraxis: the accident that dared not speak its name until Freud authorized it. The Freudian slip – whose very name is a giveaway – is the accident that is meant to happen.

II

His basic question was: 'Can we ever find within determinism a way out of it?'

Sartre, *Mallarmé, or The Poet of Nothingness*

The Psychopathology of Everyday Life, first published as a book in 1904, has always been one of Freud's most popular works – although it is perhaps more accurate to say that the ideas in the book are among Freud's most popular, because most people find the experience of reading the book through rather wearing. But *The Psychopathology of Everyday Life* – the Mistake Book, as I will call it, to bring it in line with the Dream Book and the Joke Book – has been through more German editions and foreign translations than any of Freud's other books apart from the *Introductory Lectures on Psycho-Analysis*. And as Freud's English editor and translator James Strachey tells us, it is like *The Interpretation of Dreams* and *Three Essays on the Theory of Sexuality* in that Freud added fresh material to virtually every new edition published during his lifetime. This seems particularly interesting given the fact that, as Strachey remarks in his introduction to *The Standard Edition*, 'Almost the whole of the basic explanations and theories were already present in the earliest edition.' In fact, unusually for him, Strachey betrays some slightly bemused exasperation with Freud about this. 'No doubt he felt particular pleasure,' Strachey writes, 'both in the anecdotes themselves and in being presented with such widespread confirmation of his views. But the reader cannot help feeling sometimes that the wealth of new examples interrupts and even confuses the mainstream of the underlying argument.' Why then, in this book, subtitled *Forgetting, Slips of the Tongue, Bungled Actions, Superstitions and Errors*, are there so many examples? Why is so much evidence needed?

In a way it is not surprising, given Freud's professional allegiances and the uncertain status of his new and unusual science, that he should want to accumulate evidence as proof, even though in this case, as Strachey says, the quantity diminishes the quality. In so far as the Mistake Book is written in a specific genre – it was first

CONTINGENCY FOR BEGINNERS

published in a journal called the *Monograph for Psychiatry and Neurology* – it observes the conventions of a certain kind of scientific treatise. If one answer to the question of the book's excess has to do with genre, the equally obvious psychoanalytic answer would be that the insistence of the book betrays a doubt in Freud's mind; that the material evokes a resistance both in the writer and in the imagined audience that requires tenacious overcoming. It is as though Freud is saying, 'There really are lots of mistakes and accidents in life, and they really are meaningful, often in a sexual way.' Given Freud's interpretations of parapraxes, it is not surprising that he thinks we need persuading; but we all do, of course, know that life is full of errors and accidents. However, if the errors and accidents are meaningful in the way he proposes, they cease to be errors and accidents. With something akin to Freud's logic of dreams, the book describes a large number of accidents to prove that there is no such thing as an accident. By the end of the book, if we get through it, we have been absolved of error and introduced to the psychoanalytic world of multiple plots. We are not continually making mistakes, we are continually making alternative lives. But why can't we, as Freud suggested six years later in his book on Leonardo, consider chance to be 'worthy of determining our fate'? It may not be that all accidents are meaningful, but that meaning is made out of accidents. Freud uses psychoanalytic theory to turn accidents, apparently chance events, into significant intentions. But the excessive evidence of the Mistake Book may also be to counter the anxiety that chance is determining our fate and the potential loss of meaning this could entail. Freud, after all, has managed to make accidents entertaining.

The Mistake Book, a virtual encyclopaedia of errors and accidents, reveals with scientific sobriety the slapstick of everyday life; in which what Freud calls 'seemingly accidental clumsy movements', in all their minuscule violence and chaos, 'prove to be governed by an intention, and achieve their aim, with a certainty which cannot in general be credited to our conscious voluntary movements'. 'Falling, stumbling and slipping,' he writes, 'need not always be interpreted as purely accidental miscarriages of motor action.' He reveals that we are not making fools of ourselves, but that on the contrary we are as competent as we dream we are. We are suffering from an excess of meaningful intentions. Accidents become, in Freud's version, ways of securing unconscious gratifications, either self-punishment or other muffled fulfilment of forbidden wishes. And 'there is no sphere,' he writes, 'in which the view that accidental actions are really intentional will command a more ready belief than that of sexuality.'

Accidents become disowned intentions; other voices speak through our mistakes. So the idea of accident – of the apparently unintended, the contingent – gives us access to otherwise unavailable desires or parts of the self, depending on one's language commitments. Accidents become the best way, indeed the only way, of doing some things. And conversely, without a notion of accident or contingency we would not be able sufficiently to disown them to make them known. Freud is showing us, in other words, not only that accidents are meaningful but how we use the idea of accident in the production of meanings that are most forbidden. Error is legitimate criminality. We are at our most transgressive when we fail. The Mistake Book contains, that is to say, both descriptions of what people use accidents to do, and what Freud can do by redescribing these accidents. And one of the many things he can then do by redescribing accidents in this particular way is to make them revelations of personal history. As psychoanalysis turns instinct into personal history, so there is no such thing as a mistake, only the continual disclosure of the past. If a parapraxis is a self-inflicted accident, why would one want to inflict such an accident on oneself? And Freud's remarkable answer is: to gratify, in compromised form, a forbidden desire, but also to recover the past, to link us to our history. There is a history that our competence conceals.

By way of concluding his book, Freud states:

There is one thing which the severest and the mildest cases all have in common, and which is equally found in parapraxes and chance actions: the phenomena can be traced back to incompletely suppressed psychical material, which, although pushed away by consciousness, has nevertheless not been robbed of all capacity for expressing itself.

Suppressed desires are suppressed histories, or suppressed histories that were in the making. Through psychoanalytic interpretation Freud takes the luck out of accidents and makes them available as non-mystical sources of meaning. What looked like accident or chance was in fact voices from the past pressing for recognition; there are lives inside us competing to be lived. We must assume from what Freud says here that the 'suppressed psychical material' wants to express itself – that there are personal histories inside us, in conflict but clamouring for recognition. Accidents are reminders of unfinished business, that we are living too few of our lives.

III

It is a matter of agreement between us and the baby that we will never ask the question: 'Did you conceive of this or was it presented to you from without?' The important point is that no decision on this point is expected.

D. W. Winnicott, 'Transitional Objects and
Transitional Phenomena'

Freud invented a method, a treatment, for the recovery of the past through reappropriation – to use the wrong word – of desire. Transformation, however circumscribed by the modesty of his therapeutic ambitions, involved the recovery through the transference of the possibilities of desire. But Freud also knew, because he was not an orthodox Freudian, that all sorts of experiences can remind us of who we are; that if chance is worthy of determining our fate anything might serve to transform one's life; that the past, as Proust devoted nearly twenty years of writing to show, can return by accident. But the Proustian accident, unlike the Freudian accident, does not appear to come from inside.

In the Overture to *Swann's Way* Proust writes:

One day in winter, on my return home my mother, seeing that I was cold, offered me some tea, a thing I did not ordinarily take. I declined at first and then for no particular reason, changed my mind. She sent for one of those squat, plump little cakes called 'petits madeleines' . . . no sooner had the warm liquid mixed with the crumbs touched my palate than a shudder ran through me and I stopped, intent upon the extraordinary thing that was happening.

The extraordinary thing that was happening, brought on by the most famous cakes in literary history, was the memory of Combray, a crucial piece of his past. Proust conveys both the simplicity, the absolute ordinariness, of the event, and how it could easily have not happened. His mother needn't have offered him tea, she might not have had those cakes, he needn't have had any and so on. Proust makes us feel that in that moment of hesitation – 'I declined at first and then for no particular reason, changed my mind' – his life and the writing of his extraordinary book were in the balance without, of course, his knowing it. It was, from his point of view, an entirely gratuitous event.

Secular epiphanies like this reveal the past, but one's personal history is an elusive god. In the world of Proust's novel there is always a tantalizing quality about people's lives, as though time were flirting with them. Our recovery of the protean past, and the selves we have buried there, cannot be arranged. 'There is a large element of chance in these matters,' Proust writes, 'and a second chance occurrence, that of our own death, often prevents us from awaiting for any length of time the favours of the first.' Proust's writing, as an essential parallel text to Freud's, provides an anti-psychoanalytic version of psychoanalysis. From a Proustian point of view the analyst is someone with whom one might, with a bit of luck, through the transference, stumble on a bit of the past. Proust writes:

It is a labour in vain to attempt to recapture it, all the efforts of our intellect must prove futile. The past is hidden somewhere outside the realm, beyond the reach of intellect, in some material object (in the sensation which that material object will give us) of which we have no inkling. And it depends on chance whether we come upon this object before we ourselves die.

'Depending on chance' is, of course, an interesting phrase. For Proust there is no organizing, no technique, for securing access to the past. The past is disclosed by coincidences that are in themselves meaningless: a smell, a tune, a taste. And there is no knowing beforehand which or when it might be. Both Proust and Freud, in quite different ways, make us think about contingency, as they elaborate their instructive accidents. Proust's accidental encounter with the madeleines – an encounter which in his view might never have happened – prompts an involuntary memory that transfigures his sense of himself and the shape of his life. It presents him with a new future. But the past that is inside us is not, for Proust, busily and furtively arranging for its own disclosure, is not seeking attention. It is not even, he implies, waiting to be found; though it is there, somewhere, in some 'material object', if we are lucky or unlucky enough to come across it. And we will probably only come across it when we are doing something else; we cannot organize a quest for the past, nor is the past pursuing us with its essential messages and unfinished projects.

For Freud the accident disclosed a counter-intention; and this counter-intention is an insufficiently repressed desire, a piece of urgent personal history wanting to be lived out, even in its compromised form. But the desire is not wanting, so to speak, to be decoded as history; it is wanting some version of gratification. The desire seeks satisfaction, but the psychoanalyst makes history. Freudian interpretation aims to extend the realm of intention, and diminish the empire of contingency.

Proust's secular epiphany becomes, in Freudian terms, another piece of unconscious calculation. Endorsing a paper by Otto Rank, Freud writes: 'Often not only losing objects but also finding them appears to be (psychologically) determined . . . It is obvious that in cases of losing, the object is already provided; in cases of finding it has first to be looked for.' All finding in Freud is a looking for, and an already having seen, a refinding. What is intimated in the Proustian scenario and is repressed – indeed is nonsensical, from a psychoanalytic point of view – is the idea that we are not looking but that we may find.

For the purposes of this paper I want to use Proust and Freud as figures for two possible versions of the self; so I don't mean Proust and Freud in their real complexity but rather those aspects of them represented by my two examples. Staged in this way the comparison reveals, I think, an important omission or disavowal in psychoanalytic theory (though I think psychoanalysis has repressed the Proustian in Freud). I want to say that there are two versions of the self that psychoanalysis, despite its dualism and commitment to conflict, always tries to resolve into one. One version of the self, the Freudian, knows, in the psychoanalytic sense, what it wants and is always wanting; we can call this 'unconscious desire'.

But there is another version of the self – not defensive, indeed radically undefended – that is not about knowing what it wants or is wanting (and that brings with it the question: why is it so difficult for us to really believe that we don't know what we want?). This version of the self – for which wanting is not the game – lives its contingency without contesting it. One could say it simply abides by its contingency. But in certain environments this version of the self can only be lived either as despair – my life is out of my control and that's what's wrong with it – or as scepticism – I don't know what I want and therefore doubt my capacity to know anything. Acknowledgement of the contingent self – that self which has no contracts to make and that is linked with one's own death in a way that the self of unconscious desire never can be – entails, I think, the belated recovery, or processing, of the earliest forms of experience.

Early emotional experience may be imagined as being like a series of accidents – unarranged events like hunger or sleepiness – that are gradually redescribed as more than coincidence. A person's relationship to coincidence – or to the idea of coincidence, or chance or luck – is a complicated link to this earlier self. Development in its non-progressivist sense means taking one's chances. Coincidences belong to those who can use them.

IV

Something has to be done to get us free of our memories and choices.

John Cage (interview)

Coincidence simply means two things happening together, 'occurrence or existence at the same time'. But from a Freudian point of view, discussion of coincidence is inevitably tainted with notions of the paranormal, or the kind of mystical animism that psychoanalysts tend to pathologize. Freud clearly could not have written a book called *Synchronicity: An Acausal Connecting Principle*. The four pages on coincidence in the Mistake Book are a brief testament to Freud's new-found ability to 'resolve' coincidences, like most other apparent accidents. That our lives might be simply a series or collection of coincidences seems peculiarly unacceptable (though it could, of course, be comforting). Indeed, the word 'accident' usually signifies something going wrong. If we began to think of Oedipus, for example, as just extremely unlucky, psychoanalysis would be a very different thing. The play, after all, is full of extraordinary coincidences.

It is, I think, of interest that in Winnicott's description development begins with instincts experienced as contingent events, and their gratification as a coincidence (like the 'overlapping of two lines'). For the infant, he writes, 'the instincts are not yet clearly defined as internal to the infant, the instincts can be as much external as can a clap of thunder or a hit'. If the instincts feel to the infant like contingent events, then the mother's task, in the Winnicottian picture, is the personalizing or humanizing of an original and formative contingency. Instinctual experience, through the complementary relationship with the mother, becomes a discernible process, with something like a beginning, a middle and an end, or at least, a pause. So the question of how one recognizes coincidences and comes to use them as such can be linked with Winnicott's description of the process of illusionment. In *Paediatrics and Psychiatry* (1948) he writes:

Initially there is a condition which could be described at one and the same time as absolute independence and absolute dependence. There is no feeling of dependence, and therefore that dependence must be absolute. Let us say that out of this state the infant is disturbed by instinct tension which is called hunger. I would say that the infant is ready to believe in something that could exist, i.e. there has developed in the infant a readiness to hallucinate an object; but that is rather a direction of expectancy than an object in itself. At this moment the mother comes along with her breast (I say breast for simplification of description), and places it so that the infant finds it. Here is another direction, this time towards instead of away from the infant. It is a tricky matter whether or not the mother and infant 'click'. At the start the mother allows the infant to dominate, and if she fails to do this the infant's subjective object will fail to have superimposed on it the objectively perceived breast. Ought we not to say that fitting in with the infant's impulse the mother allows the baby the illusion that what is there is the thing created by the baby; as a result there is not only the physical experience of instinctual satisfaction, but also an emotional union, and the beginning of a belief in reality as something about which one can have illusions.

For the infant, desire is of a piece with satisfaction. For hunger to be virtually synonymous with being fed is, from the infant's point of view, no coincidence; from the observer's point of view it is as though one thing, the infant's scream of hunger, causes another, the mother's wish to feed. As waiting becomes a processible and therefore a tolerable experience for the child, the question arises: is being fed the consequence of being hungry, like cause and effect, or is it simply coincidental with being hungry? The answer is that both descriptions are available but one is much harder to take than the other.

At first, Winnicott writes, 'there is an overlap between what the mother supplies and what the child might conceive of'. But once the capacity for illusionment has been secured through sufficiently attentive care, the mother has the 'job' of disillusioning the child. It is what Winnicott calls 'the good-enough environmental provision' that enables the child to 'cope with the immense shock of loss of omnipotence'.

This immense shock occurs whenever the mother's presence is no longer coincident with the child's need (which in absolute terms, of course, it never can be). Given good enough care the child accumulates a belief that he or she can create the coincidences he or she needs – what Winnicott calls 'a belief in reality as something about which he can have illusions'. From the infant's point of view, at the earliest stage, there is no coincidence because there are not yet two things to coincide; there is simply the infant's need. But once there is a glimpse that well-being or satisfaction is a cooperative venture, then it might seem as if – or be reconstructed as if – the infant or child causes his satisfaction through the clamour of demand. The child is no longer just the site of contingent instincts, but the agent of their actual appeasement. But it is integral to the process of disillusionment, the immense shock Winnicott writes about, that the child has to get beyond believing that the consequences of his actions are commensurate with his intentions. Desire is not an insurance policy for satisfaction. The mother is not his machine and neither is his body. Desires and needs – like thoughts and dreams – are as contingent as their gratification. The extent to which we socially regulate hunger suggests that appetite was once experienced as something of a surprise. (Though we, in that absurd phrase, eat between meals, we don't think between thoughts.)

For the sake of this essay I want to over-simplify and abstract the familiar process of illusion-and-disillusionment that in Winnicott's view organizes our lives. Infants, after all, have always been useful in psychoanalysis to attribute things to because they don't answer back. I want to impute states of mind to infants as a figurative way of asserting something that I think is of interest. So, from a psychoanalytic point of view, in the process of disillusionment it is as if the infant – and later the adult – has three choices. Either the infant is omnipotent, or the mother is omnipotent, or neither of them is; with this third option, which we can call the *Depressive Position*, there is, among other things, the acknowledgement that there is no such thing as omnipotence. People stop finding or being deities and have to do something else together. I want to suggest that there is a fourth choice – which looks as though it's somewhere between belief in omnipotence and the abrogation of that belief – though in actuality I think it is something quite different. It is called acknowledgement of contingency. It can be called luck, fortune, accident, coincidence, and is sometimes experienced and described as a kind of non-intentional or random agency. There is actually nothing behind it making it happen – though we can personalize it by projection – and its presence, in and of itself, says nothing about our power. It neither diminishes nor enlarges us, but we can use it to do both. Because it includes both the body and whatever is felt not to be the body, it is neither internal nor external; a bit like Winnicott's imagining of the infant's earliest experience of instinct. It would sound absurd to talk of a stage of contingency, or a Contingency Position, because what I am referring to is the enemy of fixity (of reification) but is always there. But as with the Depressive Position, or whatever one's preferred life-aim, psychoanalysis could be a process of understanding the obstacles to its full acknowledgement.

What are the preconditions, in terms of early experience, that allow the contingent self to emerge as such? What kinds of defence (defences are essentially contingency plans) blind one to coincidence? What prevents us from living, to repeat my earlier question, confidently as though our lives are a series of accidents? What is the cost of not considering chance to be worthy of determining our fate? And what happens when what I am calling the contingent self is repressed or turned away from, since, from a psychoanalytic point of view, as Joseph Smith reminds us, 'Whatever is turned away from is marked as a danger to be faced or a loss to be mourned'?

Acknowledgement of the contingency of the self – and the contingent self that lives this acknowledgement – need not be exclusively a disillusioning or depressive experience, because somewhere one has never had illusions about it; in adult life it is contesting one's contingency that is productive of disabling illusion. (Classical tragedy could never be the preferred genre of the contingent self.) This contingent self, for example, is unable to engage in that bemusing activity that Leslie Farber once called 'willing what cannot be willed'. From the point of view of the contingent self, desiring – being drawn to someone or something – could only mean creating the conditions for a coincidence. (Or to put it another way:

we cannot make our relationships work; we can only make our compromises work.) And the idea of the contingent self has interesting consequences for our moral sense, because it is through our morality, as Bernard Williams has suggested, that we often try to make our lives 'immune from luck'. The contingent self enjoins us to imagine a life without blaming, a life exempt from the languages of effort and self-control.

The contingent self 'knows' nothing in the conventional sense; this is not a deficit, though, but a definition; because in the conventional sense there is nothing for it to know. Or perhaps I am closer to what I mean by saying that the contingent self is a weak epistemologist because it knows only one thing, and it is a paradoxical kind of knowledge. It knows that emotional experience is new at every moment; and since all our equipment to prepare ourselves for the future comes from the past, it is redundant and ironic. That is, we are all beginners at contingency because it is the only thing we can be.

2

Freud and the Uses of Forgetting

I

Remembering everything is a form of madness.
Brian Friel, *Translations*

People come for psychoanalytic treatment because they are remembering in a way that does not free them to forget. From a psychoanalytic point of view symptoms are reminders – 'indications,' Freud writes in his essay 'Repression', 'of a return of the repressed'. A form of involuntary and disguised memory, symptoms are mnemonics of desire; and desire, for Freud – what he referred to as 'instinctual life' – is unforgettable. Repression, indeed all the mechanisms of defence that he described – the tropes of distribution and self-protection – are ways of retaining things by getting rid of them. The unconscious, that is to say, is what we know about when defences (like forgetting) break down. In symptoms, in dreams, in slips of the tongue, in free-association and, of course, in memories themselves we are reminded of our disowned counterparts.

It is as though there are areas of our lives about which we can pretend to lose, or never evolve, our memory. And these areas can be called – depending on one's psychoanalytic language commitments – desires, thoughts, histories, trauma, parts of the self. This category of the unacceptable, or unbearable, is the target for psychoanalytic interpretation, which ideally frees the patient to resume contact with what he has never actually lost but merely hidden away, or been unable to process, or both. He is encouraged to remember that he has forgotten these things, that he has actively mislaid them, for what might be called aesthetic reasons; that they were felt to be incompatible with whatever he had come to believe was good or desirable for or about himself.

Freud finds the analogy that he thinks of as the origin for this process in what he calls in his paper 'Negation' 'the language of the oldest – the oral instinctual impulses'. Judgement, or aesthetic valuation, is fundamentally a question of whether something is edible. But in talking about judgement in this way Freud is also giving us, by implication, one of his many pictures of memory and forgetting:

[T]he judgement is, 'I should like to eat this', or 'I should like to spit it out'; and, put more generally: 'I should like to take this into myself and to keep that out.' That is to say, 'It shall be inside me' or 'it shall be outside me' . . . the original pleasure-ego wants to introject into itself everything that is good and to eject from itself everything that is bad. What is bad, what is alien to the ego and what is external are, to begin with, identical.

Everything bad is put outside by projection, or into the outside that is inside – the unconscious – by repression. You can, so to speak, forget outside or forget inside. But is forgetting – a later, more developmentally sophisticated stage than the one described here – more like eating something or like spitting it out? Just as you can only repress something once you have acknowledged it, similarly you can only spit something out once you have tasted it. If Freud is describing here his paradigm for judgement he is also describing two forms of forgetting: if you spit something out you dispense with it once and for all; if you eat something you forget it through a process called digestion. Spat out it will be, as it were, metabolized by the world in a future you hope to have exempted yourself from; taken in, it will be metabolized by your body, and fuel your future. The question becomes not: what do I want to forget and what do I want to remember?, but: which form of forgetting do I want to use? The picture of spitting something out, taken literally, adds to the repertoire a paradoxical notion, an absolute forgetting: that which can be put beyond the reach of memory, that which cannot be redeemed – in the language of the second-oldest instinctual impulses, an 'immaculate evacuation'.

There may be a cure for symptoms but there is, from a psychoanalytic point of view, no cure for memory. The past, ghost-written as desire, is driving us into the future; in fact symptoms, in this view, are a person's always unsuccessful attempts at self-cure for memory. And yet Freud intimates in his paper 'Negation' that there is a forgetting, which is a way of remembering, which becomes repression and that he encourages us to call 'eating'; and that there is a forgetting that is its own negation, that leaves nothing to remember. I want to suggest in this paper that Freud was in a continual dilemma as to which of these alternatives best represented the aims of psychoanalytic treatment. His disillusion with hypnosis as a cathartic treatment was an episode and not merely a watershed in his insistent preoccupation with the uses of forgetting. Was psychoanalysis exorcism or recycling? Can the past be forgotten, and then be turned into something that doesn't need forgetting?

One of what Richard Wollheim refers to as Freud's 'two momentous discoveries' – the other being his loss of faith in the seduction theory – directly raises the question of whether it is possible, in psychoanalytic terms, to spit out one's desire. 'Memories,' Wollheim writes, 'are found incompatible and repressed not because of the events that they are of but because of the impulses expressed in the events that they are of.' We use memories to forget with. Memory, in other words, was what Freud was to call 'screen-memory'; and these screen-memories were screens because memory, Freud had begun to believe, was *of* desire. Since desire was, by Oedipal definition, forbidden, 'the falsified memory,' Freud writes in his paper 'Screen-Memory', 'is the first that we become aware of'. Memories become forms of forgetting. 'It may indeed be questioned,' he continues, 'whether we have any memories at all from our childhood; memories relating to our childhood may be all that we possess.'

If memories are more like dreams than pieces of reliable documentary evidence, and are disguised representations of forbidden desire, it is as though desire can only be remembered by being successfully forgotten; which in this context means, represented by a sufficiently censored dreamable dream, or an often banal replacement-memory. Forgetting, in its versions of disguise, makes desire accessible by making it tolerable. We can only desire because we can hide things from ourselves. The defences, as described by Freud, are

24

a repertoire of forms of forgetting. But if desire, because of the threat of castration, can lead only to a furtive double life of concealment what, then, is the aim of psychoanalytic interpretation? The re-cycling of desire or the dispelling of it? If there was – as Ernest Jones suggested, with his powerful but now repressed concept of Aphini-sis – a dread of the death of desire, perhaps also there was a wish to kill desire, to be able to forget instinctual life; a wish that psychoana-lysis may (or can) be unwittingly complicit with? If, as Freud's description of the ego as a defensive structure suggests, we only pretend to forget, then what kind of remembering is psychoanalysis aiming to promote? And one answer would be: psychoanalysis is a cure by means of the kind of remembering that makes forgetting possible.

So in this picture of psychoanalysis Freud's later, and more obscure, notion of the Death Instinct is a way of describing a part of the self that wants to make memory impossible, that creates states of mind in which there is nothing left to remember; the Death Instinct was Freud's sublime of forgetting. If the body – that illimitable complexity of the self that the word signifies – is always in excess of the individual's capacity for representation, then the Death Instinct is that which shatters the possibility of representation.

In Freud's view man is the animal driven to forget, and driven by forgetting. If Freud's analysis of hysteria convinced him that we are never good enough at forgetting, it was his analysis of the Ratman that prompted him, perhaps unwittingly, to acknowledge the more paradoxical uses of forgetting; to give us his pictures of what forgetting might entail, for better or worse.

II

Death is not a splitter.
William Kerrigan, *Hamlet's Perfection*

Once Freud had located the unconscious content of the Ratman's pervasive sense of guilt – that his 'criminal wishes' were actually directed against his father – the Ratman, in the following session, turned his doubts about himself against psychoanalysis and its father. When his now-famous patient 'ventured', as Freud puts it delicately, 'to bring forward a few doubts' about the efficacy of psychoanalytic interpretation, of making the unconscious conscious, Freud gives him a curiously ambiguous account of the therapeutic value of remembering what one has tried to forget. It is as though the Ratman reminds Freud of his own uncertainty, of his own ambivalence about remembering, which his work with hysterics had obliged him to forget. Beginning his lecture to the Ratman, Freud writes:

I then made some short observations upon the psychological differences between the conscious and the unconscious, and upon the fact that everything conscious was subject to a process of wearing away, while what was unconscious was relatively unchangeable; and I illustrated my remarks by pointing to the antiques standing about in my room. They were, in fact, I said, only objects found in a tomb, and their burial had been their preservation; the destruction of Pompeii was only beginning now that it had been dug up. – Was there any guarantee, he next enquired, of what one's attitude would be towards what was discovered? One man, he thought, would no doubt behave in such a way as to get the better of his self-reproach, but another would not. – No, I said, it followed from the nature of the circumstances that in every case the affect would be overcome – for the most part during the progress of the work itself. Every effort was made to preserve Pompeii, whereas people were anxious to be rid of tormenting ideas like his.

If Freud had revealed to the Ratman his repressed, and so forgotten, murderous wishes towards his father, he suggests here that memory itself can be a form of murder, a way of disposing of things. 'The destruction of Pompeii was only beginning,' he reassures the Ratman, 'now that it had been dug up.' On the one hand, Freud says, forgetting, like burial, is a preservative; a kind of storage. And, of course, in his example of Pompeii, it is the storage of what has already been damaged. But on the other hand, remembering, like excavation, does something paradoxical: by linking the fragments – whether it be of the patient's story, or the shards of the city – it makes possible imaginative reconstruction; and yet this very reconstruction contributes, or even causes, the final destruction and disappearance of the material. What has made the reconstruction possible destroys the evidence (and from a psychoanalytic point of view this might make us wonder, for example, what happens to the dream once you have interpreted it, and what you want to happen to it).

The Ratman's question to Freud, after he has given him the example of Pompeii, obliquely registers the dilemma Freud has presented him with. He has compared his highly valued antiques, and the great city of Pompeii which he clearly considers worth preserving, with the Ratman's repressed death-wishes towards his father which he clearly considers worth, as Freud puts it, 'overcoming'. You render such wishes redundant, or at least relatively powerless, by making them conscious. But what if wishes, like antiques, should be preserved? How can Freud possibly forget his antiques once they are in his consulting room? His analogies produce an instructive muddle: is remembering a form of forgetting, or forgetting a form of remembering? If everything conscious, as Freud said, 'is subject to a process of wearing away', then isn't remembering a form of depletion, or even dissipation? And isn't Freud feeling guilty that his acquisition of the antiques contributes to their decay? It is as though one is evacuating the past, emptying oneself of it by remembering it. (It is perhaps worth noting here that it is a common clinical experience that bereaved people fear that talking about the person they have lost will dispel their contact with them; as though real remembering entails real loss.)

The alternatives that Freud offers the Ratman – remembering as a wearing away, or the repression of forgetting as 'relatively unchangeable' storage – are a vivid representation of Freud's perplexed preoccupation with the uses of forgetting. In fact, he presents the Ratman with what is at best a paradox and at its worst a double-bind: remembering is a way of killing off the past, and therefore so is psychoanalysis when it works. Either the most significant bits of one's past are unconscious, and only available in the compromised form of symptoms and dreams; or the past is released through interpretation, into oblivion (this is like a gloss on Rilke's famous remark that he would never have psychoanalysis because if he lost his devils he would lose his angels). Is the aim of psychoanalysis to make the past – the problematic past – available for disposal? If to remember is to relinquish, then memory may be a process akin to mourning; and forgetting may be either a refusal to mourn – a defence, as it were, against one's own entropy – or its completion. You can only forget when there is nothing to remember. Pompeii may have started to disintegrate only when it was dug up, but the antiques in Freud's consulting room, as I have said, were not apparently diminished by being taken from their tomb. By comparing the fate of Pompeii with his own collection of antiquities, he makes a distinction that he fails to note: some things, like Pompeii, may be protected by being buried and forgotten, and some things may be destroyed by being dug up and remembered, like Pompeii and one's unacceptable wishes; but there are other things from the past that are, in fact, sustained by being recontextualized.

As a Jew in Vienna at the turn of the century, Freud may well have identified with the fate of his, by definition, non-Jewish antiquities that had changed places and come so far. His lecture to the Ratman, and to the reader of the case-history, suggests that, despite his describing psychoanalysis as a cure by memory, there were things about the past that were, in a sense, nurtured by being forgotten. It has been the value of forgetting that psychoanalysis after Freud has most often repressed. Freud could describe a pathology of forgetting, but not an art. And yet his lecture to the Ratman represents, I think, his fundamental ambivalence about memory – his commitment to the uses of forgetting, and to the definition of its most benign and various forms. For Freud to have addressed more explicitly his ambivalence about remembering would have involved him in confronting his ambivalence about psychoanalysis itself – something every psychoanalyst has to work hard to disguise. For Freud, the aim of analysis was not to remember, but to establish sufficient states of forgetting.

III

Memories are killing.
Samuel Beckett, *The Expelled*

If Freud described symptoms as forms of forgetting, and so a cure based on remembering, he produced – as a mirror-image, so to speak – a method of treatment, an explanation of artistic creation, and an account of sexual development based on the capacity to forget. Free-floating attention, the sublimation that is art, the fundamental configurations of the Oedipus complex, all depend upon the trope of forgetting. What Freud refers to as the 'defences' are all imaginative ways of losing one's memory, of pretending to oneself that the past has no future; that distinctively psychoanalytic forgetting (of concealment) that is the only way to remember. Psychoanalysis is, in fact, a phenomenology of processes – repression, repetition, transference, memory, dreams – that cannot begin without a forgetting. There are, in other words, two ghosts in this machine: the unconscious, and the capacity to forget. We are the creatures who refuse to remember who we are; and yet, from a psychoanalytic point of view, there can be nothing human without competent forgetting. If a life, in psychoanalytic terms, can be described as a relationship between the unconscious and a repertoire of forgettings, this relationship can only be understood, in psychoanalytic treatment, if the analyst has learnt the art of free-floating attention.

Psychoanalysis, as a technique that aims to facilitate by interpretation the memory that is desire, depends, in Freud's view, on the analyst's ability to forget; to be able to tolerate not wilfully keeping things in his mind. And this, though Freud does not put it like this, is an act of faith. It implies a belief that there is a process inside the

29

analyst that gets to work by not trying to remember; and for which conscious, as opposed to pre-conscious or unconscious, memory is a saboteur. 'It must not be forgotten,' he writes in 'Recommendations to Physicians Practising Psychoanalysis', using the pertinent word, 'that the things one hears are for the most part things whose meaning is only recognized later on'; the making of meaning, he suggests, depends upon deferral, on a certain kind of storage. 'The analyst,' he writes, 'should simply listen, and not bother about whether he is keeping anything in mind', because 'a conscious determination to recollect the point would probably have resulted in failure'.

Listening, Freud says, is informed by forgetting; to try to remember is not to hear in the sense that he is proposing. In his encyclopaedia article on psychoanalysis of 1923, he writes:

Experience soon showed that the attitude which the analytic physician could most advantageously adopt was to surrender himself to his own unconscious mental activity, in a state of evenly suspended attention, to avoid as far as possible reflection and the construction of conscious expectations, not to try to fix anything that he heard particularly in his memory, and by these means to catch the drift of the patient's unconscious with his own unconscious.

In this picture, memory, as a function of the ego, is an obstacle: this surrendering' of the analyst to 'his own unconscious mental activity' so as to 'catch the drift of the patient's unconscious with his own' implies that conscious active remembering is a defence against contact; that memory obstructs communication. It is as though there is an unconscious analysing instrument that can only function when memory is abrogated (the Kleinian psychoanalyst Wilfred Bion advocated that the analyst should engage in the psychoanalytic session 'without memory or desire', but he had both to remember to do that, and want to). Understanding can happen – the analyst can 'catch the drift' of the patient's unconscious, a phrase which catches the drift of this kind of understanding – in the space cleared by relinquishing memory.

'Surrendering to one's unconscious' means temporarily forgetting who one is; Freud, that is to say, with the kind of instructive lucidity which can make it all sound like practical common sense, presents his listeners with something very paradoxical. The patient free-associates – every association being a memory, coming from the past – and the analyst does something complementary that Freud calls, 'simply listening'. And yet he makes something quite clear that he cannot elaborate: that it is only when two people forget themselves, in each other's presence, that they can recognize each other. Because we can only communicate underground – only recognize each other in spite of ourselves, unconscious to unconscious – communication entails, indeed necessitates, a version of forgetting.

By explaining free-floating or evenly suspended attention, Freud is trying to describe a version of memory – or rather, a form of forgetting – that does not mystify contact between people. But there is, it should be noted, a curious conviction informing his method: that unconsciouses, so to speak, can catch the drift of each other; that there is recognition somewhere even if it does not lie in trying to remember what people say. So in this picture once you have forgotten, once you've stopped trying particularly to 'fix' anything you hear in your memory, what have you got down to, or what do you start with? I assume it is not an accident that this is so difficult to imagine. One possible imagining, though it is bland in the range of analogy it suggests, is that when we can sufficiently forget – or forget, as Freud says, our 'reflection and the construction of conscious expectations' – we can process each other, meaning that we can make sense of each other, or at least the kinds of sense that psychoanalysis requires of us or that we may require of each other. Certainly, Freud intimates that particular kinds of sense–making are inextricable from, and impossible without, certain kinds of forgetting; it is as if people can only meet in anonymous encounters. And psychoanalytic theories are imaginative constructions of what happens in the gap between recognition and remembering – the gap we make by the act of forgetting.

Freud sometimes calls what happens in the gap we call forgetting, 'dream-work'; and at other times, though he does not use this phrase, 'art-work'. The making of a dream, like the making of a work of art, in his account, is essentially a process of reworking, and you can't remember something, of course, until it has happened to you, or at least until something has happened to you. 'What memories, hysteria and works of art have in common,' Sarah Kofman writes in *The Childhood of Art*, 'is that they are phantasmal constructions from memory traces, and have a plastic or theatrical form.' And these reworkings, these phantasmal constructions, are akin to that protracted unconscious free-floating attention that Freud prescribed for the analyst. What the analyst does from outside, the dreamer and the artist do from inside: a sustained, forgetful self-listening. Each of them is finding ways of making the previously unacceptable accessible through redescription or redepiction. It is almost as though Freud is saying that the dreamer and the artist (and the ordinary rememberer) already have something like an analyst inside them, 'simply listening'; and that a person comes for analysis when this inner analyst can no longer sustain evenly suspended attention. That this internal figure has forgotten how to forget and needs to be reminded (not, it should be said, by a real analyst, which can only be internal, but by his external representative, a provisional impostor). In analysis it is as though everything has already happened, even the analyst.

For Freud, the psychoanalyst was, among other things, a way of describing a new figure with a particular way of forgetting called 'simply listening'; and in this kind of listening, meanings – or constructions – can only be made by way of deferral. A time lag is built into the system. You cannot remember something as it is happening; and you cannot know – or rather, predict – quite what it is you will remember. One cannot learn one's personal history off by heart.

IV

If all time is eternally present
All time is unredeemable.

T. S. Eliot, 'Burnt Norton'

It is perhaps unavoidable in this context to mention Freud's concept of deferred action; though it is significantly difficult, as it clearly was for Freud, to rework it. Deferred action seems to be something we can remember but not retranscribe. Freud himself could only repeat it – admittedly in different contexts: in a letter to Wilhelm Fliess, in the Dream Book, in the Wolfman case – he could not sufficiently elaborate on it. For such an illuminating idea, it is indeed surprising that he did not devote a paper to it. It is as if the idea itself was like a trauma for him, subject only to repetition, not to modification. 'Freud uses the term "nachtraglich" repeatedly and constantly,' Jean Laplanche and J.-B. Pontalis write in their dictionary of psychoanalysis, 'often underlining it. The substantival form Nachtraglichkeit also keeps cropping up, and from very early on. Thus although he never offered a definition, much less a general theory, of the notion of deferred action, it was indisputably looked on by Freud as part of his conceptual equipment.' After mentioning that it was Lacan who 'drew attention to the importance of this term' (they give no references), they introduce their own characteristically lucid account by saying, 'we do not propose to set forth any theory of deferred action here' (Charles Rycroft, incidentally, has no entry for deferred action in his *Critical Dictionary of Psychoanalysis*). The question, intimated by Laplanche and Pontalis, is: did Freud set forth any theory of deferred action, and what might have been the problem of doing so?

In one sense Freud's theory of deferred action can be simply stated: memory is reprinted, so to speak, in accordance with later experience. As Laplanche and Pontalis put it, 'experiences, impressions and memory traces may be revised at a later date to fit in with fresh experiences or with the attainment of a new stage of development. They may, in that event, be endowed not only with a new meaning, but also with psychical effectiveness.' Freud, in a famous letter to Fliess (6 December 1896), writes of 'memory traces being subjected from time to time to a re-arrangement in accordance with fresh circumstances – to a retranscription'. Memory is like a stock of material available for revision. And these ideas of rearrangement, retranscription, revision enable Freud to make sense of two central and related preoccupations: sexual development and trauma.

'Every adolescent,' he writes in his *Project for a Scientific Psychology*, Part 2, 'has memory traces which can only be understood with the emergence of sexual feelings of his own.' It is the forgetting of infantile sexuality that makes possible, and makes sense of, adolescent sexuality and therefore of the infantile sexuality that preceded it. Just as, sometimes, a memory can only become a trauma by being remembered; 'a memory,' Freud writes, 'is repressed which has only become a trauma by deferred action'. It is as though experiences are in search of a context to make them meaningful; in fact, to make them into experiences. Something happens that we can call a 'psychic event' which then, in some form or other, is repressed, only later to be called up into meaning. Something has to be forgotten which we then get access to by revision. Remembering, at any given moment, is a process of redescription; the echo can be different each time. The past is in the remaking. Remembering is a prospective project. But it is as though we are continually remaking something that to all intents and purposes never existed; or perhaps because we are making copies without an original – a representable original – all the copies are different?

Meaning is made, according to Freud, in the revision consequent upon deferral. The status, or the state, of what is forgotten is, in his account, indeterminate, so memory is a way of inventing the past. We are compulsive revisionists with an unknowable vision. Freud is very close here to making a nonsense point, though, of course, it is often at the nonsense points that psychoanalysis seems most interesting. He is almost saying here: there's no such thing as forgetting, there's only remembering; or rather, there's no such thing as the forgotten, there's only the remembered. I want to suggest here simply that Freud could not make much of his concept of deferred action because one cannot remember without having forgotten, just as one can only defer something that already exists.

Freud is close here to a picture of psychic life as something that lives in a continual present tense: nothing is forgotten, nothing is deferred, there is just intermittent redescription. In other words, he may have needed the idea of memory and forgetting to keep the past and the future apart. With the idea of deferred action it was as though he sensed the possibility of time collapsing. The concept of deferred action was like a conceptual fetish to protect him from the 'timelessness' he ascribed to the unconscious.

V

The mind is additionally burdened with a compulsion to repeat the past, and a compulsion to get away from the compulsion to repeat the past.

Leonard Shengold, *The Boy Will Come to Nothing*

In Freud's view the individual has to forget because the consequences of remembering are too painful, or too dangerous (or, in the analyst's case, sometimes too obstructive). But the forgetting that is in the service of self-protection can sometimes remake, as a way of refinding, what it has lost. In his essay on Leonardo Freud writes:

When in the prime of life Leonardo once more encountered the smile of bliss and rapture which had once played on his mother's lips as she fondled him, he had for long been under the dominance of an inhibition which forbade him ever again to desire such caresses from the lips of women. But he had become a painter and therefore he strove to reproduce the smile with his brush, giving it to all his pictures.

He had, Freud writes, 'remained true to the content of his earliest memory'. It is as though the past, a particular memory, was pushing Leonardo into the future to look for echoes. Replication is a self-cure for loss. 'Mona Lisa's smile,' Freud writes, 'awoke something in him which had for long lain dormant in his mind – probably an old memory. This memory was of sufficient importance for him never to

35

get free of it when it had once been aroused; he was continually forced to give it new expression.' The very possibility of repetition signifies loss; one only repeats the unrepeatable.

But this initial forgetting under the aegis of the super-ego turns one kind of repetition – frequent caresses from the mother – into the other, displaced kind of repetition called art. Because Leonardo was coerced to forget – for fear of castration by the father – he had to find a substitute called remembering, reproducing the smile, as Freud, or rather his editor and translator James Strachey, put it, 'conjured up on the lips of his female subjects'. For Freud the logic of the Oedipus complex dictates that men must forget what they want (the mother) in order to remember something they can supposedly 'have' (other women). And according to the normative logic of this, women have to forget what they want (the mother) in order to find and be found by the father, whom they also have to forget in order to more successfully desire; they have to twice forget.

Leonardo, like everyone else – though, of course, Leonardo was also not like everyone else (psychoanalytic writing finds it difficult to show that everyone else is not like everyone else) – was in search of those substitutes that create the illusion of unique experience. But in order to find substitutes he had to forget what he had lost, make it absent. Forgetting is a way of describing the remaking involved in substitution (and by the same token, the most dangerous insights, or revelations, are those one cannot forget: they become fetishes rather than objects for use, for forgetting). To make a substitute is to make a difference. Forgetting is the precondition for symbolization. It instigates the work – the dream-work – that goes on behind the scenes. The substitution we call symbolism is a reminder that what we call the past only happened once. And yet there is, of course, something that Freud refers to as repetition – indeed, a repetition compulsion that he increasingly regarded as a prime mover, or rather prime paralyser, of the psyche. But repetition for Freud is what happens when something cannot be remembered. 'Forgetting impressions, scenes or experiences,' he writes in 'Remembering, Repeating and Working Through', 'always reduces itself to shutting them off . . . The patient does not remember anything of what he has forgotten and repressed, but acts it out. He reproduces it not as a memory but as an action; he repeats it without, of course, knowing he is repeating it.' Freud discovered, in other words, that people were suffering not from their memories, but from their forgettings. They were forgetting in the wrong way, in ways that disabled them.

If a trauma is, by definition, that which you cannot experience until you remember, then repetition is evidence of an unwillingness – or, more disturbingly, an inability – to forget. The aim of psychoanalysis was to make emotional experience from the past available for transformation, subject to dream-work; available, that is, for the kind of forgetting that would put it beyond the repetition compulsion. 'In the end,' Freud writes, 'we understand' that the patient's repetition compulsion 'is his way of remembering . . . the patient yields to the compulsion to repeat, which now replaces the impulse to remember.' This formulation brings with it the questions: what kind of actions would we be performing if we were not remembering; what would our lives look like without repetition? In our repetitions we have found a way of remembering something by never knowing what it is; and by not knowing we make it unforgettable. Those who can't, do; those who can, remember (or dream). And, as in the case of the Ratman, this leads Freud to formulate what might be called an exorcist aim for psychoanalysis: 'it is a triumph of the treatment,' he writes with uncharacteristic triumphalism, 'if [the analyst] can bring it about that something that the patient wishes to discharge in action is *disposed of* through the work of remembering' (my italics).

Ideally, one rids oneself of the repetitive past through analysis, but does that make the analyst the accomplice of the Death Instinct, which ultimately disposes of everything and whose aim, Freud writes in *An Outline of Psychoanalysis*, 'is to undo connections and so to destroy things'? If repetition puts memory on hold, the Death Instinct kills it. If the aim of the organism, as Freud says, is to die in its own way, is this because it is remembering how to die – as though there were a 'death-memory', so to speak – or because it is forgetting how to live? The Death Instinct, as I suggested earlier, is Freud's figure for the most sophisticated forms of forgetting, perhaps the kind of forgetting that the analyst is in search of on behalf of the patient. The only way to truly forget the past is to dispose of it, to kill it, and the only way one can do that with any assurance is by dying.

3
On Love

Some people would never have fallen in love if they had never heard of love.

La Rochefoucauld

If sex is the way out of the family, falling in love is the route back, the one-way ticket that is always a return. From a psychoanalytic point of view these miracles of affinity are echoes of our first fascinations. Such states of absorption are memory in its most immediate form, the sense of uniqueness the uncanny sign of the past. What is being recruited, or rather, evoked – what makes these transforming experiences possible – is the knowledge and desire of childhood. When we fall in love we are remembering how to fall in love. And by retrieving these earlier versions of ourselves we achieve a kind of visionary competence.

But if falling in love is always a reminder, for Freud, it is a reminder of an impossibility. 'Childhood love is boundless,' he writes, 'it demands exclusive possession, it is not content with less than all. But it has a second characteristic: it has, in point of fact, no aim and is incapable of obtaining complete satisfaction; and principally for that reason it is doomed to end in disappointment.' We are now bewitched – and terrorized – by this story of insatiability, of infinite lack; it is our modern sublime, parodically appropriated in Jacques Lacan's remark that love is giving something you haven't got to someone who doesn't exist. But Freud's description of the child here is his version of Faust – the hero re-created by Goethe, the 'genius' of Freud's native language – the legendary figure for whom knowledge and desire are synonymous; and for whom their equation, their contract, spells death. But this originally Platonic muddle of the lover and the knower – as though they are comparable pursuits – gives each of them an impossible project. As though each has to do both in order to do either. In this story intimacy is privileged (or enviable) information. The analyst, Lacan says, in his well known formulation, is the one who is supposed to know; not, as he might have said, the one who is supposed to love. It is assumed that knowing is prior to or inclusive of loving. (Later he was to say: 'The one whom I suppose to know, I love.' Which is, of course, different again.) Once loving has been described as wanting, we have to find something to want, and this is where knowledge is supposed to come in. Falling in love is conventionally a madness for some philosophers, psychoanalysts and poets because, among other things, it irredeemably ironizes any distinction between certainty and scepticism.

'Transference', 'repression', 'fetishism', 'narcissism', 'the riddle of femininity' – all these key psychoanalytic concepts confirm the sense that in psychoanalysis love is a problem of knowledge. That lovers are like detectives: they are trying to find something out that will make all the difference. And the stories that psychoanalysis tells about love tend to confirm a traditional progress narrative about the acquisition of wisdom (wisdom, of course, is always counter-erotic). Lovers begin as prolifically inventive, producing enthralling illusions about each other (recycled from the past), only to be disappointed into truth. The madness of love is a journey from anti- (or dis-)foundationalism on to the rocks of conviction, so to speak. Psychoanalysis, in other words, endorses the view that falling in love is not a good way of getting to know someone (as opposed, say, to thinking of it as simply another way, not invalidated by subsequent events). Psychoanalysis offers us instead the romance of disillusionment in which falling in love is the (sometimes necessary) prelude to a better but diminished – better because diminished – thing; a more realistic appreciation of oneself and the other person (to which the rejoinder of the aesthete can be: If this is 'real', then let's make something else). In this sobering story, the fluency of 'idealization' – usually a pejorative, and always a cover story in psychoanalysis – is replaced by the haltings of ambivalence. After all the excitement, there are the revelations of dismay. Frustration is the aura of the real. But it may be that in this twilight home of disappointment, which psychoanalysis promotes, people are not suffering from their knowledge, but from losing a more ruthless capacity for self and/or other reinvention. It is not truth that they have gained but their versionality, so to speak, that they have lost.

Freud and Proust are alert in complementary ways to the senses in which knowing people – or certain kinds of knowledge about people – can be counter-erotic; that the unconscious intention of certain forms of familiarity is to kill desire. It is not simply that elusiveness, or jealousy, sustains desire, but that certain ways of knowing people diminish their interest for us; and that this may be their abiding wish. So we have to watch out for the ways people invite us – or allow us – to know them; and also alert ourselves to the possibility that knowing may be too tendentious, too canny, a model for loving.

Lovers, of course, are notoriously frantic epistemologists, second only to paranoiacs (and analysts) as readers of signs and wonders. But what would falling in love look like if knowledge of oneself or another, of oneself as another, was not the aim or the result? What would we be doing together if we were not getting to know each other? Another way of saying this might be to imagine a meeting or a relationship without (answerable) questions.

It seems as though the loved, or the desired, is that which it is impossible for us not to be interested in. But because our languages of love are versions of theology and epistemology, they are relentlessly redemptive and enlightening. 'How do I know if I know someone?' is a very different question from 'How do I know if I love or desire someone?' Some people would never have known if they had never heard of knowing.

4

On Success

A lecture to student counsellors

I

Don't wish too hard, or you'll get what you want.
Jewish proverb

John Stuart Mill's extraordinary education has become a kind of fable of pedagogic ambition, and of the way in which parental demand can structure a child's life. Taught exclusively by his father, and having no contact with other children apart from his own siblings whom he had to teach, Mill started learning Greek when he was three, and Latin when he was eight. Between the ages of eight and twelve he learned 'elementary geometry and algebra thoroughly, the differential calculus and other portions of the higher mathematics'. As well as reading at this time a good deal of the most important classical literature, what he refers to as his 'private' reading was mostly history, which he also wrote (in the form of a history of Roman government).

At twelve he began learning logic – Aristotle and Hobbes – and when he was thirteen his father gave him what he calls 'a complete course in political economy'. His father, Mill wrote in his *Autobiography*, 'exerted an amount of labour, care and perseverance rarely, if ever, employed for a similar purpose, in endeavouring to give, according to his own conception, the highest order of intellectual education'. 'If I have accomplished anything,' Mill concludes without obvious misgivings, 'I owe it, among other fortunate circumstances, to the fact that through the early training bestowed on me by my father, I started, I may fairly say, with an advantage of a quarter of a century over my contemporaries.' That is to say, by the age of fifteen he had the learning of a man in his late thirties; 'the experiment was,' as Isaiah Berlin has written, 'in a sense, an appalling success'.

One's history, of course, never begins with oneself; everyone's life, in a sense, is the afterthought of unknowable previous generations. James Mill, J. S. Mill's father, acquired a formal education only because he came to the notice of what, in this context, we could call a substitute father, a patron, Sir John Stuart, who sent him to the University of Edinburgh. Mill records in his *Autobiography* that his father was 'the son of a petty tradesman and (I believe) small farmer'. (For us, of course, in this transgenerational story, the absence of significant mothers is striking.) The implication of Mill's brief account of his grandfather as a petty tradesman is that the family history is a kind of progress narrative, a success story of sorts.

And yet the ultimate success of the story seems to have depended on its breaking down: at the age of twenty Mill suffered a catastrophic disillusionment. And again it involved fathers not being good enough to get their sons where they wanted to go. But like all disillusionments, it was made from a history of illusionments; an implicit belief in belief itself. Well prepared by his father's educational project, in 1822 at the age of sixteen Mill read Dumont's *Traité de Législation* – a French translation of the work of his father's good friend Jeremy Bentham. 'The reading of this book,' Mill writes in his *Autobiography*, 'was an epoch in my life; one of the turning points in my mental history.' Reading this book, and Bentham himself, gave Mill – as what we call an adolescent – 'what might truly be called an object in life: to be a reformer of the world. My conception of my own happiness was entirely identified with this object . . . my whole reliance was placed on this.' From an accumulation of fathers living and dead (all the books he records reading are, of course, by men) he had acquired a project: to reform the world according to Bentham's Utilitarian principle of the greatest happiness for the greatest number.

Like all ideals, Mill's gave him that most paradoxical thing, a picture of the future. It was, as he says, his object in life; the least flirtatious of men, he was entirely identified with it and placed his 'whole reliance' on it. And all of these, of course, would be ways in which a psychoanalyst might describe a child's relation to a parent; then in adolescence, to put it at its most reductive, parents are replaced by ideals, and sexual desire is partly usurped by moral principle and ambition. Indeed, Mill describes his new-found 'object in life' in ways that are particularly revealing from a psychoanalytic point of view. He was made happy in this project, he writes, 'through placing my happiness in something durable and distant, in which some progress might be always making, while it could never be exhausted by complete attainment'. As with belief in a god, the durability of this object depends upon its distance. Just as we only identify with what we don't understand, authority – of a person or an ideal – is constituted by unfamiliarity. The paradox that Mill presents us with – and that may be integral to fantasies of success (the attainment of ideals) – is that fantasies are reliable *because* they cannot be achieved; that both the person and his or her ideal may fear being 'exhausted by complete attainment'. That success entails a fear of success; that something will be depleted by its realization. It is as though we need to know the end of the story, but have to ensure that we don't experience it. Mill's description of placing his happiness in 'something durable and distant' suggests the way in which those beliefs we call our ideals, our fantasies of success, are hypnotic like the horizon. And there is an implicit idea of the self here as something that needs a strong belief, a commitment, to organize it and hold it together. But our success stories, in which our problems are solved and our desires gratified, may be forms of self-hypnosis. In other words, the risk – as in psychotherapy or counselling itself – is that we use our solutions as ways of pre-empting experience of the problem (listening for the answer is not listening). If I eat every time I feel hungry I may never find out what my hunger is (for). For several years Mill could successfully devote himself to his project because, as he puts it, it 'seemed enough to fill up an interesting and animated existence'. And then, as I have said, in his twentieth year he suffered a disillusionment, a breakdown, which he describes as the breaking of a spell, an awakening:

[T]he time came when I awakened from this as from a dream. It was in the autumn of 1826. I was in a dull state of nerves, such as everybody is occasionally liable to; unsusceptible to enjoyment or pleasurable excitement; one of those moods when what is pleasure at other times becomes insipid or indifferent; the state, I should think, in which converts to Methodism usually are, when smitten by their first 'conviction of sin'. In this frame of mind it occurred to me to put the question directly to myself, 'Suppose that all your objects in life were realised; that all the changes in institutions and opinions which you are looking forward to, could be completely effected at this very instant; would this be a great joy and happiness to you?' And an irrepressible self-consciousness distinctly answered, 'No'. At this my heart sank within me; the whole foundation on which my life was constructed fell down. All my happiness was to have been found in the continual pursuit of this end. The end had ceased to charm, and how could there ever again be any interest in the means? I seemed to have nothing left to live for.

It is easy to see this as, so to speak, a traditional Oedipal crisis; Mill compares it to a Methodist's first conviction of sin against God; later in his account he reminds himself of Macbeth who, of course, killed a king. And he begins to recover from this crisis – 'a small ray of light broke in upon my gloom' – when he starts reading Marmontel's *Memoirs* and 'came to the passage which relates his father's death, the distressed position of the family, and the sudden inspiration by which he, then a mere boy, felt and made them feel that he would be everything to them – would supply the place of all that they had lost'. After reading this account of a son replacing a father, Mill describes himself as literally coming back to life: 'from this moment my burthen grew lighter. The oppression of the thought that all feeling was dead within me, was gone. I was no longer hopeless; I was not a stick or a stone.'

Clearly, one cannot psychoanalyse a writer from his text; one can only appropriate him. But it is nevertheless plausible, despite the fact that Mill does not say it, that his crisis, among other things, was a protest against the life his father had organized for him; an attempt to renegotiate it. The question Mill puts directly to himself – if all his ambitions in life were realized, would he be happy? – was a question he dared not ask of his father; his breakdown – like most breakdowns, given a sufficiently attentive environment – was also a breakthrough. And one of the many things that tend to break through in such crises are repressed questions addressed to the parents, or to the parents internalized as parts of oneself. In psychoanalytic language one can say that the children carry, often in the form of symptoms, the parents' repressed doubts about their own ideals and ambitions; this is one of the things Freud meant when he suggested that 'a child's super-ego is in fact constructed on the model not of its parents but of its parents' super-ego'. Just as every internal prohibition represents an ambition – a moral aim for the ego – so every symptom is a transgenerational task. A crisis is always also on behalf of someone else, even if that someone else is part of oneself. It is as though the generations – each subject contingently to different economic, political and historical con- ditions – are processing each other's ambitions. And university is, of course, for some people essentially a crisis of ambition.

John Stuart Mill's crisis was prompted, finally, by a simple imaginative act: he fast-forwarded his life and looked back at it from the position of having achieved his ambitions; he imagined that he had already become his own ideal. Having lived by the lure of an endlessly deferred future – having organized his life around the demand of a specific ambition – he made the wished-for future present and killed his aspiring self. And once, in his mind, this future had already happened, the foundation of his life was destroyed. Mill, that is to say, here does consciously what Freud says we do each night unconsciously, in our dreams: he imaginat- ively fulfils a wish (in psychoanalytic terms dreams are our para- digm for success). And at this point, as though it were a conscious nightmare, he awakens to his own despair; he has nothing left to live for; he has become inanimate, like a stone.

Now that he has realized that success would be a form of failure for him, what has Mill woken up to? It would be reassuring to say that he has simply rediscovered a piece of traditional wisdom: that it is better to travel hopefully than to arrive. But actually he has discovered something that seems now more psychoanalytic, and pertinent to our present subject: that sometimes, with some ambitions, you can *only* travel hopefully if you ensure you never arrive (hope is only ever false in retrospect). That in order to hope – or, as Freud would say, wish – you need an object; and these objects, these ideals that encode our fantasies of success, though they derive from past experiences, are set in the future. They are aims, targets for desire; they have to be separate from us – they have to keep their distance – in order to make a journey of it. (No one says, as perhaps they should, 'I'm aiming to be what I am already.') Ambitions, in other words, are ways of locating – or rather, ways of describing – possible futures and possible future selves. Without belief in the future, the idea of success would disappear.

So to have ambitions – and therefore fantasies (conscious and unconscious) of what it would be to succeed or fail – one needs, firstly, an object of desire, an ideal, a state of the world or of oneself sufficiently separate from oneself to aspire to. So one needs to have perceived a lack, of sorts, in oneself. Secondly, one needs a belief in Time as a promising medium to do things in; one needs to be able to suffer the pains and pleasures of anticipation and deferral. And thirdly, as Mill's example shows, one needs a tolerable relationship to satisfaction; and this involves something that Freud uniquely problematized: belief in the accuracy, the possibility, of one's desire. For Freud, as we will see, knowing what one wants can be a contradiction in terms; and this means that success and failure often double for each other.

The need for a separate object, the commitment to waiting in Time, and the relationship to satisfaction – all these ingredients of success (and failure) reveal our ambitions, from a psychoanalytic point of view, as versions of our erotic life, in which satisfaction is always conflictual. Ambitions can be described as wishes, and therefore derivatives of instinctual life. To talk about one's ambitions is to find a respectable way, an unembarrassing way, of talking about what one wants (which is not always respectable). Ambitions are more or less culturally legitimated desires. Nothing is less disreputable than the wish to get to university – or the wish for academic success. But these wishes may be ways of encoding, or disguising, more problematic desires – like, for example, the wish to consolidate, or deconstruct, a precarious sexual identity cobbled together in adolescence. So it is to the *use* of ideals, and to the relationship to satisfaction, to success – the material of any therapeutic encounter – that I want to turn now.

II

fear a too great consistency
A. R. Ammons, 'One: Many'

One of the papers in a series, 'Some Character Types Met With in Psychoanalytic Work', that Freud wrote in 1916 is entitled 'Those Wrecked by Success'. In it he uses the examples of Macbeth and Ibsen's Rosmersholm to explain something that defies common sense: that people can fall ill 'upon the fulfilment of a wish and put an end to all enjoyment of it'; that 'people occasionally fall ill precisely when a deeply rooted and long cherished wish has come to fulfilment'. It is not that they discover that they didn't really want what they have now succeeded in getting, but rather that having got it they now need to punish themselves with the suffering of an illness. There is, Freud intimates, nothing like success to show us that we are not quite who we think we are. In his view it is not that the wish is necessarily wrong, nor the object chosen for its gratification; but rather that, from a psychoanalytic point of view, we are always doing at least two if not three (or more) things at once.

In order to make sense of the experience that wanting is always conflictual – that people can be wrecked by success – Freud suggests that we imagine our lives as a story in which three parts of ourselves are always involved; that in doing any one thing we have at least three projects: we are satisfying a desire, we are sustaining a sense of moral well-being, and we are ensuring our survival. In this useful fiction the id is productive of desire, the super-ego is the carrier of our ethical ideals, and the ego tries to make these often conflicting demands compatible with keeping going. 'Analytic work,' Freud writes, with blithe self-confidence, 'has no difficulty in showing us that it is forces of conscience which forbid the subject to gain the long hoped for advantage from the fortunate change in reality.' The super-ego is an essentialist, and always has a fixed view of the ego; like all fixed views, it can only ultimately be sustained by intimidation. Having changed reality in pursuit of success, we realize that we are at cross-purposes with ourselves. 'For a neurosis to be generated,' Freud writes, 'there must be a conflict between a person's libidinal wishes, and the part of his personality we call the ego.' And since there is always a conflict, ambition spells self-division. Success can make people feel guilty; but guilt is also something one can hide in (from oneself).

It is easy to forget that an ambition begins as a wish, and that a wish has a history. Wanting something (like academic success) or someone connects us with the past. My success – the fulfilment of a wish – is always an echo of previous encounters with my own desire. My ambition, so to speak, as a baby to be warm and sufficiently nurtured can be linked with my ambition to get a good degree. Satisfactions can be described as both repeating and modifying earlier satisfactions: pleasures are echoes. From a psychoanalytic point of view, we are always talking of a person's relationship to his or her own wishes, a relationship that has evolved over time. Frustration and satisfaction become synonymous with, or rather precursors of, our ideas of failure and success: the child is very much alive in the young aspiring adult. 'People fall ill of a neurosis,' Freud writes, 'as a result of frustration.' The picture becomes complicated, as I have said, when frustration for one part of the self, say, the super-ego, is satisfaction for another part, the id. In this picture one kind of success can be another kind of failure. In psychotherapy one always has to remember that anyone who is failing at one thing is always succeeding at another. The therapist, or counsellor, is useful as someone who can show the patient the paradoxical nature of his acts. If I fail as a student to have a girlfriend, I succeed at keeping myself as someone who loves only in the family. If I fail my exams I successfully maintain myself as someone who is not ready for the next stage. If I can't write my essay, I can show myself to be capable of refusing a demand by a figure of authority. In this context the aim of the therapy is not so much to help people make more competent choices as to show them how many choices they are (unconsciously) making.

So if we are to think of success from a psychodynamic point of view, we have to bear in mind three things which are inevitably connected. Firstly, it can be useful to think of ourselves as multiple personalities; of our internal worlds as more like a novel than a monologue. Each character, or part of ourselves, has different projects, and different criteria of success; so some people, for example, live as though they would prefer to be morally right than sexually satisfied, or clever rather than ordinary. In these cases it is as though an internal democracy has become a meritocracy; certain internal voices become muted because a repertoire of ways of being has been turned into a set of alternatives (in actuality, one can be clever *and* ordinary). Conflict requires the forging of incompatibles. The second point that follows from this is that because our different selves have different projects, success and failure are inextricable; success for one self can feel like failure for another, and vice versa. We are always doing at least two things at once, and this can mean that the art of psychotherapy is turning what feel like contradictions – incompatibilities – into paradoxes. This does not entail ironing out the conflicts, but rather extending the repertoire of ways of describing them.

So a useful interpretation in this context might be something like: up until now you have been getting your sexual satisfaction by being morally right; there may be other ways of doing both things. Or, if you could be clever *and* ordinary, what would your life look like? These forms of redescription are revisions of the past. And this leads me to the third point, which is that these internal selves and their relationship have a history; that we have grown up in particular families in particular cultures, in sexed and gendered bodies, and subject, of course, to the multiple contingencies – economic, political, psychological – of any life. A person's fantasies of success are only the most recent versions of an elaborate personal history of such fantasies. If our earliest success is our own survival – our development into people who can have fantasies of success – we acquire, in the language of our mother tongue, the ideals of our culture. Fantasies of success are both given to us – our inheritance but not our invention – and, much like our gender identities, from which they are inextricable, constructed. And this leaves us, I think, with two questions pertinent to therapy. How do we make ideals for ourselves, those success stories that we try to live by? And secondly – and in some ways more problematic – how do we make them our own? How do we get to feel that to some extent we have chosen them – that they formulate what matters most to us – rather than had them imposed upon us? Ideals should feel like affinities, not impositions. It is striking how tyrannical – hypnotic and intransigent – people's ideals can be. And this is particularly vivid, I think, during adolescence and young adulthood.

Clearly, these issues reach a kind of crisis around the initiation rite of going to university, and leaving it. And what I am talking about, any adolescent – and any adult old enough to go on being an adolescent – will recognize. It is the difference between doing something that I believe is right and doing something because if I don't I will be punished. It is the difference between doing what I want – what makes me feel alive and can fill me with anticipation – and doing what other people want me to want. University, in other words, can be a crisis for the compliant self; and, of course, a crisis for the compliant self of the student counsellor or therapist who has to deal with such crises. Is the student counsellor to comply with the demands of the university institution and get the student back to productive work as soon as possible? Or comply with the student, understanding his or her symptom as an intelligent critique of the university? And what does the counsellor do when it feels like this kind of choice? The counsellor, like the student, has to answer a fundamental question: who am I working for? Success for the counselling treatment can mean failure for the university. The successful student counsellor may have to be a double agent, and is always a kind of spy.

III

For the moment I want merely to underline the words the actual disorder of experience.

William Arrowsmith, 'Turbulence in the Humanities'

It has become a conventional formulation, in the jargon of psycho-analytic theory, that people suffer when the disparity between their ego and their ego-ideal becomes excessive; that is to say, suffering turns up when there is too great a distance – too big a gap – between who a person feels himslf to be and who he wants to be. When my ideal or preferred versions of myself begin to seem remote – or exclusively embodied by other people – so-called symptoms can be both a way of registering the distress and an attempt to mobilize resources. In fact, one could say that people come for any kind of psychotherapy or counselling because there is a problem in their relationship to success; because someone is letting someone else down, and that someone else can be a part of the self. Psychother-apy is about refinding the future.

Because we have come to think of ourselves as creatures who *aspire* – whether it be to survival or something grander – it is difficult to imagine (or describe) our lives without conscious and uncons-cious ideals. So I would like to try and work out why it is so difficult to imagine a (non-cynical) life without ideals, those objects we use to feel successful with (is a life without ambition a life without a future, or a life without a particular kind of future?). If, for example, my ambition in life is to see what happens to me, what kind of future am I imagining for myself? In this context we have to remember that the only contact we have with the future, so to speak, is in the form of wishes. But firstly, I want to look at the question of success – the conflict of ambition – from a developmental perspective.

Developmental theories offer us a repertoire of what can be called success stories – and success-anxieties. Developmental theories are the success stories against which we fail. Indeed, the idea of development itself – with its language of 'stages' and 'achievements' and 'fixation-points' – involves the idea of progress, of an ambition for something. And when we are faced with this barrage of theories of developmental competence, it can be easy to forget that the so-called patient or student might have quite different theories of his or her own of what a good life is; everyone has, and is, his or her own developmental theory. There is, of course, no rule that people have to grow up; there are just consequences to not doing so (and each person has a different sense of what this entails). It may, for example, be rather misleading to think that the child's *ambition* is to become an adult. Freud himself suggested that it was the child's ambition to become like the grown-ups; he didn't mention the fact that this also seems to be the grown-ups' wish.

Since every crisis about success, from a psychoanalytic point of view, has developmental antecedents, is full of reminders, it may be worth describing a repertoire of developmental puzzles. I want to suggest that these puzzles can be organized around a fundamental dilemma, that easily becomes (or perhaps is) a muddle; that after the earliest stages of infancy – the pre-linguistic stages – there is a fundamental ongoing internal relationship between desire and self-sufficiency. Development, one could say, is the continual process of working out what one cannot provide for oneself; and then one's relationship to such acknowledgements. There is a project of self-sufficiency and a project of wanting (these, of course, are conscious and unconscious fantasies); and in so far as these projects are felt to be incompatible, a person has an insoluble dilemma. If I am eager to learn something, but reading books about it exposes my lack of knowledge, the more I learn the less I seem to know. The books might seem like a mother who already seems to have everything I want. Since dependency, or the ways we have so far described it, seems such a pervasive conflict – no one ever says, for example, 'He's very good at being dependent on her' – at any transitional stage spurious alternatives are likely to turn up. Is success satisfying one's desire or escaping from it? Why, if I said I had an ambition to become more dependent, would I, at least in this culture, be politically and psychologically disparaged?

We can think of success, at any developmental stage, as being related to issues of self-sufficiency; and of wanting, of independence and dependence as the extremes on some imaginary spectrum. 'Success,' one of my adolescent patients said to me, 'is having everything you want.' I said, 'What will you want then?' and he said, 'Nothing.' Then there was a pause as he thought. After a few minutes he said, as though brightening up, 'After I've got everything I'll have to find someone else to give me some new ideas!' If we are living, at least in fantasy, between the extremes of having (or being) everything and the idea of there being something else, what are the available forms of success from a developmental point of view? Nearly all kinds of learning involve acknowledging what one does not yet know, and depending on a source outside oneself to acquire that knowledge. Successful learning is successful, or tolerable, dependence.

The psychoanalytic distinction between two-person and three-person relationships – between the pre-Oedipal and the Oedipal – can be useful here, because each brings with it different kinds of success and failure, different compromises and conflicts, different versions of dependence. Whether or not we believe in their chronology, they are ways of adding to our repertoire of kinds of relationship. From a psychoanalytic point of view these early relationships are the circumstances in which we begin to construct our ideals and depend on them, to formulate our wishes and watch them in action. So I want to build up a picture of what it would be, in psychodynamic terms, to be a pre-Oedipal and an Oedipal success, and consider how this can be linked to the conflicts and confusions of student life.

What are the ambitions of the infant and child, and what does it mean for them to fail? These pre-Oedipal and Oedipal issues can be usefully over-simplified by talking about envy and rivalry. We can say, for example, if we believe in these kinds of psychoanalytic story, that reading a book is a later version of feeding from a mother, a kind of visual eating. Or at least we can usefully describe the problems of reading in terms of this pre-Oedipal two-person mother–child relationship. A successful feed depends upon a number of factors: firstly, the coming together of the child's actual hunger with a mother ready and willing to feed. By the same token, perhaps, we can only really read – that is, take it all in and digest it – if we are really interested. Otherwise, we read with growing resentment; that is, with a compliant version of ourselves. The reading gets done, but not by us. So a student might come to a counsellor to recover, or rediscover, his appetite; to understand the obstacles to taking things in, and to work out what he or she is hungry for.

If there is real appetite, or curiosity, around, then quite quickly for the child there is the dawning awareness that these wants depend upon an external object for both recognition and satisfaction; and that this external object – the mother, father or a substitute parent – is both beyond the control of the child and seems, especially at times of acutest need, to have or be everything the child wants. So there is the shock of dependence and the disillusionment of not ruling the world. It is easy, in other words, for the child to envy the mother; and this envy – the spoiling of what is felt to belong to oneself – can get in the way. Indeed, the need for the mother might feel, or be made to feel, so unbearable that the need itself has to be destroyed. If somebody you are longing to see makes you wait too long for them, it is extremely difficult to appreciate them when they finally arrive; and to recuperate your desire for them.

All this infantile eating and envying might seem a long way from the student at university who finds himself or herself unable to study. And yet the one who knows, or seems to know – the teacher – might be experienced like a mother, or a father, as an object of envy. The frenzy of need – of felt inadequacy – baffles the learning experience. Or the student, aware somewhere in himself of his own envy, may, by the same token, be very fearful of becoming a successful student through fear of the envy of others. People can go to remarkable lengths to avert the catastrophe of their own success; or to ensure that they are not seen, even by themselves, to be, or to be trying to be, successful. It is certainly useful in the psychotherapy of adolescents to help them find ways of managing other people's envy of them as well as their own. If a book or a teacher can be experienced as being like a mother – and so has echoes of an earlier relationship – then in psychotherapy or counselling we are trying to understand the obstacles in the relationship. The exchange – the taking in and the being taken in by – is in some way being sabotaged.

A first-year undergraduate I saw for psychotherapy, who had developed an anxiety about remembering during her A levels, came to see me because she had become phobic about going into the university library. Going into the library, she said, was 'too much for her' and she felt faint. I said, 'Too much of what?' She said she 'couldn't take it all in'. I suggested that she had a belief that she had to take it *all* in. She then became huffy with me; it was a bit like a rather pious mother telling her delinquent child to be conscientious. I described what I thought was happening between us and asked her – she was a literature student – if she knew Oscar Wilde's remark, 'If a thing's worth doing, it's worth doing badly'? She was amused by this but then asked me, having recovered herself, what that had to do with anything. I suggested to her that going into the library felt like someone placing a huge meal in front of her and telling her that she had to finish her plateful; and that her faintness was a rage about this. And she replied, 'Perhaps I should blow up the library.' In this situation a person might feel that they have either to blow up the library, or blow up the need for the library. This student told me that when she found herself enjoying a book she would start on a fault-finding mission because 'the book was too good'. As with the library, it was as if her primary task was managing her greed. In a sense, she wanted it so much she couldn't take it in. She said to me at one point, as a joke: 'I really envy the library, it knows everything already.'

If there is envy *of* the desired object in the earliest relationship, there is rivalry *for* the desired object in the later three-person relationship. The child realizes, in other words, not only that the mother seems to have what he or she needs, but that there are rivals in competition for her – the father and perhaps other siblings. From a psychodynamic point of view, acquiring, in whatever sense, the object of desire becomes the precursor for – the original picture of – success. Rivalry means competition, and competition brings with it winners and losers, and we have all had the experience of being both. Everybody knows what it feels like to be left out, and the first people who can leave us out – in fact, can't help but leave us out – are our parents. They do things together that exclude us and the ways we find of managing this formative experience have important repercussions. It may, for example, feel safer to be left out than to do the damage necessary to get in. And every student who gets to university has, somewhere, to cope with his or her triumph over all those who did not, or who never had the opportunity even to compete.

If the successful pre-Oedipal infant can enjoy, or at least tolerate, the intensity of his appetite, the successful Oedipal child has to enjoy, or at least tolerate, his or her triumphs. To put it another way: he or she has to learn to share without sacrificing his or her passion. For the Oedipal child – or for that part of ourselves – success always means (unconsciously) someone else's failure; and this can feel intolerable, or worthy of punishment. Failure can sometimes feel like the only appropriate punishment for success.

A twenty-two-year-old patient – a graduate student – told me that she had bought a suit she really liked to go to the first seminar of the term. She felt very attractive in it and when she got there two of her female friends commented on how nice she looked. But instead of this confirming her sense of herself she suddenly became very 'jittery and self-conscious'. I suggested that she had heard this as though they had said to her, 'You look more attractive than us.' She replied that, unusually for her, she had made herself 'invisible' in the seminar. The conversation then rambled, as it does, until eventually, as part of an apparently inconsequential story, she described a memory of her mother and brother sitting on a sofa together at home and her feeling 'like a television set that no one wanted to turn on'. I wondered if it felt too dangerous to be turned on, to be so special that everyone would look at her? She said, 'If they all look at me, who'll look after me?' It was as though, for her, successful competition could feel like abandonment. Or that in order to be looked after she had to keep herself left out.

Envy and rivalry as essential ingredients of our failures and successes come from a picture of ourselves as acquisitive creatures driven by animal appetites and moral greeds. And this is a picture that psychoanalysis – and all the therapies derived from it – both endorses and partly created. Of any theory one can usefully ask; what is the drama that the theory is a caption for. Theories, that is to say, are interpretations of dreams. But I want to suggest, by way of conclusion, that it may be too limiting to think of ourselves and our clients with only this picture in mind. It is particularly difficult to entertain alternatives in a culture so bewitched both by the idea of success and by such a limited definition of what it entails. Because the idea of the enviable life has now replaced the idea of the good life, it may be difficult to hear, or to listen to, the parts of our patients or students that are not interested in success. There are, as we know, people around for whom being successful has not been a success. But there may also be people around – and I would guess there are a lot of them at universities – for whom success itself is a distraction, but for whom there is no language available to describe a good life free of success. We police ourselves with purposes. Our ambitions – our ideals and success stories that lure us into the future – can too easily become ways of not living in the present, or of not being present at the event, a blackmail of distraction; ways, that is, of disowning, or demeaning, the actual disorder of experience. Believing in the future can be a great deadener. Perhaps we have been too successful at success and failure, and should now start doing something else.

5
Besides Good and Evil

It gets more and more simplistic:
Good and Bad, evil and bad; what else do we know?
Flavours that keep us from caring too long.
John Ashbery, 'Posture of Unease'

Only someone entranced by the possibilities of his own goodness could now find a use for the notion of evil. It is a word, we assume, that the 'patient' is more likely to use than the analyst. And yet evil is still integral to the vocabulary of anthropology, of politics, of theology – even perhaps of literature – while psychoanalysis is distinguished, ironically, as the art of the unacceptable that is phobic about the word. If, as Freud concluded in his review of *The Mysteries of Sleep*, 'unconscious mental activity deserves to be called "daemonic" but scarcely divine', then where in psychoanalysis can we find this forbidden signifier? The word that so recently organized our moral vocabulary seems suddenly to have vanished.

In the compulsive banality of binary oppositions it is, after all, only a Bad object that Melanie Klein opposes to her Good object, not an Evil one. Freud does not refer to the Death Instinct as a force of evil (though he does, in 'The Uncanny', link the Evil Eye with envy). Even the perverse core of the personality outlined in *Three Essays on the Theory of Sexuality* is exempt from such a description. Despite the horror of the history that is contemporaneous with his invention of psychoanalysis, evil is simply not a word Freud is given to using. But it was, of course, essential to his post-Enlightenment project to find a way of talking about the unacceptable without allying it to the supernatural.

And it was also part of Freud's disingenuous rationalism to disclaim any ethical preoccupations. Writing to Oskar Pfister in

1918, he states quite clearly, in a famous passage: 'ethics are remote from me . . . I do not break my head very much about good and evil, but I have found little that is "good" about human beings on the whole. In my experience most of them are trash, no matter whether they publicly subscribe to this or that ethical doctrine or none at all.' For Freud this is uncharacteristically extreme. It is one thing though to say that there is little that is good about people, and even that they are 'trash', but quite another to say that they are evil. Freud, as we know, was not drawn to these particular grand absolutes but to the astonishing resourcefulness, however immoral, of the human subject's capacity for compromise amidst enduring conflict – compromise, which includes, as the *Oxford English Dictionary* tells us, the sense of 'a putting in peril, exposure to risk or suspicion'.

In the clinical situation we think of the conventional abstractions, the moral pieties in the 'patient's' discourse, as a defensive refusal of imaginative – that is to say, passionate – elaboration. A defence is always a concession to the banal; repetition or cliché – lack of invention – can be an envious attack on the language. The use of words like 'good', 'bad', 'happy' and so on function in the analytic setting as an invitation to the analyst. They bring with them, apparently, no risk or suspicion of exposure. In the attempt to simulate a consensus – an always collusive denial of difference – the bland becomes a version of the enigmatic. 'Evil', however, is still not a bland term (there is, of course, no comparable intensifier of the good); it signifies now either a kitsch excitement or a most disturbing conviction about the self. But what would lead a person now to ascribe the word 'evil' to his self-experience? Or in what context could an analyst find himself, however casually, using such a word?

When Winnicott, for example, writes of a patient that 'fantasying possesses her like an evil spirit', we know that, for him, evil might be that which sabotages the developmental process; fantasying, in Winnicott's personal idiom, is an attempted self-cure through daydream that signifies a breakdown of the holding environment; a breakdown in which a person feels the need to insulate herself, in a fantasy, from exchange. But it is only because the developmental process functions as an acknowledged good that evil can find a place. In Freud, of course, there is no developmental process as such, and so there is no explicit definition of what constitutes a proper life. Unconscious desire is that which at every turn disrupts – or rather, disfigures – any story of the predictable life (it is this which makes interpretation in psychoanalysis tentative and provisional). Developmental theory, by trying to pre-empt the issue – the issue of the unconscious – does that most ludicrous but reassuring thing: it provides a map for a country that is, as it were, making itself up as it goes along, but always disappearing from view. It is the developmental theory of object-relations, however, that can accommodate the concept of evil. It was once, after all, familiar territory.

In fact, in Winnicott's work, it could be argued, psychoanalysis was incorporated into a Christian empiricist tradition. Indeed, the unconscious complicity of object-relations with Christianity has never been sufficiently remarked upon. In two contemporary case-histories, for example – Masud Khan's 'The Evil Hand' and Frances Tustin's 'The Rhythm of Safety', both concerned with evil (Khan with dismay, Tustin without apparent misgivings) – we see both writers, as they reframe the word, being led to similar conclusions. A sense of evil was something that two quite different kinds of patient were left with after, or reactive to, a catastrophic disillusionment; a breakdown of reciprocity that was in excess of the person's developmental needs. Evil, in a sense, was soluble in the good-enough mothering of analytic treatment. In these extraordinary, redemptive case-histories we find perversion (in Khan's paper) and a degree of autism (in Tustin's) constituted by – that is to say, as personal solutions to – failures of holding. They are consequences of relationship, not original states of being, as they might be in Freud. Psychoanalysis becomes a new theology of mothering; and the treatment, in this context, is the reconstruction of an absent provision.

Paradise Lost, we may remember, one of Freud's favourite poems, is a story of contested disillusionment; and symptomatology is always the questioning – the refusal – of a disillusionment. But in *Paradise Lost*, the disillusionment was with the Father.

II

. . . it is evident that the phrase, original sin, is a pleonasm . . .
S. T. Coleridge, *Aids to Reflection*

Disillusionment is always premature. (And if a person believes that he has lost something, then he must have had a prior fantasy of ownership.) It is the mother's 'job', as Winnicott would say, to make it tolerable, to present the world in manageable doses to the infant and child. But it is at the Stage of Concern (which Winnicott derives from Klein's Depressive Position) that the infant inherits, it is assumed, the distinction between good and evil. Ignoring the question of language – believing, that is, that bodily 'experience' is merely translated into language and not constituted by it – and making pre-Oedipal reparation to the mother the pivot of development, Klein simply mapped back on to infancy Kant's profoundly anti-Freudian categorical imperative of the moral life. Development depended, she stipulated, on the infant coming to recognize – suffering the recognition – that the mother was, in that most baffling, that most morally stupefying phrase, an end in herself, and not merely a means to an end. Or rather, by becoming an end in herself, one might say, she becomes the proper, the acceptable, means to the infant's development. This then sets the seal, provides the all too familiar, all too human, moral paradigm for adult sexual relations.

There is, it is suggested, a simple sequence of events (though it is an old story) at a certain stage of development a feeling of guilt or concern begins to appear after the wholehearted instinctual experience of a feed. But once the reparative gesture – a smile, a gift – has been successfully acknowledged by the mother, Winnicott writes, 'The breast (body, mother) is now mended, and the day's work is done. Tomorrow's instincts can be awaited with limited fear. Sufficient unto the day is the evil thereof.' Though in one sense a representative statement – one Freud could not have made – it includes a revealing allusion. On the one hand Winnicott is making, albeit in explicitly Christian terms, the conventional object-relations point. Desire is eventually experienced by the infant as 'bad' (because felt to be damaging to the loved object) until the mother, by allowing the restitutive gesture, confers acceptability on it. But on the other hand the biblical allusion, returned to its context, brings with it, ironically, the conventional Christian idea that need, or desire itself, is evil because it signifies a lack of faith in God, or even a doubt about his existence. It represents, in short, a confusion of priorities:

Therefore take no thought, saying, What shall we eat? or, What shall we drink? or Wherewithal shall we be clothed? (For after all these things do the Gentiles seek:) for your heavenly Father knoweth that ye have need of all these things. But seek ye first the Kingdom of God, and his righteousness; and all these things shall be added unto you. Take therefore no thought for the morrow: for the morrow shall take thought for the things of itself. Sufficient unto the day is the evil thereof. (Matthew 6:31–4)

These are certainly questions that might concern the child; the answers, one imagines, a child would find less satisfying. Where Winnicott puts the mother at the centre, here we find the mother ablated and the deified father put in her place. And here it is not a question of reparation but of disowning desire. Winnicott's casual quotation is a shard from which we could construct some of the contradictions in the buried history of British psychoanalysis. One thing, however, is clear: in object-relations theory, 'evil', though rarely used, is a viable term, whereas in Freud's writing it is not. In Freud, man is unacceptable to himself, but not evil.

Freud's work was an attempt to rescue desire, with its traditional evil inflection, from a theological (or animistic) context. In proposing the radical unacceptability of the self in a new guise, the split in the human subject, Freud did not invoke the traditional concept of evil (as Jung did) because in writing about the unconscious and infantile sexuality he was writing of something different, of something that could not be accommodated by that moral vocabulary; of something, in fact, that put the implied narratives of a life, sanctioned by a Christian cosmology, in question. Psychoanalysis was a new language for the unacceptable; and for the senses in which the acceptable is always being shattered. It was part of the appeal of object-relations, I think, to assume that Freud's dual-instinct theories were merely a modern redescription of the Christian allegory. For the baby, Winnicott writes, 'ill-health is identical with doubt about oneself . . . it is a matter of the balance of forces of "good" and "evil" within, and this is true for the infant and for the psychosomatic sufferer, and for the more sophisticated philosophical doubter'. Winnicott is good at reminding us that philosophers were babies; but evil, in this account, is whatever in the infant has the potential to destroy the nurturing link with the mother. Goodness is that which sustains life, and life is in the balance between the forces of light and the forces of darkness.

With the theoretical icon of the mother and child Winnicott sometimes uses psychoanalysis to redescribe a traditional theology which can include the notions of good and evil. Freud's dualisms, however, elude the Christian paradigm of conflict (compromise is not redemption). How could the struggle between Eros and Thanatos be a version of good versus evil when, as Freud wrote, it was the function of the component instincts 'to assure that the organism shall follow its own path to death, and to ward off any possible ways of returning to inorganic existence other than those which are immanent in the organism itself . . . What we are left with is the fact that the organism wishes to die only in its own fashion'? Death, the obsessional thinks, is the exemplary decision. But the paradox of Freud's belief here reveals the obsessionality, the either/or nature of our traditional moral orientation. The categories of good and evil are no longer viable objects of thought. What would it be to live a life without – not in defiance of – these categories?

We are left, in fact, not with Nietzsche's prospective question: what is beyond good and evil? but with a retrospective – that is, a psychoanalytic – question: what have we used the conflict between good and evil – even in our so-called reconstructions of primitive mental states – to stop ourselves thinking? Freud, of course, did not answer this question; he merely posed it by way of a possible answer.

6

The Telling of Selves

Notes on Psychoanalysis and Autobiography

I

Whenever I read an autobiography I tend to start halfway
through, when the chap's grown up and it becomes interesting.
Philip Larkin, in an interview with John Haffenden

'The patient is not cured because he remembers,' Lacan writes in his
Écrits, 'he remembers because he is cured.' A successful psychoanalysis, that is to say, makes memory possible, but with a specific
end in view – the patient's recovery. The analyst analyses the
obstacles to memory – the defences – and one of the obstacles to
memory, from a psychoanalytic point of view, is memory itself. 'The
falsified memory,' Freud writes in his 1899 paper 'Screen-Memory',
'is the first that we become aware of.' What might once have been
thought of as a memory – an internal picture or story of the past – is
not actually a memory, in his view, until it has been interpreted;
until it has been interpreted it can be what he calls a screen-memory,
a waking dream of the past.

Exploring the question of why so many childhood memories are
merely banal, Freud suggests that the experiences of childhood, the
significant experiences, 'are omitted rather than forgotten'; 'the
essential elements of an experience,' he writes, 'are represented in
memory by the inessential elements of the same experience'. The
banal is a cover story. By imaginative acts of substitution we repress
and replace whatever has been unacceptable. As a consequence of
this, he writes, 'the impressions which are of most significance for
our whole future usually leave no mnemic images behind them'.
These apparently trivial or uninteresting screen-memories are comparable, Freud goes on, to hysterical symptoms and to dreams

65

because they use the process of displacement as disguise; and like symptoms and dreams they disclose through concealment. 'Not only some but all of what is essential from childhood,' he writes in 'Remembering, Repeating and Working Through', 'has been retained in these memories. It is simply a question of knowing how to extract it out of them by analysis. They represent the forgotten years of childhood as adequately as the manifest content of a dream represents the dream-thoughts.'

Of course, 'all of what is essential from childhood' is predetermined by how one constructs childhood; in psychoanalysis the desires of childhood are the target of interpretation. More like a dream than a piece of documentary evidence, the screen-memory is a disguised representation of unconscious desire. And because, in this account, memory is of desire, and desire is forbidden, the most vivid element in an ordinary memory may be the least revealing. By the unconscious logic of what Freud calls the primary process there are continual shifts and reversals of emphasis going on. Once he had made the dream the model for memory he could then question whether, as he put it in 'Screen-Memory', 'we have any memories at all from our childhood; memories relating *to* our childhood may be all that we possess'. With the advent of psychoanalysis it was memory as much as childhood that lost its innocence.

Freud's account of screen-memories – and memory as dream and symptom, as construction – presents a paradox for the modern autobiographer: the memories least likely to be recorded are the most significant ones, and they are significant *because* they are the least interesting; but for their significance to be revealed requires a psychoanalyst. So the autobiographer is doubly disabled. Without psychoanalytic interpretation there is no personal history, only its concealment. According to this view, those who want to continue misleading themselves about the past write autobiographies; those who want to know themselves and their history have psychoanalysis. It seems rather unlikely, though, that pre-Freudian autobiographies are really dream-books, and that post-Freudian autobiography is impossible. There is, of course, no progress here but rather histories of constituting genres of self-telling, and the kinds of selves implied by such projects. All psychoanalysis can produce is the life-stories told and constructed in psychoanalysis. Psychoanalysis, as theory and therapy, can never be useful – despite Freud's commitment to the progressivism of Science – as a way of putting us closer to the Truth. But it can be useful in the way it adds to our repertoire of ways of thinking about the past (in Freud's work thinking *is* the processing of the past). With concepts like deferred action, the notion of screen-memories – and memory as dream – Freud multiplied our ways of remembering; and he made one kind of memory – the psychoanalytically legitimated one – dependent upon a certain kind of interpretation. This, perhaps inevitably, has interesting consequences for the connections between psychoanalysis and autobiography.

The material that makes psychoanalytic interpretation possible – the stuff from which analyst and patient reconstruct the past – is free-association. Lacan's telling formulation, 'the patient is not cured because he remembers, he remembers because he is cured', is, in fact, an echo of an earlier remark by Sandor Ferenczi: 'The patient is not cured by free-associating, he is cured when he can free-associate.' Free-association is memory in its most incoherent and therefore fluent form; because of repression, the past can only return as disarray in de-narrativized fragments. And the analysis reveals the patient's unofficial repertoire of incoherence. Free-association, in a psychoanalytic context, is integral to the process of remembering because, Freud writes in *The Interpretation of Dreams*, 'when conscious purposive ideas are abandoned, concealed purposive ideas assume control of the current of ideas'. Our unspoken lives press for recognition in fragments, in our pauses, our errors and our puns. It is the continuity of our life-stories that we use to conceal the past; through free-association the patient's story loses its composition and becomes more like a collage in which our favourite words unwittingly find alternative contexts. The radical nature of Freud's project is clear if one imagines what it would be like to live in a world in which everyone was able – had the capacity – to free-associate, to say whatever happened to come into their mind at any given moment.

Once the patient has agreed to what Freud called the 'golden rule' of analysis – that he will say, in spite of himself, whatever comes into his mind – he is participating in a ritual for reconstructing the past (but the past, that is, as psychoanalysis constructs it), out of disparate pieces. In psychoanalysis life-stories fragment in the telling; in order to be read, interpreted, they have to be unreadable. The patient has to refuse himself the conventional satisfactions of narrative. Abrogating his need for beginnings, middles and ends, he often has to become a very bad story-teller and make a nonsense of his life. Giving himself up to another person's punctuation, the patient recreates something of the process of being parented.

And this raises the question of whether psychoanalysis enables the patient to tolerate anti-narrative – the kind of apparently random material that might make a written autobiography unreadable – or simply exchanges one story for another that is, at least provisionally, better. The patient presents a dream or a memory and the analyst invites him to associate to particular details; and then at some point in all this licensed digression the analyst will punctuate the patient's story with a comment (psychoanalysis is essentially a theory of interruption). In the double act of a psychoanalysis the analyst and the patient's observing ego, in relationship to a third object called the patient's speech, confer a different version of intelligibility on the patient's story (the editor of an autobiography is doing something quite different). The fragmentariness of his or her associations entails the making of links; a psychoanalysis is as much about the making of gaps as about the making of links. Each retelling excludes in a different way. By filling in the newly made gaps with informed guesswork, they reconstruct the patient's past (it can be like trying to reconstruct a football match from the result). The patient can remember only when he or she can free-associate; and free-association, at least initially, makes sense only as part of a dialogue. Just as, at the beginning, one's life was made viable, was given a certain continuity, by the responsive presence of at least one other person, so in psychoanalytic treatment it takes two to make a life-story.

II

And yet the ways we miss our lives are life.
Randall Jarrell, 'A Girl in a Library'

The quotations from Freud, Ferenczi and Lacan articulate the necessary connection, from a psychoanalytic point of view, between free-association, the constructions of memory, and the notion of cure. Despite the new kind of resolute suspicion that Freud's work creates about autobiographical narrative – the suggestion that we trust the untold tale, not the teller – psychoanalysis is clearly akin to autobiography in the sense that it involves a self-telling, and the belief that there is nowhere else to go but the past for the story of our lives. Every analysis, in a sense, is about the obstacles to memory: people come for psychoanalysis because the way they are remembering their lives has become too painful; the stories they are telling themselves have become too coercive and restrictive. In so far as they have a dominant story about who they are, they have a repetitive story. And repetition, for Freud, is forgetting in its most spellbinding form. 'The patient,' he writes in 'Remembering, Repeating and Working Through', 'does not remember anything of what he has forgotten and repressed', but acts it out. He reproduces it not as a memory but as an action; he repeats it, without, of course, knowing that he is repeating it.' This might make us wonder what the completely remembered life would look like. And it makes one of the aims of psychoanalysis to produce a story of the past – a reconstructed life-history – that makes the past available, as a resource to be thought about rather than a persecution to be endlessly re-enacted. There is, as it were, no future in repetition. The aim of analysis is not to recover the past, but to make recovery of the past possible, the past that is frozen in repetition; and in this sense psychoanalysis might be more of a prelude to autobiography. A way of creating the internal conditions that would make it possible. It is worth wondering, at any given moment, what kind of object the past is for us – what kind of resistance it requires – and so what kind of relationship we can have with it. The past that repeats itself was unique in every instant, and yet memories like resistances, as Freud wrote in the case of Little Hans 'are sometimes in the nature of stereotyped motifs'. Psychoanalysis itself of course is not exempt from such stereotyped motifs; a case history is often identifiable by its use of them.

But as I have been suggesting, psychoanalysis differentiates itself from the writing that is autobiography in three obvious ways. Firstly, psychoanalysis is, at least explicitly, a deliberate attempt at a cure which can be, but need not be, an ingredient in the writing of an autobiography. Memory is assumed to have a function, in fact a purpose: that is, to release futures – the possible futures that are wishes and desires. Telling one's life-story in the context of psycho-analytic treatment is a means to a particular kind of end, even if the end is both unconscious and unknowable, and changes, as it usually does, in the course of the treatment. Once you have the notion of cure in the picture you have to have a world in which there can be something wrong with people. So some psychoanalysts use norma-tive developmental stories so that they can find things wrong with people. The life-story the patient tells is matched against a kind of master-plot of human development; and here the risks, clearly, are of pathologizing in order to limit variety (after all, any person might be a new kind of person). So the question is: given his or her training – whatever its theoretical allegiances – what is the repertoire of life-stories the analyst can allow, or allow himself to hear, and consider plausible? What are the acceptable shapes of a life that the analyst, by virtue of his profession and of his conscious and unconscious aesthetic preferences, finds himself promoting? At what point, in listening to a life-story, does he call the police? Everybody sets a limit to the stories they can be told; and in that sense there is a repertoire of the stories one is likely to hear.

It is always worth asking of any psychoanalytic writer: if the world he or she values came into being, what would it feel like to live in it? (If Lacan, for example, had cured us all, what kind of world would we be living in?) Each psychoanalytic theorist is telling us, implicitly and explicitly, his or her version of what a good life-story is; so, for example, a Kleinian good life-story would not be one inspired and gratified by revenge; a Winnicottian good life-story would not be defined by its states of conviction but by the quality of its transitions; and so on. In choosing a psychoanalyst of one persuasion or another, one is choosing the kind of life one wants to end up speaking. By defining itself as a form of cure, psychoanalysis, even in its least essentialist versions, cannot help sponsoring very specific ways of describing and redescribing a life-story. Despite the fact that the unconscious is a way of representing a part of the self that is always revising our life-stories, psychoanalysis as a theory and a therapy unavoidably promotes and institutionalizes the idea of the exemplary life (the modern autobiographer assumes his life is interesting, but not usually exemplary). 'The important question,' as the philosopher Donald Davidson has remarked, 'becomes: whom, if anybody, does this theory interpret?' As a professionalized genre of self-telling – autobiography, unlike psychoanalysis, could never be a profession – psychoanalysis cannot, of course, get outside the conventions of its genre. It has to go to autobiographies, biographies and novels to find other ways of plotting lives. Psychoanalysis is autobiography by other means. A psychoanalytic autobiography, like a Freudian poem, should be a contradiction in terms.

This sense of the constraints imposed by the genre leads inevitably to the second significant difference between autobiography and psychoanalysis: psychoanalysis is self-telling to, and in the presence of, a particular other person, the analyst. The analyst's reticence invites the patient to recreate him or her from the significant figures in the patient's past. Transference – this unwitting repetition of early relationships – reveals the way one is continually inventing and reinventing the people one is talking to (in Paul Van Heeswyk's phrase, transference is 'an outrageous misunderstanding'). The patient, that is to say, not only does the talking but thinks he has made the listener. Interpreting the patient's life-story means, among other things, revealing the implied listeners to it. (And it might be an interesting question to ask of an autobiography: who is its implied ideal reader, and what is the catastrophic reading it is trying to avert?) Psychoanalysts of most persuasions would, I think, share the assumption that when a person speaks someone is always being talked to, and that there is a demand in the communication. In a psychoanalysis the patient recapitulates, in disguised form, a history of demands, and the relationships in which these demands were made and modified. By having a recipient present the patient, unlike the autobiographer, is in a position to go on talking to someone about this simple fact, integral to what they are saying: that a life-story is wishful and so is always a demand. The patient, like the autobiographer, wants something, but he does his wanting in a very different context. The autobiographer spreads out his audience, most of whom are anonymous.

The psychoanalytic question, at any given moment in the story, is: what is the unconscious nature of this demand and who is it addressed to? And these questions – though they could never be posed as such – bring in their wake other, related questions: what kind of person do you unconsciously believe you will turn the analyst into by telling him or her *this* version of yourself? What is the version of yourself that you present organized to stop people thinking about you? What are the catastrophes associated with your repressed repertoire of life-stories?

The material associated with these questions constitutes the psychoanalytic conversation. Whereas the dialogues that may have informed the writing of an autobiography are inaudible, the dialogues that have informed the patient's life-story are repeated in a new and continuing dialogue. There is an immediacy in the exchange that can, for example, show the patient that he is always answering the questions he wants to be asked; or that, unconsciously, he is always speaking to the same three people. But this very immediacy of the dialogue – or at least, the possibility of dialogue – only produces that particular life-story told in the actual, rather than the imaginary, presence of another person. And however supposedly anonymous the analyst's psychoanalytic technique encourages him to be, the life-story told is, in a sense, specific to the particular relationship. With a different analyst one would speak different life-stories.

The life-stories told in analysis are occasional – as is any piece of writing, but in a different sense – and made in the circumstances of a special relationship. 'One shouldn't write one autobiography,' the French psychoanalyst J.-B. Pontalis wrote, 'but ten of them, or a hundred because, while we have only one life we have innumerable ways of recounting that life to ourselves.' Perhaps we have even more innumerable ways, so to speak, of recounting our lives to people other than ourselves? It is of interest that while people tell their life-stories to other people, or write them by themselves, there is no familiar genre of speaking one's life-story to oneself. Dreaming may be our only truly solitary form of autobiography.

Even if, as Freud suggests, memories are akin to dreams, we don't find ourselves asking: did I dream that right? Whereas memories often make us wonder about distortion. Once Freud had promised himself psychoanalysis as a new 'science', it was interrogated – and it interrogated itself, for the kind of truth-claims it could make on behalf of its method. But towards the end of his life, sounding, for once, more like the American poet Wallace Stevens, Freud was making very unscientific statements about the kinds of reconstructions of the past that worked in analysis. 'Constructions in analysis,' he wrote in the paper of that title, making a significant concession to the fictive nature of the project, 'can be inaccurate but sufficient.' Constructions in autobiography can be inaccurate but sufficient. The difference, of course, is that the inaccuracy and the sufficiency are subject only to one person's criteria, however unconscious. In writing an autobiography there can be no comparable co-evolving of this sense of sufficiency. One may be as much beholden to the genre and its tradition – to the previous autobiographies one has read – as to the putative truth of the recovered, or rather written, past. Indeed one's sense of truth, of accuracy, is at least partly constituted by the genre. Both written autobiography and psychoanalysis are genres of self-telling, but the constraints of the psychoanalytic genre are more defined because it is a professionalized social practice.

And this brings us to one element of perhaps the most obvious difference between psychoanalysis and autobiography. In psychoanalysis one arranges, and pays, to co-construct one's life-stories by engaging in a nominally therapeutic conversation. Autobiographies are written, and only when they are ghost-written do they in any sense begin to bridge this significant gap between the written and the spoken in the telling of lives. The fact that autobiographies *are* written makes them accessible as a genre (and in oral cultures the public telling of lives also makes them available but to a more circumscribed group); it is difficult to imagine someone writing an autobiography without having read one.

But you cannot, and never will be able to, read or witness a psychoanalysis; you can only read or hear about one. You become an autobiographer by having lived enough of a life, by having read some autobiographies, and by happening to live in a culture that has a kind of book called an autobiography. Traditionally – along similar lines – you become an analyst by having been a patient; but how do you become a patient? How do you know if you are doing it properly? (In what sense, if any, is finishing an analysis comparable to finishing an autobiography?) The analyst has privileged access to the rules of the genre – and to the kinds of process it involves – and initiates the patient into a very specific way of talking and of being responded to. And even if the analyst and the patient keep notes, there is a strong sense in which a psychoanalysis leaves no evidence. The patient and the analyst, as people living their lives, are subject to public evaluation; but the analysis, unlike a written autobiography, is not. It is, by definition, a self-telling in private (despite the fact that the idea of the unconscious makes guaranteed confidentiality impossible). The analyst may write a case-history and the patient may write his account of the treatment – as Freud and the Wolfman did – but these will be different from a biography and an autobiography because, among other things, the analyst and the patient are writing up a conversation: and this is true even if, as is mostly the case, there is very little actual dialogue in the account. By being spoken and being private, a psychoanalysis exempts itself from certain kinds of evaluation; it can never be read, it can only be gossiped about. Psychoanalytic practice is always hearsay.

So if we ask: what kind of autobiographical performance is an analysis? we can say – once we have said that every analysis is different though some are more different than others – that it is one performed in the presence of, and in cooperation with, another person, nominally skilled in a certain genre of self-telling; with no necessary recourse to, or inclusion of, third parties; the conscious aim not being the production of a text for circulation (and what the analysis wants to give to, or exchange with, the world in which it is taking place is often not articulated). And the autobiographer, unlike the patient, may be paid for telling his story.

Psychoanalysis adds to the stock of available life-stories mostly through theories about life-stories; there are surprisingly few case-histories or fully fledged autobiographies by patients or analysts (It is of interest how impersonal Freud's *An Autobiographical Study* is). And as an autobiographical performance, psychoanalysis is inevitably – indeed, formally – selective in its attentions: childhood memories, dreams, mistakes, the vagaries of erotic life; where there is conflict, wherever continuity is disturbed or composure undermined, our other lives are in the making. And from a psychoanalytic point of view our lives are always other lives (and always in the making). The psychoanalyst, in other words, like the patient and the autobiographer, is always having to manage the fact that too many autobiographies make a life; that one's autobiography might be different at every moment. Perhaps it is not surprising how few autobiographies individual people write, given how many they speak. There is no cure for multiple plots.

There are surprisingly few occasions – or rituals – in which people are expected or invited to tell the story of their lives from wherever they think the beginning is; or to tell the even odder story that is their dream. And the difference between living a life and telling it can feel like the difference between a dream and its account. The autobiographical narrative and the psychoanalytic dialogue both confront us with a simple puzzling question: in what sense is living a life like telling a story? The dream, we should remember, is addressed to oneself; there is no one else who can tell it.

II
PSYCHOANALYSIS REVIEWED

7
Depression

The idea that literature, or any other discipline like boxing or song-writing, could modify psychoanalytic theory – that it could be a two-way street – has always been problematic for psychoanalysts. There is, of course, no reason to think a psychoanalyst's interpretation of a boxing match would necessarily be more revealing than a boxer's account of a psychoanalytic session. But psychoanalysts have worked on the rather misleading principle that psychoanalysis is useful or interesting only if it is in some sense right, rather than believing that it is another good way of speaking about certain things like love and loss and memory, as songs can be (and that, also like songs, it is only ever as good as it sounds). For most psychoanalysts, including Freud, great artists tend to provide either vivid illustration or prestigious confirmation of psychoanalytic insights. Melanie Klein, for example, found nothing she didn't already know in the *Oresteia*, and even Lacan found *Hamlet* reassuring.

Great theorists, unlike great artists, whether they intend to or not, always make us believe in progress. So it can sometimes seem in psychoanalytic writing that Western – and occasionally Eastern – culture has reached its triumphant conclusion in a handful of psychoanalytic formulations. Dominated today by masterful voices promoting the impossibility of mastery and the virtues of difference, psychoanalysis has been far less willing than literary studies, or anthropology, or philosophy, to acknowledge a multiplicity of interesting cultural conversations (believing in the centrality of the Oedipus complex makes the whole notion of pluralism, and of pragmatism in relation to psychoanalysis, extremely tricky). And yet it is surely at its most compelling, as it is in the work of Julia Kristeva – who came to psychoanalysis from linguistics – when it knows itself to be in a world of complementary and not only competitive languages. In Kristeva's writing, despite the sometimes tortuous difficulty of her style, hero-worship and pluralism no longer seem incompatible. In fact, her work is in no way prejudicial in the sense that she does not simulate incompatiblities. She reads Dostoevsky, and Marguerite Duras, and Holbein's *The Body of the Dead Christ in the Tomb* – in three of the most brilliant chapters in her book *Black Sun: Depression and Melancholia* (1989) – after Freud but not for Freud. David Aberbach, by contrast, in his book *Surviving Trauma: Loss, Literature and Psychoanalysis* (1990), is oddly impressed by how much Great Writers in the past knew about loss without having read John Bowlby.

If new disciplines like psychoanalysis thrive initially on fantasies of purity, they can only be sustained by what looks like contamination. And it is not surprising, given the radical uncertainty of the clinical enterprise – and talking with people who are trying to find states of mind they prefer *is* different from literary criticism – that people have been eager to become analysts of an identifiable and usually monotheistic persuasion. The theoretical preoccupation in certain British and American versions of psychoanalysis with fantasies of boundaries and separateness and the self as a unique possession reflects this fear of jumble, and the terrors of exchange that can make the idea of the self into a prison. People's lives as miscellaneous and contingent but still, or for that reason, narratable is the irony that confronts the analyst who is himself equipped with his own favourite stories to deal with this. But psychoanalysis as the understanding game, rather than a redescription game, is always threatened by its own rhetoric of spurious profundity, 'deep' being the word psychoanalysts often use when they want to indicate that they think something is Very Important. There is the thrill of hermetic, separatist idioms, and the extensive repertoire of ways of dealing with dissenting voices. And then there is also, of course, the thorny question of what it is that psychoanalysts can claim to know.

When Freud wrote in his famous essay 'Dostoevsky and Parricide' that 'before the problem of the creative artist, analysis must, alas, lay down its arms', he seemed to be suggesting that there was some kind of war between psychoanalysis and art. And also that the creative artist was in some sense a problem, at least for psychoanalysis. Art may not be soluble in terms of psychoanalysis – it is difficult to see now why anyone should want it to be – but it is interesting to see what kind of object it is for different psychoanalysts, both how they find themselves using it in their writing and what kind of relationship they have with it. If psychoanalysts could think of themselves as the makers of sentences rather than of truths they would feel less at odds with – feel less need to privilege and covertly disparage – what Freud called 'Creative Writers'.

The idealization of art and artists among psychoanalysts who write is always accompanied by its shadow of envy; and it is of interest that psychoanalysis has never found a place for the idea of inspiration. But from quite early in Freud's work – both in its genesis and in its content – the connection between creativity and mourning did find a place in psychoanalytic theory, one Melanie Klein was among the first to elaborate. Freud began to believe that lives were about achieving loss, eventually one's own loss, so to speak, in death; and that art could be in some way integral to this process, a culturally sophisticated form of bereavement. A work of art was a work of mourning – and mourning itself was an art. So after Freud and Klein it becomes possible to think, as Julia Kristeva suggests in one of many striking sentences in *Black Sun*, that 'my depression points to my not knowing how to lose – I have perhaps been unable to find a valid compensation for my loss?' Compensation comes only, in Kristeva's view, in renewing the possibilities of communication, in the commitment to language. The acquisition of language is the only way of learning how to lose. 'The Freudian way,' she writes, 'aims at planning for the advent and formulation of sexual desire . . . for named sexual desire ensures securing the subject to the other, and consequently, to meaning.' Her translator Leon Roudiez, who in *Black Sun* produces a mostly fluent version of a difficult text, translates *arrimage* as 'secures'. The French term, *arrimer*, which is nautical in origin, also means 'to stow'. It is through desire, in language, Kristeva is saying, that the potential for connection between people is stored and kept safe. It is this, for very good reasons of his own, that the depressed person refuses and

attacks. 'The depressed person,' she writes, only apparently changing the context, 'is a radical sullen atheist.'

Black Sun opens – and it is more like a drama than a treatise – with
an inquiry into depression as an absence of interest, and with the
paradoxical sense that to write about depression or melancholia is to
write words about a state of mind in which words can be virtually
meaningless:

> For those who are racked by melancholia, writing about it would only
> have meaning if writing sprang out of that very melancholia. I am trying
> to address an abyss of sorrow, a non-communicable grief that at times,
> and often on a long-term basis, lays claim upon us to the extent of
> having us lose all interest in words, actions, and even life itself. Such
> despair is not a revulsion that would imply my being capable of desire
> and creativity, negative indeed but present. Within depression, if my
> existence is on the verge of collapsing, its lack of meaning is not tragic – it
> appears obvious to me, glaring and inescapable.

Depression is a self-cure for the terrors of aliveness, of being alive
to one's losses and therefore to one's desires. From a psychoanalytic
point of view, imagination – the capacity for representation – begins,
or rather, is initiated, by the experience of loss; and the first loss
appears to be of the mother. It is only in the absence of that first
essential object that the infant or child will have to give thought to
the mother. He will cope with the absence, which should be
temporary, by imagining her presence. It is only in the space created
by the mother's absence that she can be desired and therefore
imagined. Knowing people is what we do to them when they are not
there. And language in Kristeva's view – and the view of the
versions of psychoanalysis she uses – is the way of managing loss by
making it up. 'Signs are arbitrary,' she writes, 'because language
starts with a negation of loss, along with the depression occasioned
by mourning.' 'Arbitrary' because they are what happen to stand in
for the absent mother – as though the child is implicitly saying, 'I
haven't lost her because I have the words for her' – and a negation of
loss because they are a pretended substitute. If my mother and I are
the same, of the same mind, so to speak, I would not need a word for
her or for what I wanted; and because my desire would then be

strictly commensurate with its satisfaction, there would be no desire. It is through loss that I come to want something, and to imagine, even though it is a controversial thought, that there might be an I doing the wanting. But it is only in the medium of language that such constructions become possible.

The child, it seems, depends on his mother; but his development into a separate speaking being depends upon what might be called sufficient loss. And loss is literally figured out in language. 'If I did not agree to lose mother,' Kristeva writes, bringing in the notion of choice, 'I could neither imagine nor name her.' Without language, and without the pain of acknowledged absence this entails, there is no desire. So from this point of view psychoanalysis becomes a way of understanding the obstacles to symbolization, to the conversations that are being refused. The realm of the unspoken comes to represent, among other things, the unwillingness to mourn, or to relinquish primary involvements. 'By analysing – that is, by dissolving – the denial mechanisms wherein depressive persons are stuck,' Kristeva writes with beguiling confidence, 'analytic cure can implement a genuine graft of symbolic potential.' In psychoanalysis you cannot, of course, force people to be interested, but you can show them that there are interesting things around, that they are making more sense than they can let themselves know. As part of this graft of symbolic potential – horticulture is always preferable to militancy in psychoanalysis – she proposes that 'vowels, consonants or syllables may be extracted from the signifying sequence' of the depressed patient's language and construed by the analyst in the service of new meanings. The analyst, in other words, can make sense of the patient's language by listening to it as though it were nonsense poetry. If the analyst looks after the sound the sense can be taken care of. And this becomes necessary because, in psychoanalytic terms, defence mechanisms, like the denial Kristeva refers to, are forms of anaesthetic, unconsciously sustained poverties of language that pre-empt a knowledge of feeling. The desolate apathy of depression is less painful than the meanings it attempts to blank off. The possibility of meaning, the release of curiosity, is what the depression works to deny.

People organize their lives to avoid the imagined catastrophe of certain conversations; and they come to analysis, however fluent they may be, because they are unable to speak. But some people, of course, have had unspeakable experiences, or experiences that have been made unspeakable by the absence of a listener. *Black Sun* and *Surviving Trauma*, through very different versions of psychoanalysis – one, broadly speaking, linguistic and the other empirical – attempt to describe, and in Aberbach's book causally explain, such experiences. Another way of putting the difference between them – the language difference, so to speak – is that Kristeva sees that 'aesthetic and particularly literary creation, and also religious discourse in its imaginary fictional essence . . . constitute a very faithful semiological representation of the subject's battle with semiological collapse': the artist, in her view, can be the one who is 'the most relentless in his struggle against the symbolic abdication that blankets him'. Aberbach, on the other hand, worries 'the question of whether, or to what extent, loss might account for the mystery of the creative gift'. The mystery, I think, is in the 'whether'.

It is not clear from Aberbach's book in what sense our lives would be better if we understood more about 'the mystery of the creative gift'. But since it is impossible to imagine a life without loss, and equally impossible not to notice that the 'gift' is rather unevenly distributed, Aberbach's question may be a lost cause. Unlike *Black Sun*, *Surviving Trauma* is easily accessible, and by the same token coercive in its very simplicity. Psychoanalysis always short-changes us with its larger abstractions, and words like 'love' and 'loss' and 'hate' assume exactly the consensus of meaning that is always in question. But Aberbach uses the word 'loss' in the restricted context of John Bowlby's work on this subject, if that's what it is (it is the title of the third volume of Bowlby's influential trilogy, *Attachment*, *Separation* and *Loss*, but that doesn't necessarily make it a subject, either). Aberbach simply takes Bowlby's standardized picture of healthy as opposed to pathological mourning – Bowlby was the first psychoanalyst to outline a normative mourning process from an empirical standpoint, and acknowledge that children could suffer such things – and uses it to explain a catalogue of quotations from great literature, and the lives of a number of great men and women. After a psychoanalytic reading of Keats like the one Aberbach offers in *Surviving Trauma*, one longs for a Keatsian impression of psychoanalysis. Figures as diverse as St John of the Cross, Descartes, Spinoza, Rousseau, Wordsworth, Coleridge, Krishnamurti, Conrad, to mention only a few, are all deemed to be suffering from, or really writing about, unresolved grief (it is only in books that grief or transference, or an Oedipus complex, or anything else, ever gets 'resolved').

All this levelling could be harmless enough were it not for Aberbach's apparently untroubled commitment to what he calls 'normal social life', and slightly more ominously, 'normal social functioning'. John Lennon, for example, comes out of this rather badly. 'The enormous numbers of styles and faces with which he experimented,' Aberbach writes, as the last hundred years of cultural change drop from view, 'testify to the insecurity of his self-image, and his songs reflect this variety.' It is his assumption that a secure self-image is something we all want – or more absurdly, could even have – that is pernicious, because it pathologizes variety, the styles and faces that any version of the normal precludes and often disparages. All the normative versions of psychoanalysis generate nostalgic bad faith by implying that one's life could have been better if only one had been born into a different family. John Lennon's life would not have been better if his parents hadn't separated, because it wouldn't have been his life. And a self-image is always exactly that – an image. It is a fundamentally useful Freudian insight that we are never coincident with – the same as – the images we have of ourselves. And in a certain sense there are no selves, only families of images that we sometimes choose to think of, or collect, as a self-image. It is not that Aberbach need subscribe to these views, which are as contentious as his, but his work is impoverished by not even acknowledging their existence. 'Even the soundest among us,' Kristeva writes, 'knows just the same that a firm identity remains a fiction' (the original French *une identité ferme* includes the sense of *ferme* as both 'firm' and 'closed', or 'locked'). Kristeva, almost by virtue of the difficulty of her text, returns us to Freud's really interesting question, one which Aberbach assumes Bowlby has already answered, but which has a complexity that inevitably eludes Bowlby's empiricism: what is there to lose?

Mourning, Freud wrote in 'Mourning and Melancholia', is an entirely appropriate response to the loss of a loved person through death or separation, but in melancholia 'a loss . . . has occurred, but one cannot see clearly what it is that has been lost, and it is all the more reasonable to suppose that the patient cannot consciously perceive what he has lost either'. In a revealing and understated way in *Black Sun* Kristeva often obscures Freud's distinction. Not denying that there is a difference between an actual rupture between people and a prevailing mood of despondency, she keeps open the question – a question that would be meaningless to someone grief-stricken by a bereavement – of what it is that has been lost. Is the trauma, for example, constituted for the child by the excessive absence of the mother, or by a breakdown or refusal of the possibilities of representation? Is what is lost the mother (or lover) as an object, or the belief in language as a substitute for her? 'The speech of the depressed,' Kristeva writes, 'is to them like an alien skin; melancholy persons are foreigners in their maternal tongue. They have lost the meaning – the value – of their mother-tongue for want of losing the mother.' So part of the value of language is the struggle we have to believe in it. And by its commitment to the possibilities of meaning, psychoanalysis, as Kristeva says of works of art, 'can lead us to establish relations with ourselves and others that are less destructive, more soothing'. There is no cure, but there are ways of talking.

The Holocaust and the other terrors of recent history inevitably haunt both these books. 'Those monstrous and painful sights,' Kristeva writes, 'damage our systems of perception and representation, our symbolic means find themselves hollowed out, nearly wiped out, paralysed.' Aberbach, in a frightening chapter on survivor literature, reiterates Bettelheim's point that the people who survived best in concentration camps were those who were most able to numb themselves. Learning not to feel things is obviously integral to development, and in the face of such horror the only viable self-protection may be to be muted, to relinquish or sabotage any capacity for representation. But if it is our destructiveness that makes us speechless, the risk is that our speechlessness makes us more destructive, and particularly of ourselves. Julia Kristeva, who has written in *Black Sun* one of the very best psychoanalytic books on depression and melancholia – which is, by the same token, a celebration, in unpromising circumstances, of the erotics of plurality – should have what her book shows is impossible, the last word: 'For if it is true that those who are slaves to their moods, beings drowned in their sorrows, reveal a number of psychic or cognitive frailties, it is equally true that a diversification of moods, variety in sadness, refinement in sorrow or mourning are the imprint of a humankind that is surely not triumphant but subtle, ready to fight, and creative.'

8
Anna Freud

Psychoanalysts after Freud have to acknowledge that the founder of psychoanalysis was never properly trained. He was not psychoanalysed in the conventional sense – that is, by someone else – and there was no one to tell him whether what he was doing with his patients was appropriate. That Freud, paradoxically, was the first 'wild' analyst is one of the difficult facts in the history of psychoanalysis. It is easy to forget that in what is still its most creative period – roughly between 1893 and 1939 – when Freud, Jung, Sandor Ferenczi, Karl Abraham, Klein and Anna Freud herself were learning what they thought of as the 'new science', they had no formal training. Later generations of analysts dealt with their envy of Freud and his early followers by making their trainings increasingly rigorous, by demanding and fostering the kind of compliance – usually referred to as 'conviction' – that tended to stifle originality. Psychoanalytic training became a symptom from which a lot of people never recovered.

Not surprisingly, most of the dissensions in psychoanalysis after Freud's death arose around this vexed question of training. Since she devoted her life to protecting her father's legacy, Anna Freud was to be involved, often unwillingly, in what soon became known as the politics of psychoanalysis. After the devastation of the Second World War, the generation of psychoanalysts that emigrated to London would think of psychoanalysis as something they belonged to and that belonged to them. When they talked about psychoanalysis they were always talking about something else and Anna was, inevitably, in a privileged position in this fraught conversation. In Freud's absence psychoanalytic groups increasingly organized themselves around different canons of acceptable interpretation. And pscyhoanalysis, which, at least in theory, makes hero- and heroine-worship impossible, found new leaders, all of whom claimed to be protecting Freud's legacy. As Elisabeth Young-Bruehl's careful work, *Anna Freud: A Biography* (1989), shows, Anna was not only the daughter of an extraordinary man – a father who made himself indispensable, and not only to his own children – she was also the daughter of a growing controversy. Freud called her, in one of his more daunting pieces of mythologizing, 'his Antigone'. It is one thing to be Antigone to one's father, but to be Antigone to his Movement may have been a distraction for Anna as well as a destiny. Oedipus, after all, did not start a new profession.

Freud managed to live virtually half his life – what he came to think of as the more significant half – without psychoanalysis. Anna lived her whole life in its shadow. Young-Bruehl's compelling account enables us to consider what it would be like to live a life committed to psychoanalysis, as Anna Freud was perhaps the first person to do. She would regret towards the end that they had 'not yet discovered the secret of how to raise . . . men and women who make use of psychoanalysis to its very limits . . . for a way of living'. But devotion is always a parody of its object. Since psychoanalysis has undermined piety Anna Freud's life is necessarily one of strange and unprecedented ironies, not least of which is the fact that when she was a young woman her father psychoanalysed her (it is usually the fantasy that one is being analysed by one's father that has to be analysed). A father's ordinary ambivalence about his daughter – we see Freud, in Young-Bruehl's vivid account, worrying about Anna's social timidity but suspicious of any interest she showed in men – is enacted for the first time in the new scenario of analysis, in which Anna is obliged to report her masturbation fantasies. 'Papa himself requires that when one speaks with him one does not stop after telling half of the information.' To have been psychoanalysed by one's father would not qualify today as any kind of psychoanalytic training. With biographies such as Young-Bruehl's we can begin to see how really bizarre psychoanalytic history is.

Instead of freeing her for Love and Work, as Freud in his more enthusiastic moments believed it could do, psychoanalysis seems to have strengthened Anna's resolution to do one at the cost of the other. 'Maybe we have all learned how to work too well,' she wrote wistfully to her old friend and colleague August Aichorn, when she was in her fifties, 'and done rather poorly in learning to loaf.' Nursing her father through several terrible illnesses including his last, organizing their flight from Vienna in 1939, and then setting up her own child analytic training in London after the war, left little time for loafing. And loafing is certainly not taught, though it should be, in any of the recognized training institutions. It is, nevertheless, a pertinent regret and cannot be unrelated to the absence in her life of sexual relationships or, indeed, to longings for a life outside psychoanalysis. Anna Freud, as far as we can know, was the first and probably the last chaste analyst. If sexuality, as Freud showed, is the only route out of the family – faced with the three-person relationship of the Oedipus complex, the child is forced to realize that he or she can do everything else with the parents, except the one thing he or she most wants to do – then there is a sense in which, despite her extraordinary character, something in Anna never came to life. All this is only tactfully implied by Young-Bruehl, and perhaps that is as it should be. To construe the possible connections between Anna's capacity to frustrate herself and the fact that she was manifestly one of the very few great analysts after Freud becomes a perilous invitation to a biographer. Young-Bruehl's honourable wish to report without unnecessary judgement leads her, however, to moments of grotesque Dickensian humour. Unable to knit at the end of her life because her hands shook, Anna 'mocked herself,' Young-Bruehl writes, 'for the good sublimation behaviour she had demanded of them when she was young: "Look at what that hand did, it is angry because I controlled it for so long." '

Though the biography is divided into two parts of almost equal length, entitled 'Vienna' and 'London', it is the first part, or more exactly, the period up to Freud's death, that is the more revealing. When she read the account by Max Schur, Freud's physician, of what he called 'the last chapter' of Freud's life, dealing with his terminal illness, Anna said of it: 'There is contained my whole biography.' In fact, she lived with great resourcefulness for another forty-three years, but the story revolves continually around her father. And what is not glossed over here is Freud's complicity in keeping his daughter for himself. When Ernest Jones, for example, began to take a bit of a shine to Anna, Freud sent him a letter, Young-Bruehl reports, 'suggesting that the courtship was inappropriate because Anna was too young and not yet interested in men' – she was nineteen – and a further letter to Anna making himself quite clear. 'I have no thought of granting you,' he wrote, 'the freedom of choice your two sisters enjoyed. For it has so happened that you have lived more intimately with us than they, and I would like to believe that you would find it more difficult to make such a decision for life without our – in this case my – consent.' When Anna met a man she was interested in she would tend to give him to her father, usually for psychoanalytic instruction. Even Lou Andreas-Salomé, whom she admired and confided in, wrote to Freud, after one of Anna's visits, celebrating her asceticism. 'Altogether Anna has stirred up quite a storm of passion here,' she writes in 1922, when Anna is twenty-seven, 'but nevertheless returns home totally unseared by these flames. Nor should I be at all surprised if this sequence of events were to be constantly repeated, so much does she enjoy every homecoming.' There was, she was constantly being reminded, no place like home. And home, of course, would be one of the many things that would never be the same again after Freud. In Young-Bruehl's story there is certainly a suggestion that Freud was to blame for the sins of his daughter. Or rather, in Anna's case, for the sins she was unable to commit.

Anna Freud was born in Vienna in December 1895. Five months earlier something more momentous than the birth of a sixth child had happened to her father. 'Do you really believe,' Freud wrote to his collaborator Wilhelm Fliess, 'that some day on this house one will read on a marble tablet: "Here revealed itself, on 24 July 1895, the secret of the dream to Dr Sigm. Freud"?' At this crucial time of his life, troubled by an array of symptoms, Freud was preoccupied by the need to earn a living for his growing family while persisting with his self-analysis. The year after Anna's birth his father died and he used the word 'psychoanalysis' for the first time in print (in

French). These were years of real and necessary self-absorption for him. Mrs Freud's absence, as all biographers of the Freud family have found, is more puzzling. It has always been a revealing gap, so to speak, in the story, but we do at least know that at the time of Anna's birth Martha Freud was exhausted by her five other children, four of whom were under five. According to Young-Bruehl, Anna never made a close or pleasurable relationship with her mother, and was really nurtured by their Catholic nurse Josefine. Quite definitely Josefine's favourite, Anna described her after her funeral as 'the oldest relation and the most genuine of my childhood'. Throughout her adult life Anna would seek intimate relationships with powerful older women and would have remarkably little to say in her theoretical work about mother–daughter relationships.

After Anna's birth the Freuds, for the first time in their married life, did not spend their holiday together. And this period of Anna's early years coincided with their use of a new form of contraception, the one that was to be at the heart of the psychoanalytic enterprise and was called abstinence. The year after her birth the now infamous Aunt Minna, Martha's sister, moved into the family home; she was another woman whom Freud liked but who never took to Anna. The last of the Freud children, Anna was the accidental latecomer, the one who, judging from some of Young-Bruehl's upsetting evidence, had to struggle especially hard to find a real place in her parents' minds. From the picture that Young-Bruehl builds up of Anna's early family life it seems that the Freud parents had to work at their sense of Anna's specialness. It sounds, that is to say, as if she was more an object of devotion than desire, and this became one of the stories of her life. At the age of fifty-eight, writing to Ernest Jones about his biography of her father, she is struck by the fact that his 'descriptions bring it home to me what a long and full life he had before my time, that I really only appeared somewhere in the middle as a very insignificant item'.

From the very beginning, it seems, the spoils had been divided. Freud had named their previous child, his adored Sophie, after Sophie Schwab, an attractive niece of his revered Hebrew teacher, Professor Hammerschlag. Anna was named after the professor's 'very intelligent but quite plain daughter'. This Anna, who was widowed after a year of marriage, was, as Anna Freud would be, a schoolteacher and a patient of Freud's. Anna always hated her name, thinking of it as common and plain, while 'Sophie' was 'lovely and sophisticated'. (Freud's peculiar but touching attempt to console her by pointing out that her name was a palindrome could easily have been heard by her as implying that her body was the same back to front.) 'The two young Freuds,' Young-Bruehl writes, 'developed their version of a common sisterly division of territories: "beauty" and "brains"!' There is something too jaunty about this, but lives *are* cast in such early divisions of emotional labour. What one is loved for in the family becomes a fate.

'Annerl is turning to a charming child,' Freud wrote to Fliess, 'she is of the same type as Martin, physically and mentally.' Anna deleted this passage from the first edition of the Fliess letters. She must have known very early the agony of sexual jealousy: that it is not a question of rivalry – competitions, after all, can be won – but of something far worse. It confronts us with the impossibility of being someone else. 'Brains' and 'beauty' are dismaying alternatives, and because no one is ever given the choice we all know which we would prefer. Never made to feel beautiful in the family, Anna was left with her intelligence and the lack of something 'feminine' that her father was drawn to in Sophie. She would not be the last person to find that psychoanalysis was a relief from the mystique of beauty.

'She felt herself to be lacking,' Young-Bruehl writes, 'the slim waist and trim ankles that her sister had, and as she grew into her adolescence she favoured the long-skirted traditional country dress, the dirndl, that disguised her waist and covered her thick ankles. She also developed a slightly hunched forward posture – one that hours sitting over knitting aggravated – of the sort adolescents use for hiding.' Young-Bruehl organizes some of the early part of her book around a conventional over-simplification derived from the nineteenth-century novel. Anna is the heroine whose exceptional character is the consequence of her undesirability, of the fact that she has had to do more work. She was, apparently, 'such a daydreamer that even her father was startled by the elaborateness of her creations'. In her imagination, she was daring and dreamy, full of spirit, identifying with the male heroes in her stories; in public she was timid and cramped. She is presented as someone bold *and* inhibited – 'an adventurous, fearless girl who was also very prim and orderly' – but also as someone trapped in the banality of opposites, a biography that is not allowed to turn into a novel. The use of this kind of presiding conflict as an explanatory device too easily replaces a more subtle or nuanced sense of the complexity of Anna's character. One could be left thinking that depth is the only resource of those who are not shallow enough to be attractive.

As an adolescent, Anna would sit in on the famous Wednesday meetings where Freud and his newly formed circle discussed psychoanalysis. She may not have been out dancing but she was the only woman present while a group of older men, led by her father, engaged in a new kind of conversation about the significance of sexuality. For a seventeen-year-old, not to mention for the men who talked in her presence, this must have been a heady atmosphere; it certainly makes sense of Young-Bruehl's contention that in Anna 'the good girl caution and conservativeness . . . were always coupled with her verve'. If she was, as we are told here, 'very self-conscious about not being feminine or femininely attractive enough', it wouldn't have taken her long to work out what it was about her that could engage her father. For Freud, the dream was their nightly rendezvous. In 1915, during the bleak war years, Anna, having qualified as a teacher, began to translate psychoanalytic articles into German, and wonder what she really wanted to do with her life, now that she was the last remaining child at home. And her father began, 'when he thought it appropriate', as Young-Bruehl adds in parentheses, occasionally to interpret her dreams.

If dreams are the way we tell ourselves secrets about ourselves at night, they also represent the impenetrable privacy of the self. No one can know what someone else's dream means, though they can, with the dreamer's assistance, say more or less interesting things about it. But in dream interpretation the margin of error is also the margin of freedom: the interpreter can never capture the dream or the dreamer. Telling one's dreams to someone else is a form of flirtation because the dream invites a curiosity that will always be frustrated. For Anna to offer her dreams to her father, the man to whom, supposedly, the secret of dreams had revealed itself, may have been as much an act of unconscious defiance as one of surrender and enlightenment. In Young-Bruehl's fascinating account of Anna's struggles during these formative years – taken mostly from diaries and letters – it is possible to detect considerable but veiled hostility to her father as The One Who Knows. One fortnight when Freud was too ill to analyse her she wrote to a friend: 'These two weeks I have lived as I did in the time before I became an analyst . . . with the poetry of Rilke and daydreams and weaving. That, too, is an Anna, but without any Interpreter.'

Psychoanalysts, and psychoanalytic theory itself, create a problem for modern biographers, especially when they want to interpret their subject's dreams or provide a plausible account of their subject's own psychoanalysis. Dreams, by (Freudian) definition, require the associations of the dreamer – which can hardly be reconstructed by someone else; and an analysis, like all forms of coupledom however well documented, is always hermetic to outsiders. This need not preclude speculation – most great literature, after all, is conjecture about couples – but it can create timidity in the biographer of a famous psychoanalyst when faced with what is loosely known as the analytic community. This putative community has not been keen to let outsiders speculate about its idols, as though its members needed to protect themselves from their own doubts as from more vulgar forms of questioning. The link between Anna Freud's lifelong celibacy and her analysis with her father is worthy of, indeed invites, thoughtful consideration (puerile consideration would not be the end of the world). But the idealization that Anna sometimes suffered from in her lifetime – the idealization that is a refusal to know someone – has continued in retrospective accounts. Young-Bruehl provides the evidence to rectify this without quite daring to guess at possibilities.

In Young-Bruehl's intriguing account of Anna'a analysis with her father, which began in 1920, it seems as though the one thing that her father refused to recognize – and her biographer is unwilling to dwell on in the evidence presented – is Anna's insistent but thwarted attempt to get out of the net of understanding that psychoanalysis, in the person of her father, provided. Of course, so-called training analyses rarely cure people of psychoanalysis. But there is still a daunting sense of Anna having submitted to a tyrannical version of Truth in the absence of compelling alternatives. Young-Bruehl implies in her ambiguous summary that Anna's analysis and her life afterwards were an education in a Christian version of the stoicism – that most peculiar and unprepossessing virtue – that Freud was idealized for after the Jones biography. Young-Bruehl writes:

She developed a habit of finding acceptable outlets for unacceptable impulses and wishes, ultimately altruistically surrendering her wishes to others. The processes of sublimating and surrendering did not, of course, mean that her drives were depleted – she had the awesome, somewhat compulsive energy that is characteristic of chaste people with burning faith or compelling causes . . . she was able to have a scientific interest in sexuality, but not be actively sexual in either a heterosexual or a homosexual mode.

Anyone who heard Anna Freud at one of her Wednesday meetings at what was then called the Hampstead Clinic would not have thought of her as the Mother Theresa of psychoanalysis. But given that Anna Freud was an object of emulation for generations of analysts there are ironies here that should not be muffled. Freud had used psychoanalysis to make a powerful critique of burning faiths and compelling causes. He had revealed the origins in childhood of certain kinds of belief. After the war Anna would turn her father's achievement into an object of such belief. In her theoretical work there would be little criticism of him, and she would make what is still the finest contribution to the psychoanalytic understanding of passivity.

From about 1920 to his death in 1939 Anna was Freud's devoted nurse and colleague and was therefore soon embroiled in the frenetic rivalries of the psychoanalytic horde. 'I am only under my father's influence,' she wrote ingenuously, 'and for the rest I try to think of myself as an independent person and to figure things out for myself.' There was, by the sound of things, a lot of trying, but there was also a lot of natural wit, an unofficial cunning that the biography every so often catches. So when Otto Rank, for example, begins to get critical of her father she is scandalized – partly from envy of his freedom to do so – but figures out something rather shrewd of her own. 'Rank,' she writes to her colleague, Max Eitingon, 'is very advanced compared to all of us in his understanding that human relations exist for the sole purpose of being ruined.' She could never allow herself to be disillusioned about her father; and as the political situation worsened in Vienna there would be a growing external focus for any free-floating discontent.

Young-Bruehl provides a lucid narrative of the difficult pre-war years in the course of which the complicated psychoanalytic movement became international, and the dialogue between Anna and her father was to constitute some of their most important theoretical work. She is particularly interesting about the extent to which they both used material from her analysis as clinical illustration in their sometimes complementary papers. But despite, or because of, their devotion to each other, Freud's contempt for Anna is something that shows up again and again, albeit obliquely and often unremarked, in Young-Bruehl's temperate version of their relationship. 'If the day comes when there is no more psychoanalysis you can be a seamstress in Tel Aviv,' Freud used to say to Anna – it was, we are told, one of his 'favourite little jokes'. When, towards the end of her analysis, Anna went for a holiday to Germany, Freud makes what Young-Bruehl calls 'another very candid statement' about her in a letter to Lou Andreas-Salomé: 'I have long felt sorry for her for still being at home with us old folks . . . but on the other hand, if she really were to go away, I should feel myself as deprived as I do now, and as I should do if I had to give up smoking!' No one, presumably, wants to be a cigar. The first book of his that Freud ever gave to Anna was *Moses and Monotheism*, published in the year of his death.

After the years in Vienna and the account of Anna's extraordinary courage in dealing with the Nazis before their much deferred emigration, the second half of Young-Bruehl's biography, covering the years in London, is less engrossing. And this in itself is revealing because they were in fact years of exceptional achievement for Anna, as well as a period of protracted mourning. Working at first with refugee children, she also established links between the analytic community and schools as well as setting up what is now called the Anna Freud Centre to train child analysts. It was then that she wrote her most distinguished psychoanalytic papers – including 'About Losing and Being Lost', which everyone should read regardless of their interest in psychoanalysis – and consolidated the most intimate relationship of her adult life with her colleague Dorothy Burlingham. She began to be able to enjoy, at least occasionally, her celebrity, and overcame her father's prejudice about America by forming sustained professional and friendly links with American analysts, who would play an increasingly important role in her psychoanalytic projects. Her elaborate and problematic relationship with Melanie Klein, the Institute of Psychoanalysis in London and the International, revealing as they are in the detail with which Young-Bruehl reconstructs them, are mostly of interest to anthropologists of the psychoanalytic movement. In a sense, she blossomed as her life narrowed; she turned into a centre of psychoanalysis. 'Her expectations were often exhausting to her correspondents, except for those who were unconflicted in their identification with her and the cause.'

The abiding and complicated enchantment between Anna and her father produced, in her own theoretical work, a protracted meditation, unrivalled in the psychoanalytic literature and possibly elsewhere, on submission, on the nature of passivity and what she called 'emotional surrender'. Her sense of what it is to be a child is resonant in all her writing. She could make psychoanalytic theory sound like common sense, the refused common sense that it must be without sacrificing its radical oddity. But for her there was always one sacrifice that was the heart of the matter. As she wrote of the post-Oedipal child in *Psychoanalysis for Teachers and Parents* (1935), 'the originality of the child, together with a great deal of his energy and talents, are sacrificed to being "good" . . . It is as if the parents said: You can certainly go away, but you must take us with you.' The war between originality and being good, between leaving home and finding nowhere else to go, was to dominate her life. When Oscar Nemon's statue of Freud was unveiled in 1971, Anna 'very pointedly made sure that her children from the Hampstead Nursery School did attend, and then she sent pictures of them looking up at her father's presence and image to all of her friends and colleagues'. One can't help wondering what the children made of it. But then a lot of us are still looking up to her father.

9
Perversion

It was part of Freud's disingenuous rationalism to assert that psychoanalysis could never be any kind of *Weltanschauung*, that it was exempt from traditional moral questions like whether virtue can be taught, or whether we need to know what we are doing in order to be good. Confronted, however, with patients who claimed to have been seduced as children by parents or other adults, Freud very quickly came up against his own personal preferences – which he would later call resistances – and the normative standards of his culture. There were clearly certain things which were deemed absolutely unacceptable for adults to do to children and these could only be adequately described in terms of sexuality. Freud's first patients, though, were mostly women who claimed to have been seduced by their fathers. It is Estela Welldon's point in her often sympathetic book, *Mother, Madonna, Whore: The Idealization and Denigration of Motherhood* (1988), that maternal incest may be more pervasive than Freud was able to recognize.

Psychoanalysis began, however, with the really very puzzling question of the difference between adults and children: that is, the significance of the link between desire and the capacity for reproduction (a link, of course, complicated by the manufacture of increasingly efficient methods of contraception). Children, Freud realized, desire – but without possibility. They are, as Winnicott once famously said, all dressed up with nowhere to go. With the advent of psychoanalysis the growing child has continued to model himself on the adults, while the adults are theoretically modelled on the child. After the disappointments of the Oedipal drama, adults are children manqués. Because Freud also realized that the lives of both adults and children were dominated by the work of wishing (and one advantage of this is that we can usefully ask of any psychoanalytic theory what wishes it tries to satisfy). He discovered not only the actuality of incestuous seduction, but also the child's fantasized wish to seduce and be seduced by the parents. Psychoanalysis was, initially, a phenomenology of malign – that is, inappropriate – seduction. And since it began in relation to the parents it was not clear what the (relatively) non-incestuous varieties might be. 'Seduction' has always been a dirty word in psychoanalysis, and there is even now a paucity of psychoanalytic accounts of good seductions, despite the fact that psychoanalysis is able to address that most disabling of symptoms, the unwillingness to seduce or be seduced. The present horror and righteous indignation about the prevalence of child sexual abuse, which Welldon's book forthrightly examines, should not be allowed to leave such things in the dark.

In the *Three Essays on the Theory of Sexuality* Freud described, for both sexes, a perverse core to the personality as the essence of an infantile sexuality which was by inclination keenly seductive. But the notion of seduction with which Freud started, and the concept of perversion to which it led him, inevitably brought with them the more traditional idea of a True Path. To seduce is to lead away, and a perversion, by definition, deviates from a norm, though the crucial irony of Freud's account in the *Three Essays* was that perversion in childhood *was* the norm. Was perversion, in fact, perverse? In Welldon's account, perversions are the consequence of 'faulty mothering'. They are expedient solutions to a traumatic personal history, distortions of what, in a better world, is a potentially more satisfying and straightforward developmental process. Psychoanalysis, as Freud conceived of it, however, was always a critique of the straightforward life, and indeed of any tyrannical intimations of perfection. It was exactly his sense of how equivocal a process a life was that drove him to some necessary complications which Welldon's approach leaves to one side. For example, the case-histories she presents are used simply to illustrate her theoretical proposals. Her patients' lives have a misleading inevitability, an absence, from the analyst's point of view, of accident or genuine perplexity. It begins to seem that having a life could involve not making a mess. A familiar psychoanalytic knowingness sets in which is singularly unimpressed by loose ends.

For Freud, the story of a life was always the story of a life in disarray. By 1905 he had evolved, in a sense, two theories which were in many ways at odds with each other and whose legacy of useful contradiction is alive in contemporary psychoanalysis. On the one hand, in the *Three Essays*, he devised a rudimentary developmental theory of oral, anal and phallic stages which gravitated towards the Oedipal drama and gave what he considered to be empirically verifiable shape – a story-line, perhaps even a purpose – to the bemusing project of growing up. This involved unifying the perverse parts of the personality towards their putative aim of 'genital maturity'. On the other hand, in the Dream Book and the Joke Book, Freud constituted an unconscious that was 'timeless' and whose ingenious desire and insistent linguistic opportunism rendered any notions of predictability (or development) redundant. The patient is cured in psychoanalysis when, among other things, he continues to plan for the future knowing he is unable to do so.

In British psychoanalysis, with the work of Melanie Klein and Anna Freud, who were not British, and Winnicott, Bowlby and Fairbairn who were, it was the developmental theory, which Welldon uses in her book, that was taken up, often at the cost of the Freudian unconscious. A confluence of peculiarly disparate traditions, British psychoanalysis was never witty or wordly-wise. It tended to favour counter-erotic progressivist notions of growth and maturity rather than, say, Wilde's profoundly Freudian quip that only mediocrities develop. It struggled, in fact, and still struggles, to sustain itself as an empirical tradition based on 'observation' – when psychoanalysis is patently fantastic – and it has repressed the spectre of Hume as part of its ignorance of its own history. Psychoanalysis began with Freud, but something that might now be called psychology did not. And we need to know something of all this, both in order to reinstate a generous scepticism in British psychoanalysis and to provide a sufficient context to understand such a provocative book as *Mother, Madonna, Whore*. Though listening, for some reason, is something psychoanalysts have written little about, this is clearly a book written out of an impassioned listening to people with frightening stories to tell; and for a serious psychoanalytic book it has a reassuringly sensational title. But the explanations it contains are sometimes too costively neat.

'The clinical evidence,' Welldon writes in the epilogue to her book, 'supports the maxim "never underestimate the power of a mother".' Freud's version of psychoanalysis, in her view, did not give sufficient attention to the powerful influence of mothering, which, she emphasizes, 'can scarcely be overemphasized'. I should have thought there was now no more risk of psychoanalysts underestimating mothers than of their plucking the heart out of the mystery. But the mystique of the vague, modish word 'power' in this context casts a false spell on the discussion. Turning Freudian psychoanalysis inside out, Welldon finds in the child's mother the 'power' that was once vested in the child's unconscious. What is inside the child is, in this account, at least potentially good – meaning acceptable to the child – but what is outside, the mother, is seen as problematic. Only bad mothers produce hard-core Freudian children. From Welldon's point of view, it is not the human condition as constructed by Freud that is innately perverse and therefore insistently troubling; but perversion carried over into adult life is the consequence of what is grudgingly called, in this tradition of psychoanalysis, 'maternal failure'. Perversion becomes eroticized homesickness. And though this developmental account is consistently illuminating, it can also be seen as a theoretically elaborated grievance against a mother (fathers, as in the perverse scenario itself, tend not to get much of a look-in). Mothers, in fact, do not let their children down, even though both mothers and children are keen to see it this way: they simply live their lives.

It is not clear why so many of our notions of accountability – and often intelligibility – depend so exclusively upon a capacity for blame. But judgements cannot be disowned by saying one is not making judgements. Despite Welldon's disclaimers, language cannot be policed by spurious notions of analytic neutrality. If psychoanalysts are to sanctify the past – which always runs the risk of deadening the future – and mine it for 'causes', then questions of responsibility need to be given more than the short shrift they get in this book. It is not enough to have it baldly asserted that the use of a word like 'perversion' in this context implies no moral judgement, or that perverse mothering is simply something one might learn to diagnose. 'To treat patients,' Welldon writes, 'you must act on evidence not presuppositions', but – to ask what is surely by now an obvious question – how does one know what constitutes evidence, except on the basis of presupposition? With this naïve empiricism – continual recourse to 'facts' and clinical evidence and the supposedly non-moralistic use of terms – *Mother, Madonna, Whore* forgives mothers through understanding, but blames them by implication.

It is Estela Welldon's contention in this book that some mothers, for very good reasons to do with their own histories, can let their children down by turning them into perverts. It is because of 'inadequate mothering' that perverts 'are prevented from a very early age from achieving sexual, emotional maturity'. Exactly what sexual, emotional maturity is in psychoanalysis is not altogether clear, but generally speaking one rarely meets anybody who has achieved it. And descriptions of it usually produce a plethora of vague clichés about rich, fulfilling mutuality or fantasies of wholeness that are full of holes. Certainly in the perverse relationships described in this book there is an absolute absence of any shared pleasures. Certain kinds of mothering, Welldon believes, make such pleasures impossible. And these particular kinds of mothering she regards as characteristic forms of female perversion. Society's idealization of mothering, she suggests, has rendered these female perversions invisible (men have usually been considered to be the perverts and women simply the victims). But the absence of nursery places, for example, or even the advertisements for washing-powder, suggest quite the opposite: the culture is rife with the disparagement of mothers. It is, nevertheless, an interesting point that the so-called perversions are parodies, often frightening ones, of 'good' mothering. But by narrowing the focus on to mothering – even though she makes a strong and convincing case for these being multigenerational patterns, and for the importance of 'socio-psychological aspects' of the question – Welldon, in a sense, de-politicizes a useful psychoanalytic insight. Perversion is not only a compulsively enacted critique of mothering: it is also a furtive critique of the culture, a sexualized cartoon of the repertoire of relationships the culture makes possible. And the culture is made, on drastically uneven terms, by both men and women.

The ignoring of women by giving them victim status has not been helped, in Welldon's view, by psychoanalysis, which has, at least until recently, used a paradigm of male sexual development for both sexes. Freud, 'though a genius,' Welldon writes, 'was, as a man, unable to convey a full understanding of the complexities in the libidinal development of the two genders'. It was part of his 'genius' to show us that psychoanalytic theory is made with sentences, not with ideas. The nice qualification does nothing to undo the clumsy sexism of the sentence and its ludicrous assumption. How would anyone know if they had a 'full understanding' of such things? And perhaps more worrying, given the history of psychiatry since the turn of the century, what would they be doing with it if they thought they had it? Welldon exhorts us to 'return to basics. We must begin with the female body and its inherent attributes.' This presumably means that there is a land beyond History, called Biology, where the Basics live. Here femininity is constituted by the mystic proximity of two fantastic ghosts, the mind and the body.

Women, Welldon claims, 'have special problems . . . in getting to know themselves'. This must be true, given how determined men have been to exempt them from the available rituals; but it is a project to which special problems do, of course, attach themselves. The problems set the terms for what is to be known. But Welldon's explanation, if it can be called that, digs a traditional grave for women. It mires them in Nature: 'To acquire self-knowledge of their own womanhood in a way that is separate from their motherhood seems to many women a luxury that is impossible to achieve, perhaps because both their minds and their bodies are so much more involved than would be the case for men.' It is indeed difficult not to conceive of the differences between the sexes in sado-masochistic terms, the familiar language of better and worse. But dispiriting stereotypes are merely reinforced by this kind of barely literate pseudo-mystery. *Mother, Madonna, Whore* is studded with assertions about the differences between the sexes, ranging from the excitedly banal – 'There is a wide and spectacular difference in the sense of temporality in females' – to the manifestly false: 'The menopause is an exclusively female predicament.'

All this serves to obfuscate the fact that in this book Welldon has made one simple but significant new contribution to the psychoanalytic study of female perversion. And this requires, as she rightly points out, the acknowledgement of a possible difference between the sexes which more orthodox male-orientated Freudian psychoanalysis has tended to ignore. It is, of course, like all formulations of difference, a provisional, circumstantial and historically determined artefact, and not, so to speak, a revelation.

Welldon writes:

The main difference between a male and female perverse action lies in the aim. Whereas in men the act is aimed at an outside part-object – meaning a symbolic body-part, not what we think of as a person – in women it is usually against themselves, either against their bodies or against objects which they see as their own creations: their babies. In both cases bodies and babies are treated as part-objects.

This revenge, in the interests of safety and control, against what Welldon calls the mother's 'abuse of her power' evokes a perverse response in the child. But the sexes turn the tables in distinctively different ways (and by a rather unpleasant irony Welldon turns the tables on the conventional view by making women seem more powerfully, more influentially perverse than men). The mother who colonizes her child and stifles gestures of autonomy and difference breeds in him or her a virulent and sustaining resentment against any later object of desire. The child will be left, as an adult, with an often unconscious craving for the dead-end justice of revenge. Contempt will keep him or her safe from an intimacy that always threatens to belittle and trap them. But whereas 'perverse men use their penises', in Welldon's view, 'to attack and show hatred towards symbolic sources of humiliation, usually represented by part-objects . . . in the woman [perversion] will similarly be expressed through her reproductive organs'. Women turn against themselves – and their children as part of themselves – the hatred that men are able to turn against other people. This echoes, of course, the more conventional visual-aid theory of sexual difference: that because women's sexual organs are internal (which is not entirely true) they are more inward – whereas men are anatomically more outward-bound. This limited repertoire of imaginative speculation always suggests the repression of strong fantastic alternatives. But Welldon is persuasive that the boy humiliated in childhood takes revenge – perhaps also unconsciously seeks a solution to his predicament – by becoming what we think of as a pervert; the humiliated girl takes revenge by becoming a mother – in order, as Welldon puts it, to 'revenge herself against the fate of being a woman'. Perversion for both sexes is then reactive to the mostly unconscious exploitation by mothers of their children's dependence. Welldon is forceful and convincing in her claim that what perverse men do to women, perverse women do to their babies: they 'desire to engulf the other person, to dehumanize the object, and to invade, take complete control of and merge with the Other'. It is a disturbing picture because it is in exaggerated form a description of something ordinary: the need to eradicate, rather than the capacity to enjoy or be inspired by difference.

In Freud's great paper of 1915, 'Instincts and their Vicissitudes', he suggested that an instinct was subject to four main kinds of transformation: 'Reversal into its opposite. Turning round upon the subject's own self. Repression. Sublimation'. If all four are available to both sexes, why should it be the case, as Welldon's thesis implies, that women should specialize in the second, and so, by constraining their repertoire, limit their possibilities for satisfaction? Why, if it is true, do women tend to disparage themselves, when men with comparable histories disparage others? After a thorough review of the psychoanalytic literature, Welldon opts for a plausible, roughly historical explanation which is marred by the vagueness of its terms. 'Perhaps if women had a longer tradition of belonging to the power structure,' she writes, 'their attitudes to men and children would not be governed as they are now by a weakness which they strive to turn into possessiveness and control.' Relative powerlessness may produce tyrannical mothering, but it is also true that contemporary psychoanalytic notions of autonomy often sound like legitimated versions of the wish to dominate.

With that paradoxical combination of intense excitement and emotional impoverishment, perversions have become the negative ideals of development in psychoanalytic theory. Compulsive, repetitive, requiring accomplices, perversions involve – the theory tells us – an attempted denial of the differences between the sexes and the generations; and they reveal rather starkly the ways in which sexuality includes the wish to damage and dehumanize (what has become taboo, or pathologized, in psychoanalytic theory are the ways in which people are ineluctably unrelated to each other). The implied alternatives to all this are part of the therapeutic aim of psychoanalysis, which at least takes seriously the very real developmental difficulty of allowing the existence of other people. But these possible alternatives also reveal the curiously idealistic, perhaps misleadingly ambitious version of the good life that psychoanalysts after Freud have constructed. No one should underestimate, as Welldon's book makes clear, the misery of the driven, damaging life. But no one should underestimate, either, the fact that psychoanalysts have designs on their patients. Some of their designs are very interesting.

'Motherhood,' Welldon writes, 'is sometimes chosen for unconscious perverse reasons.' This may be true, but what is a good reason for having a child, and who is to say? Descriptions of motherhood like this are themselves chosen for all sorts of reasons. And psychoanalytic theory has always been the double – the not-so-secret sharer – of the symptomatology it has attempted to explain. But psychoanalysis does not have to be an omnivorous interpreting machine, or another colonial adventure. At its best, it is a way of keeping the questions of childhood alive.

10
Freud and Jones

The first chapter of Ernest Jones's misleadingly entitled auto-biography, *Free Associations*, ends with a bemusing paragraph about the Welsh 'servant who acted also as a nurse' during his early childhood: 'One of my memories of this nurse was that she taught me two words to designate the male organ, one for it in a flaccid state, the other in an erect. It was an opulence of vocabulary I have not encountered since.' As *The Complete Correspondence of Sigmund Freud and Ernest Jones 1908–1939* (1993), superbly edited by Andrew Paskauskas, shows, this childhood memory was a kind of symbolic omen, an uncanny foreshadowing of Jones's later preoccupations. The translation of psychoanalysis – both trying to get it across and turning it into English – was to be Jones's mission.

Ernest Jones has gone down in psychoanalytic history as the rather priggish servant who also acted as a nurse both to Freud and to the psychoanalytic 'movement', as it is often referred to in these revealing letters (at other times it is a 'campaign' or a 'cause'). Apparently convinced of the unimportance of being Ernest – he wrote a famous paper, 'The Inferiority Complex of the Welsh', in which he compared them unpromisingly with the Jews – Jones has always seemed rather a pompous, ridiculous figure in that 'secret ring' of early analysts: Jones the Joke, the man with no sense of humour. Who other than Ernest Jones could have defined 'cunnilingus' in the Glossary of his psychoanalytic papers as 'apposition of the mouth to the vulva'? But the man who, appropriately, contributed the term 'rationalization' to psychoanalysis (in 1908) – 'the inventing of a reason for an attitude or action the motive of which is not recognized' – also established psychoanalysis in Britain; organized, at first single-handedly, the translation of Freud's work; and was instrumental in saving many of the early analysts, including Freud himself, from the Nazis.

'You have really made the cause quite your own,' Freud writes to him in 1926, after the first twenty years of their collaboration, 'for you have achieved everything that could be made of it: a society, a journal and an institute.' But as Freud knew, fixing Jones with this kind of praise, this is the 'everything' of an ambitious bureaucrat. The cause was Freud's: Jones had simply made the arrangements. Jones may be more than the straight man in the double act of these letters, and in the tortured history of psychoanalysis, but what the correspondence does reveal is the sado-masochism of his relationship with Freud. By the same token it also reveals the new genre of 'honesty' produced by psychoanalysis, of which Jones's sometimes gruelling candour is an example, but from which Freud notably exempts himself. There are no confessions here from Freud. True to the spirit of psychoanalysis, he has no truck with the explicit, while Jones's 'honesty', true to the letter of psychoanalysis, entails boasting about vulnerability or what he considers to be personal weakness, as though telling the truth means describing all the ways in which he isn't as good as he should be. And when he is, according to him, it's thanks to Freud. 'To me it is clear that I owe my career, my livelihood, my position, and my capacity of happiness in marriage – in short everything – to you and the work you have done.' The excess of Jones's gratitude was not entirely to Freud's liking; in the complicity of these letters – Freud's composed reticence sustaining and sustained by Jones's clamorous appeals – Freud is more than willing to remind Jones of his abject self.

Jones was certainly preoccupied, in more ways than one, by what to call his potent self: 'Jones' seemed singularly unpromising. Given as he writes in one of the letters, that 'psychoanalysis is Freud', who, then, is Jones (or anyone else)? When his son was born Jones decided he would change his name because 'some names like Jones and Smith have lost the first function of a name, that is to separate them from other people'. He decided to 'amplify' his name to Beddow-Jones. Once Freud had poured elaborate and mocking scorn on this – 'I only know that you will continue to be Ernest Jones to us' – Jones, with characteristically unwitting bathos, immediately withdrew the idea: 'So I must continue to assimilate the pinpricks involved in being called Jones or 'E. Jones.' But letters, like dreams, refer to a backdrop of stories. Jones's wife, we discover, left him for someone called Jones (Herbert); and eleven years after Jones first proposed making his name more opulent Freud was to write to him of someone Jones had inquired about: 'He may be called Freud; the name is not as rare as one might wish.' Rarer, though, than Jones.

If one of the pleasures of *The Complete Correspondence* is Freud's wit, which thrives on Jones being true to his (first) name, the other is the myriad of deferred and interrupted stories that the letters contain. Any keyword – 'Women', or 'Fate', or 'Science', or 'Originality', or 'Telepathy', or 'Klein' – followed through the thirty-one years of this correspondence (the longest of any of Freud's correspondences) will disclose the multiple and conflicting histories that make up psychoanalysis. 'The readers,' Freud wrote to Jones, 'should not be induced to forget the historical moment' of any element of psychoanalytic theory; and this correspondence, for better or worse, certainly thickens the plot, making us newly suspicious of the suspicion called psychoanalysis. What it provides is a kind of source-book for the muddles and conflicts of contemporary psychoanalysis in which, though there are no longer 'heresies' and 'apostates', to use the Freud/Jones vocabulary, people still defend ideas as though they were parents. (The child, it should be remembered, always defends the bad parent more ferociously than the good.)

Jones probably did more than anyone in the early years of psychoanalysis to promote and sustain Freud's work. And his expressed view of Freud in these letters is consistently admiring, sometimes ingratiating and occasionally idolatrous ('what has made my life worth living, my relationship to you and your work'). Jones's lack of irony, so striking in these letters, is more than compensated for by Freud ('Any article of yours on the Mystery and Mythology of Flatus will be welcome'). In his autobiography, however, Jones allows himself two significant grievances against Freud which are particularly relevant to their correspondence. It was, he writes,

Freud's mistaken admiration for Jung that 'was the first indication that I had that Freud, despite his extraordinary genius in penetrating the deepest layers of the mind, was not a connoisseur of men . . . He underestimated or overestimated people over and over again on the simple criterion of liking or disliking them on personal grounds . . . [he] was prone at times to very subjective judgments.' Freud, Jones suggests, understood human nature but not individuals, the depths but not their shallow representatives, people. There is an implicit, and alarming, belief here in a 'correct' judgement of people. Jones prided himself on being a scientist, and refers in his letters to people's 'subjectivity', whatever that is, getting in the way of the work (Ferenczi, as one would expect, gets a lot of stick for this). Jones was a great believer in technique, as opposed to character, in the practice of psychoanalysis; and according to him, Freud – who does not seem to have been very interested in technique – lacked scientific rigour: he simply liked or disliked people.

The other, and clearly related, adverse judgement of Freud that Jones permits himself has to do with translation, one of the main topics of the correspondence (translation, that is, in the several senses of the word). When Jones complained to Freud about one of the early translations of his work, he apparently replied: 'better to have a good friend than a good translator'. 'I have not to this day,' Jones writes, 'been able to fathom his cavalier attitude in this matter of translations, which almost produces the impression of indifference concerning the promulgation of his work abroad.' It is as though Freud is a bit too personal and careless for Jones (one of Freud's fears, expressed in these letters, about the Kleinian version of analysis that Jones was backing was that it made 'analysis unreal and impersonal'). Of course, Freud as a casual person, liking and disliking people and preferring friends, undermines the image of Freud's stoical austerity that Jones had worked so hard to promote in his bizarre and monumental biography. These letters show him straining to keep a certain version of Freud going; when Freud gets what in Jones's view is a poor American translation of one of his papers, Jones writes: 'some of the expressions you are made to use are decidedly undignified . . . and therefore clash with our conception of you'. Jones's protectiveness is disarming, and reveals the potential of psychoanalysis as a form of dissociated knowledge. Certainly, he would have had no trouble analysing this kind of idealization in one of his patients. 'You are proof by now,' he writes to Freud in 1921, 'against misunderstandings, and can also rely on us to correct them for you.' From a psychoanalytic point of view, misunderstanding was the name of the game. With the idea of the dream-work, Freud had proposed a new paradox of knowledge: that there were misunderstandings, but no understandings. This, for the scientific Joneses, of which there were to be many, not to mention the critics of psychoanalysis, was too much.

After giving a successful talk on psychoanalysis to the British Psychological Society in 1920, Jones writes to Freud that his success 'made me think of your saying: a man is strong so long as he represents a strong idea'. But Freud realized that psychoanalysis had ironized the whole idea of the strong idea and the strong man, while still promoting them as ideals. Freud, that is to say – and perhaps he had learnt this partly from Mill – was an adept critic of his own apparently strong ideas. Criticizing something of Jones's, he speaks of 'the danger inherent in our method of concluding from faint traces, exploiting trifling signs'. When they write to each other, if it is not about business, it is about issues of competence. What you are allowed to do in the treatment and still call yourself a psychoanalyst – and who is in a position to decide – has always been the central question among psychoanalysts. So Jones's correspondence with Freud is organized around two related obsessions: how authoritative is Freud (and psychoanalysis) and who can best represent – that is, translate – his work? Because Jones is so determinedly convinced of the Truth of psychoanalysis – 'of the highest importance for the race in general and for civilization in particular' – he is mystified by Freud's casual and sometimes dismissive attitude to the translation of his work, as though Freud might even be ambivalent about Truth.

It is clear from the correspondence that Freud is often contemptuous of Jones's endless concern about translations, implying that those who can, do; those who can't, translate (edit magazines and arrange conferences). 'If you lay so great stress on the translations of my books I cannot but give in to you,' Freud writes glumly, 'but I continue to regret the amount of work it means for you and could be spent better on original research.' Given the time and the importance Jones obviously allotted to the translation of Freud's work, it must have been dismaying to receive letters in which Freud makes it quite clear that he is 'getting sick of this translation business'; that 'the whole topic of American and English translations is, so to speak, on the periphery of my interest', the implication being that anyone with any originality could not possibly take it so seriously. Translation, paradoxically – or sadistically – becomes, among other things, the stick Freud uses to beat Jones with. In a devastating crticism of Jones's book *On the Nightmare* he mentions 'that it was the sort of book that did not greatly interest [me] because it was too much a question of simply making translations from the unconscious'. Obviously, in Freud's view, there were more interesting things to do. And, as a 'wandering Jew', he may have had very mixed feelings – a combination of grandiose ambition and intransigent privacy – about the wider circulation of his work. What comes through in the correspondence is his sense of Jones's devotion to the task as often more of a symptom than a virtue, and Jones's bewildered feelings of humiliation; Jones doing his best and Freud slightly amazed that he can be bothered, but praising him occasionally. 'You probably know you have the reputation,' Jones wrote in 1938, in one of his last letters to Freud, 'of not being the easiest author to translate.' Jones's last translation, so to speak, was the unequivocally heroic one of bringing Freud and Anna to London in 1938.

Jones, it seems, was only too glad to accept Freud's estimate of him as work-horse, and propagandist. 'Nothing has taken me back to past days so much,' Jones writes in 1920, 'as that wonderful evening when you discoursed to me of your new ideas and plans; they will find a fruitful soil in me, you may be sure.' Jones was so available for Freud partly because, as he wrote in his autobiography, 'however enterprising I might be intellectually, I was not intended for a pioneer's life'. (What tends to pass for self-knowledge, and even wisdom, in psychoanalysis is a strong sense of one's personal limitations.) In his 'subjective' way Freud quickly saw – and exploited, to their mutual advantage – Jones's much flaunted doubts about himself. 'I am glad you are not one of those fellows,' Freud writes to him (in English) in the early days of their relationship, 'who want to show themselves original and totally independent when they do something in writing, but you do not despise to show yourself as interpreter of another's thoughts.'

This treads a thin line between what might have felt like accurate, and therefore reassuring, recognition and a demand on Freud's part: 'who I want you to be' cast as 'this is who you are', which is an ingredient in all psychoanalytic interpretation. The die was certainly cast early for Jones. Jung, Ferenczi, Rank and Abraham were all, as Jones knew, far more theoretically innovative than he could be; and in the end the only way he could stand his ground against Freud was on behalf of someone else's supposed originality – that of Melanie Klein. Despite what Riccardo Steiner, in a notably cautious introduction to *The Complete Correspondence*, calls the 'frankly wild analysis' of these letters, it is striking how the two correspondents keep each other in place – the same place – through all the conflict and collaboration. So Jones responds enthusiastically to Freud's sense of his lack of initiative:

My ambition is rather to know, to be 'behind the scenes' and 'in the know', rather than to find out . . . I realise that I have very little talent for originality . . . my work will be to try and work out in detail, and to find new demonstrations for the truth of, ideas others have suggested. To me work is like a woman bearing a child; to men like you, I suppose, it is more like fertilisation.

This is revealing not only of Jones's relationship to Freud, but also of his picture of women as essentially disciples and research assistants. These images matter because one of the many interesting things about the correspondence is the backdrop it provides to the formative psychoanalytic debate on female sexuality.

In the early days of psychoanalysis male sexuality was of interest but female sexuality was a 'riddle': what Freud was eventually to call, in an unfortunate pun, 'the dark continent'. Male sexuality didn't produce a flurry of controversial papers; it was, so to speak, women and children first. If translation was a 'vexed question' between Freud and Jones, women – or their psychoanalytic synonym, female sexuality – promised to have the answer to, or to be keeping the secret of, the most important theoretical conundrums. The issue of translation raised the question of who was competent, other than Freud himself, to represent psychoanalysis. The question raised by sexual difference was: who is equipped, as it were, to speak about female sexuality? It very quickly seemed as though these two questions were inextricably linked. The contest enacted in this correspondence may have been the conventional one between men – who's the expert on women? – but the uses of their so-called expertise were to have exorbitant consequences. Nothing – apart from the pathologization of homosexuality to which it is related – has been more coercive or misleading in psychoanalysis than its generalizations about women. It is baffling, in retrospect, that turning women into objects of scientific inquiry did not lead these early psychoanalysts to ask: what kind of sexual act is understanding or scientific knowledge? What was this knowledge, supposing there was such a thing, to be used for?

Psychoanalysis had to invent certain kinds of women to legitimate its practices. But every picture of a woman, like every picture of a man, is, among other things, the solution to a (largely unconscious) problem. Freud was committed, so to speak, to penis-envy; Jones to the belief, as he put it in his late paper 'Early Female Sexuality', that woman is not *un homme manqué* . . . a permanently disappointed creature struggling to console herself with secondary substitutes alien to her true nature'. Freud needed a picture of a woman who wanted to be a man, because he needed to believe he was something someone else (or other) would want to be. Jones needed a picture of a woman who wanted to be a woman, so he wouldn't have to do it for her. It is part of their legacy that we are bewitched by descriptions of sexual difference either in terms of insufficiency and lack – the sexes representing to each other what is rightfully theirs, and the (often violent) consequences of that – or in terms of an (allegedly) essential femininity, which brings with it a different kind of violence, the violence of normative standards and obligations to conform.

Jones, frequently embroiled, we infer, in what the editor of *The Complete Correspondence* quaintly calls his 'penchant for women', writes with clinical detachment about the women in his life. Freud, the enduringly married man, is usually affectionate and admiring of the women he writes about, one of whom is Jones's first wife, whom he was analysing in the early days of his relationship with Jones (Jones quite often sent people to see Freud, who was supposed to improve them in some way). One of the problems Jones had with his wife – and not only with her, alas – was that she didn't believe in psychoanalysis: 'she has terribly strong complexes against the work,' he writes in his familiar tone of ingenuous bafflement, 'and I have never had a chance of breaking her resistance'. His 'chance' came when he finally persuaded her to go to Vienna and have analysis with Freud. Confident of Freud's effect on his wife, Jones writes: 'I trust you will get a look inside this volcano of emotion, and teach her how to make a better use of its fires.' This is as concise a picture as one could wish for of Jones's picture of Freud, of his wife, and of the function of analysis.

Jones often sounds in these letters as though he is sending people to the headmaster with a bad report ('Putnam is incorrigible; he is a woman not a man'). And the Head can be quite strict: 'I was sorry too having heard you got yourself into fresh difficulties with a woman,' Freud writes to Jones (in English): 'I pity it very much that you should not master such dangerous cravings.' (For that generation, it seems, either you 'mastered' the desire or you 'mastered' the woman; it took the generation of Winnicott and Lacan to understand how Freud's idea of the unconscious made a mockery of mastery.) When Jones finds his talented colleague and ex-patient Joan Riviere unmanageable – 'it is not easy for anyone to get on well with her unless either he is in a position of acknowledged supremacy, as you are, or else is effiminate' – he sends her to Freud for correction. But this time, Jones intimates, the tamer of volcanoes will be really up against it: 'The saying here is that her visit to Vienna will be the final and most severe test of psychoanalysis, and people are most curious to see if her disdainful way of treating other people like dirt beneath her feet will undergo any modification.' In his rage Jones implies that psychoanalysis (or Freud himself) was something that he needed to protect him from being dominated by a woman.

But his wish to discipline these women – 'I think, however, that her judgments are apt to be impulsive,' he writes of the French analyst Marie Bonaparte, 'and to need a steadying influence' – was, as it always is, a complicated and painful thing. On the one hand, the women were a problem for Jones because they represented, among other things, the part of himself that refused to submit (to Freud, to psychoanalysis, to whatever he felt oppressed and coerced by). On the other, they carried his doubts about Freud, and the consequences of those doubts (Jones letting Riviere do the 'testing' he could never let himself do). Writing to Freud in 1926 about 'what in the female corresponds with castration in the male as the resolver of the Oedipus Complex', Jones comes to what now seems like a rather personal conclusion: 'After working through various layers I found as the deepest with [women] the dread of being disapproved of and deserted by the father, because this meant the loss of all hope of penis and child.' If this dread of being disapproved of and deserted by the father is the *man's* deepest fear, then perhaps he has found a way of getting women to carry it. Jones was lucky enough to find, in Melanie Klein, a woman who could tolerate the disapproval of a father.

Until Klein arrived on the scene Freud tended to treat Jones's 'problem' with women either by being outrageously patronizing – 'your understanding of your marital constellation is excellent' – or by stressing how impressed he is by, how fond of, these people whom Jones can't manage. Indeed, there is sometimes a note of glee in Freud's celebrations of them, as though the joke is on Jones ('I daresay,' he writes to Jones, 'you need not be more afraid of Mrs Riviere than of any other person'). And where Jones is more than willing, under the aegis of science and objectivity, to write about women's 'deepest' fears and needs, Freud is more circumspect. 'Everything we know,' he writes to Jones in 1928, 'about early female development seems to me unsatisfactory and uncertain.' As a parallel text to the influential theoretical papers – Jones's 'The Early Development of Female Sexuality' (1927), 'The Phallic Phase' (1933), 'Early Female Sexuality' (1935), and Freud's 'Female Sexuality' (1931) – the correspondence gives us a glimpse of the fraught lives behind the more measured 'scientific' prose. From the papers you get a sense of debate and inquiry; from the correspondence you get the sense that both men are dealing with this unmanageable thing that is sometimes called 'female sexuality', or the 'unconscious', or 'psychoanalysis' itself.

But it is Jones who has the more urgent need to sort things out, who is in search of theoretical convictions. Jones could never acknowledge the sense in which psychoanalysis, or rather, Freud's notion of the unconcious, ironized efficiency, and it was this that created the wrangle between them that is so evident in the letters. In psychoanalysis the need for certainty, and the militant competence that goes with it, leave one without an unconscious to speak of (as in much Kleinian theory). You can no more be 'in the know' about the unconscious than you can believe in it. An expert on psychoanalysis would be a person without an unconscious.

In Melanie Klein Jones found someone who knew what was in the unconscious. With Klein's arrival in London in 1926 he began to feel himself for the first time at the forefront of psychoanalytic progress – prior to this, as the letters show, he had continually felt that both he and the British Society were manifestly inferior to the continental analysts – and was clearly both troubled and exhilarated by the possibility of a split with Freud and the Vienna group. For anyone interested in British psychoanalysis – which is itself inevitably 'symptomatic' (as people used to say) of wider social issues – this is the main drama of the correspondence. The question that had been all dressed up with nowhere to go had now turned up in London: who in psychoanalysis is in a position to speak and be believed? Who has privileged access to the depths, the deepest depths? Or, to put it another way: who's in charge – Freud and his accomplice Anna, or Klein and her accomplice Jones? Within a short space of time the canon of psychoanalytic preoccupations was formed: child analysis, lay analysis (an unusual term for such a virulently anti-religious 'cause'), and female sexuality. (Just to add a bit of context to this: Freud had analysed his daughter, Anna, and Klein had analysed Jones's son; both Klein and Jones had been briefly analysed by Ferenczi; neither Anna Freud nor Melanie Klein was a doctor.) Klein represented the possibility of rupture with Freud, led by a woman.

What was revolutionary about Klein was that she succeeded where others had failed in dividing the psychoanalytic community. Ferenczi never had a following, and Jung and Adler stopped calling themselves psychoanalysts. Klein's dismaying picture of the child was, and still is, perfectly compatible with a certain strain in British culture. Her work is a kind of psychoanalytic *Pilgrim's Progress* in which Truth, Terror and Disappointment are inextricable. Jones, as one might expect, knew why some people didn't like it: opposition to Klein indicated 'nothing but resistance,' he writes to Freud, 'against accepting the reality of her conclusions concerning infantile life'. 'Disagreement' would have been a better word because it acknowledges the validity of both points of view. The question was: what can you hear when you listen to a child speak, and who is in a position to decide? Freud knew the answer: 'Melanie Klein is on the wrong track,' he writes to Jones, 'and Anna is on the right one.' Jones accused Anna of being insufficiently analysed – always the most disreputable way psychoanalysts have of disagreeing with each other – but he could also acknowledge his own doubts about it all: 'The great question of whether we in England have advanced your theory farther or whether we have made a serious mistake still remains an open one as far as I am concerned.' 'Farther' is clearly the important word here.

Both Freud and Jones thought of themselves as scientists, but they meant very different things by it; and Freud's explicit wish in these letters is to rescue psychoanalysis from being the exclusive terrain of medical scientists, like Jones himself. And it is easy to see why. But Jones does have one insight in passing – which is where most so-called insights tend to turn up – that has a different kind of rigour from his other pronouncements in these letters. 'Many analysts,' he writes to Freud, 'are sufficiently well-analysed for other activities in life, but not for doing analytic work.' Psychoanalysis might make one want to do things other than psychoanalysis. But psychoanalysts are the only people who can never be cured of their need for analysis.

11

Cross-Dressing

Describing the two sexes as opposite or complementary, rather than useful to each other for certain things but not for others, promotes the misleading idea that we are all in search of completion. Bewitched by the notion of being complete, we become obsessed by notions of sameness and difference, by thoughts of what to include and what to reject in order to keep ourselves whole. But maintaining this icon of ourselves confronts us with a paradoxical question: if we have an identity what are we identical to? It is as though we need to know where we are by never being anywhere else. And one fundamental means of orientation, of self-recognition, is the difference between the sexes, despite the fact that in practice they keep leaking into each other. Once you stop pointing to body parts and start talking, the apparent differences between men and women begin to dissipate. So if we aren't different from the opposite sex, what are we?

The one thing we never know about people when we meet them is their history, but the one thing we cannot help knowing, or assuming, is their sex. It is not clear, though, as common sense and psychoanalysis tells us, what we think we know, what we imagine the signs are telling us. Marjorie Garber suggests, in her exhilarating book, *Vested Interests: Cross-Dressing and Cultural Anxiety* (1992), that with the idea of fixed sexual identity, of being too knowingly male or female – terms, she remarks archly, 'that overwhelmingly proclaim their own inadequacy' – we may have got ourselves into something we are always trying to get out of. Indeed, what she calls the 'pitfalls of gender assignment' that her book is so loosely and lucidly about, make one wonder why it is so difficult to imagine a person now not preoccupied by difference, a person for whom the problem of difference – of identity itself, and the war between purity and danger

– has disappeared. *Vested Interests* implies, with a light but well researched touch, that our most intense erotic attachments are to our categories; that we hold ourselves together by keeping things apart. Garber wants us to wonder what our lives would look like without this project, without our endless concern about the categories of male and female. She wants to find out what we can do without, and what we might do then.

Her last book, the underrated *Shakespeare's Ghost Writers* – like *Vested Interests*, about people of uncertain status, ghosts as liminal creatures that confuse categories – asked why we need to hold on to Shakespeare, why he has such a grip on our imaginations. *Vested Interests* asks, as an echo, why we have made a fetish of sexual difference, why we have turned it into the indispensable preoccupation that keeps us and gets us going? The implication of both books is that there are some disillusionments we think we cannot bear, some things we are unable to mourn. Mourning is painful not only because it is an acknowledgement of loss, but because it confronts us with the knowledge that we never were the possessors of what we have lost, but rather, the partial inventors, which is different. Through the figure of the transvestite – the opportunist with no alternatives – Garber shows that our categories are themselves ghosts, or ghost-writers, and not the reassuring commodities which we, and a long philosophical tradition before us, pretend that they are. We don't own them, nor do they own us: we are simply attached to them. Because of the 'power of the transvestite to unsettle assumptions, structures and hierarchies', the transvestite 'tells the truth about gender'. Anti-essentialists like Garber, of course, cannot help occasionally falling back into the old language, but what distinguishes Garber as a critic is that she obviously likes all the things she demystifies and invites us to relinquish. Her truth is not told with sadistic relish: she really wants to have it both ways.

It is a convention of modern theory to show that the exception does not prove the rule, but proves that the rule is an exception; the anomalous and the marginal no longer consolidate the norm – they displace it. The transvestite, in Garber's view, disclosing the truth about gender by performing a category crisis for us, reveals the repressed norm of 'blurred gender'. Not that the sexes have some things in common, but that they are radically confused. Blurred gender is the terror that any secure sexual identity – or rather, representation of sexual identity – is trying to conceal. So despite her perhaps surprising statistics – 6 per cent of Americans are cross-dressers, 1 per cent trans-sexuals – it seems both mysterious and entirely obvious that we are not all, as far as we can tell, wearing each other's clothes. Garber, of course, cannot completely avoid the new pieties of the contemporary academic sexual enlightenment – that it is both more truthful and better not to know who you are, that it is preferable to slip, shift or float than to know, stop or stay – but her book is unusually attentive to the way in which any theory can serve as a fetish.

For Freud, psychic life, for both sexes, was organized around the catastrophe of castration; for some modern Freudian critics like Garber, it is organized around the catastrophe of certainty, of fixed and exclusive definition. In the moral world of *Vested Interests* undecidability and transgression are implicitly virtues, and like all the virtues, particularly when insisted on, they can easily begin to sound like fetishes, those things we need to believe in to avert a worse disaster, words to whistle in the dark with. Perhaps our fantasies of catastrophe are themselves fetishes; Garber is certainly mindful of the very real agonies of becoming one sex and then the other; that cheap jokes, expecially about sexual identity, can be very expensive.

Being blithe about transgression quickly becomes a way of forgetting that people actually suffer, and so of putting the (moral) emphasis in the wrong place. Prometheus didn't think that trans-gression was a good idea: he thought that élitist knowledge was unjust. Garber doesn't promote transvestites as exciting outlaws, nor does she only offer us a new orthodoxy in the guise of a radical alternative. But she admires transvestism in a way that makes her adept at showing how it is diminished and undermined by more anxiously coercive forms of interpretation. Transvestites are patho-logized (as suffering from a 'developmental disorder', often assumed to be homosexuality), normalized (as people in what she calls a 'progress narrative' going through a stage towards the rude health of heterosexuality), seen through – but not seen. Determined not to blank them out through interpretation, to snub their accounts of themselves with an apparently more sophisticated vocabulary, *Vested Interests* lets a lot of remarkable people – fictional and non-fictional, so to speak – speak for themselves. Because embarrassment is one of the hearts of the matter, it must have been tempting to be too careful, to trample the subject with sensitivity. Fortunately Garber has not tried to write an unprovocative book, so *Vested Interests* is full of good quotable lines, is written, in other words, in the spirit of Colette's winning observation, which she also quotes: 'The seduction emanating from a person of uncertain or dissimulated sex is powerful.'

Through chapters with titles like 'Cross-Dress for Success', 'Fetish Envy, *a tergo*: Red Riding Hood and the Wolf in Bed', Garber makes a powerful and seductive case for the transvestite and trans-sexual as a focal point for the way in which one category crisis always leads to another. 'The possibility of crossing racial boundaries,' she writes apropos of representations of racial stereotypes in the media, 'stirs fears of the possibility of crossing the boundaries of gender, and vice versa.' Wherever you find the transvestite, no other categories are safe: 'The appearance of a transvestite in a cultural representation,' she writes, 'signals a category crisis.' So in *Peter Pan*, the subject of one of the most telling chapters in the book, 'category crises are everywhere' – crises about class, gender and the differences between adults and children. This simple point, that one category always suggests another, leads her to some terse and revealing formulations: 'Why is Peter Pan played by a woman?' she asks. 'Because a woman will never grow up to be a man.'

For Garber, 'one of the most important aspects of cross-dressing is the way in which it offers a challenge to easy notions of binarity, putting into question the categories of "female" and "male", whether they are considered essential or constructed, biological or cultural'. It is the reassuring bind of binarism that it shrinks the repertoire; but the either/or world also produces its own kind of violence as a protest against such limited alternatives. There may be a timidity in the ease with which we choose our public toilets. The different signs on the doors, Garber suggests, satisfy 'a desire for cultural binarism rather than for biological certainty'. The way out is clearly not through these doors. The transvestite always makes a mockery of these distinctions – these familiar little signs – by always going through the wrong door. Or, to put it another way, the transvestite always gets it right whichever door he chooses. It is as though the most terrifying world is the world in which it is impossible to make a mistake.

The theoretical mistake that Garber knowingly avoids, and that would have made her book complicit with what she is trying to undo, would have been to suggest that the transvestite was merely a combination, a third sex as some kind of synthesis of the other two. (In other words, *Vested Interests* reveals the sense in which to be intelligent or intellectually respectable now, a theoretical book doesn't have to use the word 'Hegel'.) All the superordinate critical positions, all the views from outside or above that claim exemption, are a kind of covert longing for this third sex that will be able to tell us the difference. Garber – like all the most interesting cultural critics, a closet theologian – is keen to clarify her sense that the transvestite is not merely a third term that confirms the other two like a god, giving them his blessing, but is 'rather something that challenges the possibility of harmonious and stable binary symmetry'. The transvestite can make men and women look distinctly odd, peculiar in their 'naturalness', absurdly trapped in their codes of difference. The transvestite, she writes, 'as a "third" is a mode of articulation, a way of describing a space of possibility. Three puts in question the idea of one; of identity, of self-sufficiency, of self-knowledge.' And the advantage of this version is that it also puts into question the idea of using difference – in this case between the sexes, but it can be, as Garber insists, between races or classes – as a way of locating whatever we imagine, or wish, ourselves to be lacking.

When we start thinking of difference like this, difference as penis-envy, as it were, we soon find there is no difference left, only more of the same in what we thought were foreign parts. Once we experience the other sex as all we are deprived of, we begin to experience them as depriving us; thinking of the sexes as making each other whole is grounds for murder. With Garber's figure of the transvestite a space of imaginative possibility is opened up that begins to dispel the more militant, appropriative forms of identity that have become second nature. God may be dead but fantasies of self-sufficiency (or invulnerability) are not. Instead of God now, the third sex who knew the difference, or the heterosexual couple who have everything between them – a complete set of genitals – we can have the transvestite who, by crossing over, can unsettle us by provoking what Freud calls 'the laughter of unease'.

Transvestism, in Garber's compendious account, which can take in Elvis and Liberace as comfortably as it can take off cod-pieces in Renaissance drama, is remarkable for its diverse and apparently contradictory functions. The transvestites' power to unsettle is proof, if we needed it, of how precarious our categories are, and how uncertain we are as the makers of categories. It is part of the originality of *Vested Interests* to show how dressing up and cross-dressing reveal something of the bizarre logic of our senses of identity; and how a world of entitlement – of privileged positions and secure identities – conceals an underworld of (sometimes desperate) improvisation. So transvestite magazines, for example, are particularly useful, Garber suggests, for women who don't cross-dress, because they are full of good tips – 'If you have a large frame, avoid frills and busy prints', and so on (and off). The how-to guide becomes the best form of social critique; these magazines reveal 'the degree to which *all* women cross-dress as women when they produce themselves as artefacts' (this echoes Gloria Steinem's famous remark, which Garber quotes: 'I don't mind drag – women have been female impersonators for some time'). But if a man can show us how to really be a woman – that is, how to perform as a woman – perhaps a bit of cross-dressing every so often can reassure a man that he isn't really gay, or worse, really a woman.

The Bohemian Club in San Francisco, 'the most exclusive club in the United States, with 2300 members drawn from the whole of the American establishment and a waiting list thirty-three years long' – members include, to mention only the more exhausted, Henry

Kissinger and Ronald Reagan – has an annual retreat with its own musical comedy show, artfully entitled *The Low Jinks*. It has an all-male cast and an all-male audience; the biggest crowd-pleaser, one witness reported, was Bubbles Boobenheim, a drag artist dressed as a showgirl, 'who rubbed her prosthetic behind against the elevator doors at stage left'. Although it is easy and obvious to see this as misogyny and homophobia, which always go together, Garber remarks in her droll way that it is 'nonetheless curious that the means chosen to neutralise the threat of femininity and homosexuality should involve using a version of the poison as its own remedy'. It is indeed curious, although Garber doesn't quite spell it out, that I am confirmed in not being a woman if I can pretend, or enjoy others pretending, to be one; that what I really am is what I am unable to imitate. My true identity becomes something which, by definition, I cannot perform. The performance anxiety of becoming one sex or another depends upon such unpromising distinctions. There must be a reason, Garber intimates without making a meal of it, why men so often need to believe that being a man and being ridiculous are incompatible. But ideas are incompatible in a way that performances are not; the logic of language is not the same as the logic of gesture or tones and movements of voice.

Performers, therefore, are inevitably the stars of *Vested Interests* because they make a living from their parts. Among the most engaging chapters in the book are those on Shakespeare, boy-actors on the Elizabethan stage and Michael Jackson, all of whom confront us, in Garber's view, with the radical undecidability that underlies our outrage with disorder. Michael Jackson 'in performance erases and detraumatises not only the boundaries between male and female, youth and age but also that between black and white': he 'internalises cultural category crises, and in internalising them . . . makes possible a new fantasy of transcendence'. This would seem like the smart fan straining to legitimate her pleasure, were it not for the fact that it fits so well with some of the things Jackson says about himself; although he doesn't, of course, put it quite like this.

If Michael Jackson is one of the heroes and heroines of *Vested Interests* then the villains are the trans-sexual surgeons, aided by some psychoanalysts, who are seen to be violently reinforcing the problem they claim to be resolving. *Vested Interests* is at its most unsettling in Garber's discussion of the 'resistance to, or neglect of, the female to male trans-sexual' and of 'what happens when technology catches up with cultural fantasy'. Because 'women are regarded as having not sexual but cultural desires' little attention has been paid to giving them, in a literal sense, what a very small but significant minority have wanted. Phalloplasty, the 'building' of a penis for a woman, was first done as an operation in 1936. The resistance to this operation, Garber suggests, convincingly, was 'a sneaking feeling that it should not be so easy to "construct" a man – which is to say, a male body'. The problems of phalloplasty make, as it were, disarming reading: it can fall off and it does not get hard. So the trans-sexual, as Garber puts it, 'gets the name but not the game'. 'In sex reassignment surgery,' she concludes, 'there remains an implicit privileging of the phallus, a sense that a "real one" can't be made, but only born.' From her point of view, there are good political reasons why we are not very good at making penises: because we don't want to, because if you can make it it's not so real (and 'real' here means that which one is obliged to submit to). Those who believe in trans-sexual surgery and those who are appalled by it both believe they have privileged access to some deeper truth. Playing God in this context – doing the operations – certainly confirms that there is no higher authority, so the only appeal we can make is to each other. But the making of bodies is always going to be associated with the unmaking of bodies, and there are real terrors here.

Garber is surely right that 'if 'trans-sexual surgery literalises the construction of gender it is worth asking why this culture fetishizes sexual difference'. It would certainly be a relief to drop either/or distinctions, of which sexual difference is the paradigm (the other one, presumably, is the difference between being alive and being dead that sexual difference can distract us from thinking about). We could then stop talking about children 'separating' from their mothers, or adolescents 'leaving' home, or men and women needing to 'differentiate' themselves from each other; instead we could talk about people every so often finding the requisite distances to do all those things that too much closeness seems to prevent. People don't have to stop being children, they just have to be able to be adults as well. If we cultivate unbearable choices, we create imposs- ible lives.

There is, as Garber shows, an erotics of uncertainty; so the fear of relinquishing the idea of difference may be the fear of the death of desire. There is no shortage of superstition about what keeps us going, but her account of 'the real political energy to be obtained from reversing – rather than disseminating – gender signs' gives us a new way of thinking about the political connections between difference and desire. What she calls 'the anxiety of artifice' – the performance art of sexual difference – becomes the anxiety of culture. Even when we are undressed there are vested interests at work.

12
Erich Fromm

Psychoanalysis teaches people a way of hearing what they say that enables them to speak in new ways. In psychoanalytic treatment, through a process of endlessly redescribing his life to someone else, the patient, as he used to be called, gradually begins to talk differently. This entails mourning one's old vocabulary, often the words that one was brought up on; and losing some of one's favourite words for oneself can be a mixed blessing. The new vocabulary, too, is not an entirely straightforward matter. If a person ends up speaking psychoanalysis, then the treatment has failed and must be called indoctrination. If a person ends up speaking his own too idiosyncratic language, he will be deemed mad, or inauthentic, or silly. Psychoanalysis, that is to say, is torn between helping people to conform and helping them to create revolutions.

As Daniel Burston in his very useful book *The Legacy of Erich Fromm* (1991) shows, Fromm was aware of the way in which psychoanalysis too easily made people conform to what seemed to be at its inception a new and astonishing criticism of conformism. 'Consensual validation as such,' Fromm wrote, 'has no bearing whatsoever on mental health.' And yet the psychoanalysts themselves had replaced the questioning of what constituted a good life with membership in a psychoanalytic 'community' that was Olympian in its certainties and glib in its scepticism. Freud's sense that in every psychoanalysis a culture as well as an individual was being analysed quickly began to sound simple-minded, particularly in psychoanalytic circles.

Psychoanalysis as a refuge from politics was a contradiction in terms for Fromm. It could only reinforce, in insidious ways, the kinds of suffering it claimed to alleviate. In 1932 Fromm wrote:

Psychoanalysis has focused on the structure of bourgeois society and its patriarchal family as the normal situation . . . Since [the psychoanalysts] did not concern themselves with the variety of life experience, the socio-economic structure of other kinds of society, and therefore did not try to explain psychic structure as determined by social structure, they necessarily began to analogize instead of analysing.

To analogize instead of to analyse is unconsciously to reproduce in theory what you assume you are curing in practice.

Like his contemporaries Wilhelm Reich and Herbert Marcuse, Fromm knew that psychoanalysis needed Marxism – as it now needs feminism – to remind the always potentially rarefied and affluent world of psychoanalysis that people live in a world constituted by class interests and economic hierarchies. What Daniel Burston's book makes very clear, by implication and by quotation, is Fromm's sense that psychoanalysis could only become useful local know-ledge by including the insights, if not the beliefs, generated by Marxism. One did not have to believe in an inevitable historical process to see the pertinence of economic conditions for an individ-ual's development. Individual lives, he argued, get lost in the circus of grand abstractions.

It is, after all, psychoanalysis that has turned the language of feeling into jargon. Because psychoanalysts have thought it better to write psychoanalytic papers for each other than to read novels or poems, they seem always to be writing about the same two or three people with the same three or four 'problems'. It is one of the impressive ironies of Freud's work, which Fromm was quick to recognize, that people who take him seriously always go on talking about the things he talks about or the things that he leaves out. The escape from freedom, to echo one of Fromm's pertinent titles, is pervasive in psychoanalytic societies, and this has consequences for the treatment of patients. As Fromm realized, those who have conformed do not find it easy to celebrate other people's possibili-ties. Ambivalence may be central to psychoanalytic theory, but psychoanalysts – that is, psychoanalysts who love psychoanalysis – never write about what they hate about psychoanalysis. It should be part of Fromm's legacy, as Burston suggests, to keep alive the spirit of dissent, of questioning.

Fromm was born in Frankfurt in 1900, the only child of an unhappily married middle-class Jewish couple. His early intellectual interests were impressively various. He 'mixed conventional Talmudic instruction,' Burston writes, 'with mysticism, philosophy, socialism, and psychoanalysis, all in conjunction with conservative Judaism'. After studying sociology at Heidelberg, he returned to Frankfurt to edit a small Jewish newspaper, and within a year met his first analyst, Frieda Reichmann, who became his first wife. It seems a shame, in retrospect, that psychoanalysis and journalism had to part company (thinking of psychoanalysis only as unpopular knowledge diminishes both the audience and the knowledge). In 1927 Fromm began analytic training in Berlin with Hans Sachs and Theodore Reik. The Berlin Psychoanalytic Institute was unusually progressive: non-medical analysts held senior positions, and there was a free psychoanalytic clinic for poorer people. After completing his training in 1929, Fromm spent half his time practising analysis in Berlin and the other half working at the Frankfurt Institute for Social Research. Here he began his association with Max Horkheimer and Marcuse and forged strong links with what became known as the Frankfurt School. It was after his immigration to the States, in 1933, that this affiliation became problematic.

Fromm, as a member of what Burston calls Freud's 'loyal opposition', did a very unusual thing – unusual, that is, for a committed psychoanalyst. He tried genuinely to broaden the scope of psychoanalysis by integrating psychoanalytic theory into a more diverse cultural conversation that could include economics, philosophy and anthropology, among many other disciplines. This, of course, has been the enduring legacy of the Frankfurt School, of which he was an early member; but what Fromm did not do, unlike some other members of that school (and certain other psychoanalysts), was to promote those forms of mandarin intelligence that could produce convincing critiques of culture that hardly anyone in the culture was able to read.

In a consumer culture, accessibility inevitably leads to obsolescence. It was the more hermetic members of the Frankfurt School, Theodor Adorno and Walter Benjamin in particular, who had more staying power than Fromm. Those who wanted life after death had to be difficult. Fromm, however, wrote accessible and widely popular books – books that could inspire adolescents, which is always a good sign – about psychoanalysis, about psychoanalysis and Marxism, and – most interesting, I think – about psychoanalysis and Zen Buddhism. His most famous books, *The Sane Society* (1955), *The Art of Loving* (1956) and *The Anatomy of Human Destructiveness* (1973), were best-sellers; and yet, or therefore, Fromm is rarely talked about or taught by the Owners of Culture.

Psychoanalysis, when it is not hidden away as dogma, is genuinely pluralistic and democratic, in a way that Fromm appreciated, because it encourages us to take seriously those things we are inclined to dismiss. For that reason, *The Legacy of Erich Fromm* is a timely book, since Fromm's work has virtually disappeared from intelligent consideration. And with it has gone an often penetrating criticism of the idolatry that constitutes the culture industry (and the psychoanalytic community). In all his writing Fromm was trying to keep alive the possibility of being authoritative without being authoritarian. All idols, by disarming pertinent forms of criticism, distracted their worshippers from more problematic but interesting desires. And psychoanalysis, like any other cultural artefact, if it was to be useful, also had to be protected from the potential worship of its admirers. With these preoccupations, of course, Fromm was at once traditionally Jewish and radically secular.

Because psychoanalysis has one father, unlike, say, the novel or philosophy, it became a convenient oasis for rebels and conformists alike. For Freud to become a certain kind of authority, or even idol, he needed to surround himself with people who wanted a little authority in their lives. But it is often forgotten, and again Burston is informative about this, how many of the early analysts were also Marxists, or had been Marxists in their youth. Like the other great early Freudian Marxists (Reich, Paul Federn and Otto Fenichel the most notable among them), Fromm brought to psychoanalysis, among many other things, an uneasy relationship to his own authoritativeness.

They were interested in the individual, but not in the cult of the individual. The cult of the individual, by denying dependence, the multifarious links and involvements, the social context, that make a life possible, and by praising invulnerability, promoted the notion of people as obstacles to each other. For Fromm and his colleagues, certainly, the cult of the individual, by encouraging the submissions of envy, and replacing the idea of the good life with the idea of the enviable life, actually diminished the possibilities for individuality, and constricted its scope as something profoundly communal. These were not the preoccupations of the newly emerging psycho-analytic orthodoxy that by the 1960s had turned into a limited company that was, so to speak, patenting its product.

Burston suggests that the combination of Fromm's family history as a traditional (in the religious sense) middle-class Jew growing up in Germany and the events in Germany in the 1920s and 1930s made him a socialist. His 'pious upbringing' was to make him a generous admirer of unusual men and at the same time a severe critic of all forms of idolatry. For idolatry was simply a way of pre-empting a personal life. Throughout his own life, Burston tells us, Fromm retained an interest in Hasidism and the Scriptures alongside an abiding respect for Trotsky as 'revolutionary thinker, as general, as exile'.

If Burston sometimes worries that Fromm is not quite as sound as he should be – 'he is often characterized,' he writes nervously, 'as some sort of Polyanna' (intellectuals are rarely impressed by people who are happy) – the man who emerges from between the lines of his book is a vividly complicated man, indeed an extraordinary man. We need only note that Fromm's second wife was the woman with whom Walter Benjamin fled from the Nazis in 1940, and that Fromm's devoted friend Ivan Illich helped bury him when he died in 1980, to see the disparate worlds which Fromm's life connects. And his extensive writings, to which Burston gives detailed attention, are remarkable for their range and for certain insistent preoccupations. Fromm's persistent interest in idolatry, the nature of aggression, and the need for mutuality both in psychoanalytic treatment and lived life is not easy to dismiss. These rightly remain issues that are still germane to the theory and the practice of psychoanalysis, and of interest to people who do not care for it. Fromm was certainly writing for both kinds of people.

Since the most exhilarating psychoanalytic theory now idealizes incoherence, the pleasures of common sense in psychoanalysis can easily be lost. The common-sense analysts – Anna Freud, Heinz Kohut, often Fromm himself – tend to be accessible and reassuring. Their virtue is that they are often comforting, which is their vice to the more inspired bizarre analysts like Bion and Lacan, who demand not that their patients get better but that they pursue Truth. The common-sense analysts know what it is for someone to get better. For the bizarre analysts, the whole notion of getting better smacks of omniscience. After all, how could one know if someone was better unless one already knew what a good life was?

Fromm is particularly interesting in Burston's understated account because of the unusual mixture of the bizarre and the commonsensical in his work. As a writer he is calm and intelligible, but he is so wary of mystification that he never allows himself to get into a muddle, and he rarely takes the chance of being a bit weird. Still, if the common-sense analysts, unlike the bizarre analysts, never really intrigue us, they do focus our attention. So, for example, Fromm could observe lucidly, for those who were not already too knowing, that societies 'develop a system, or categories, which determine the forms of awareness. This system works, as it were, as a socially conditioned filter; experience cannot enter awareness unless it can penetrate this filter.' In Fromm's version, it was the aim of psychoanalysis to make socially proscribed emotional experience available and by so doing to modify the forms of awareness. Fromm is at his most radical in his commitment to alternatives. He never becomes a bizarre analyst, though, because he never stops wanting to help us.

At his worst Fromm had the deadly piety of the committed iconoclast, and Burston's book does not evade this. But Fromm's apparent banality could be provocative and engaging, and his writing makes us notice things. He was drawn to Zen Buddhism, I imagine, partly because of its lightness of touch, something not easily found in psychoanalytic theory. Psychoanalysis rarely makes one smile. But Fromm, I think, wanted it to provoke different forms of assent. 'One has to allow,' Freud wrote to Ferenczi in 1914, 'for a certain multiplicity of voices, even an alloy with such-and-such per cent nonsense.' Fromm's voice is a good one to have because he knew that the unalloyed voice is a contradiction in terms.

13
Guilt

When Freud insisted that psychoanalysis had nothing to do with ethical inquiry, was not in the business of moral-world making or of providing a new *Weltanschauung*, he was trying to dissociate himself from the Judaism of his forefathers, and trying to dissociate psychoanalysis from any connection with religion (or mysticism). If psychoanalysis was seen to be compatible with traditional religious belief it would lose both its scientific credibility and its apparent originality. But one is only absolutely original, of course, until one is found out.

Recontextualized in the last twenty years by historical research, and revived by literary studies, psychoanalysis, fortunately, has had all its boundaries blurred. Since it is no longer owned, and so defined, exclusively by anyone, its 'splendid isolation' has been turned into a more interesting muddled pluralism and it has now spilled into all sorts of other areas – religion, history, philosophy, politics, anthropology, among others – with which it has much in common. By joining in the conversation it has been increasingly unable to disown these family resemblances, and so has lost some of the pomposity of its own supposedly unique rigour.

Nina Coltart, who has no truck in her inspired and inspiring book *Slouching Towards Bethlehem . . . and Further Psychoanalytic Explorations* (1992) with the more excruciating purities of the profession, is quite explicit that 'psychoanalysis may be defined as a moral activity'. She believes, despite what she calls 'the sacred rules of psychoanalysis', that analysts have a lot to learn from novelists; that they are (she often thinks) all novelists manqués; and that though psychoanalysis is not a religion – and is notably insufficient if used as one – its preoccupations are of a piece with those disciplines traditionally thought of as religious.

The religion she is most interested in and practises is Buddhism (her book is worth having for the essay on psychoanalysis and Buddhism alone); and the novelist she quotes to such good effect, and with whom she shares certain affinities, is Iris Murdoch. She is interested, that is to say, in the mixing but not the muddling of traditions, and in psychoanalysis as inescapably a moral enterprise 'tending as it does towards greater freedom in the making of moral choices' – that has to work hard not to become a moralistic one. Rather like Iris Murdoch, Coltart is a kind of aesthetic pragmatist: she wants theories, which she refers to as 'tool-kits', that she can use; and she wants to get things done properly, so words like 'skill' and 'discipline' do a lot of work in her writing. But she also cares a good deal what it all sounds and looks like – she refers several times in her book to the 'ugly' parts of the personality as the ones she least likes. By being carefully but not self-consciously written, her book manages to create an illusion of common sense – masochism, for example, is 'making the best of a bad job'; 'a percentage of good manners is knowing what to do with one's body in public' – and yet the shrewd lucidity that characterizes her writing makes her recognizably a member of the independent (as opposed to the strictly Freudian or Kleinian) tradition in British psychoanalysis.

Despite Freud's disclaimers, psychoanalysis has always been about what it means to get bogged down in traditions, whether personal, familial, religious or intellectual. Traditions tend to tell us what is Good, and how we should go about protecting it; and they define the kinds of conflict we are likely to have when we do this. Like everyone else, both the psychoanalyst and her so-called patient organize their lives around their respective, and mostly unconscious, versions of the Good, what they most value and want to sustain and protect. The analyst does this with psychoanalytic theory and the patient does it with what are misleadingly called symptoms – and are in fact disablingly painful moral puzzles. (Of course the analyst has symptoms and the patient has theories, but a mystique of professional expertise is maintained by never quite spelling this out.) The repressed, the nominal focus of psychoanalysis, is not so much sexuality and violence, but alternative and problematic moral worlds. What we call sexuality and violence (or aggression) are the often unacceptable and always conflictual means we use to create these alternative worlds.

Moral-world making can be a dismaying experience. The risk for someone going to see a psychoanalyst is that one dispiriting story will meet another even more dispiriting one (every psychoanalyst should keep a copy of Nietzsche's *The Use and Abuse of History* by their beds). 'On the whole', as Nina Coltart says, 'psychoanalysis would probably agree . . . that human nature is basically nasty.' Despite two thousand years of Christianity and over a hundred years of Darwin and Freud, it still seems worth asking why one would want to have a conversation with someone who believes *that*, especially if one is in search of comfort and what William James called, in a slightly different context, 'somewhere to go from'. The equation of wisdom, or moral gravity, with pessimism has become exhausting. It is possible to believe now that it is precisely this question of Human Nature – both how we have come to believe in our particular version of it, and why we need to believe in such a thing at all – that psychoanalysis may be particularly well suited to explore. The pursuit of Truth as an absolute traditionally makes people violent. But there is covert sadism in a profession heroically committed to the bringing of bad news as Truth about Human Nature. If people are 'basically nasty', then everything about them that isn't nasty is untruthful. The endlessly reiterated boast by analysts that psychoanalysis is 'the impossible profession' is, in part, a consequence of their impoverished picture of what a person is and can be. Psychoanalysis is actually only as impossible as one makes it.

Psychoanalysis began as a persuasive picture of what Human Nature is, despite the fact that its central idea, the unconscious, describes a part of the self that is always sabotaging our favourite pictures of who we are. But psychoanalysis, which should have made all idols provisional – which sees us as compulsively irreverent, mostly of ourselves – has gone on worshipping, indeed promoting, some of the oldest idols of our emotional life. As Coltart's *Slouching towards Bethlehem* and Friedrich Ohly's *The Damned and the Elect: Guilt in Western Culture* (1992), both very persuasive books, show in a complementary way – Ohly from a literary-historical perspective and Coltart from a mostly psychoanalytic one – guilt has been the cornerstone of our Western conception of Human Nature.

A capacity for guilt seems to define our sense of what it is to be human; on this psychoanalysis and the Judaeo-Christian religions agree. Freud simply added the idea of unconscious guilt – and the violence of guilt itself – to the picture, seeing it, towards the end of his life, as a fundamental obstacle to psychoanalytic cure; the patient desperately needs his symptoms as a punishment. His symptoms are his cure. Conversely, much of what we think a person is, in his relationship with others, is bound up with our mostly unconscious sense of what guilt is. But because the notion of guilt is a virtual god-term in our moral vocabulary – a very old-fashioned kind of god-term that permits us to use the word 'we' with impunity – the question is never: does it exist? Or even: what exactly do we use the word to say? But rather: how can we arrange our lives to deal with it?

Discussions of guilt, in other words, rarely suggest that the story is all wrong – after all, who can imagine a world without punishment? – but try instead to establish what it is about ourselves that makes us feel guilty: original sin, innate destructiveness, sexuality, society? And anyone who invents an alternative story about all this will be taken to be trying to avoid guilt, to be immature, utopian or psychopathic. But trying to locate the source, or trying to improve our relationship with guilt, bewitches us into thinking that we already know what it is. So in the context of a psychoanalytic session, for example, the patient's use of the word 'guilt' – like all the most familiar moral abstractions – can be treated as an unconscious invitation to the analyst to collude in an assumed consensus of meaning. By our looking at these kinds of usage in the context of personal history, familiar words lose their coercive gravity by being more specifically contextualized. The question is no longer: what is guilt? But: what am I trying to do to myself (and others) by saying in any given situation that I feel guilty?

From Coltart's point of view – in two essays on the subject, one entitled 'Sin and the Super-ego' – two basic fears constitute our sense of guilt: fear of 'direct disapproval for transgressing the moral laws of our world', and 'fear of our potential for harm'. For Ohly, the question which belongs 'among the most enduring problems of this world' is 'How can I live with my guilt?' Guilt, in both these accounts, is a way of controlling ourselves and other people. The basic story is that someone, a God or a group of people, has made a rule which (consciously or unconsciously) matters so much to us – or to some people who matter so much to us – that when (consciously or unconsciously) we break it, we suffer. Of course, if our suffering did not come from breaking rules we would be less resourceful at improving our lives, because we would have fallen out of the reassuring world of contract. The problem isn't that if God is dead everything is permitted, but that the idea of permission disappears. Certain terms – sin (or error), guilt, punishment, redemption (or rebirth) – seem to keep stubbornly organizing our stories. How we have got to this moral cul-de-sac, and whether there is a way out of or only through it, is the subject, by implication, of both these books.

The Damned and the Elect, first published in Germany in 1976 but, as George Steiner notes, with no reference to recent German history, is about the power and promotion of exemplary stories; the way certain sequences of events are used as virtually autonomous guides inside us, as dreams from which there is no waking. In an extraordinary feat of scholarly concision Ohly compares in detail different versions of the stories of Judas, St Gregorius, Faust and Oedipus, our favourite transgressors, but in the end comes to the disappointing conclusion that 'the sequence of damnation and redemption fulfils an enduring human desire, from antiquity, through the middle ages to our own time'. Ohly illuminates a strong theme with the kind of scholarship, especially in his commentaries on medieval texts, that gives us a real glimpse of other worlds; but it is clear that he began his book with its conclusion in mind, and he has settled for it too gladly. Why is this 'sequence of damnation and redemption' such a dominant story, and what are the alternative stories it stops us thinking up? If, as Ohly says, 'all myth is bound together, above all by that most human of all constants, living with guilt', why is this what we most want to learn to live with? Or to put it another way, why has Judas, unlike, say, the Satan of *Paradise Lost*, never become a culture hero?

As Ohly shows, Judas has always been vilified for committing the ultimate sin: not betrayal but despair. By hanging himself Judas placed himself beyond God's grace, and therefore in a sense, beyond God's power. The absolute despair was the real transgression; the refusal of redemption was truly anarchic. The story suggests that despair desacralizes the world, that suicide is the only way to kill God. Judas refused God his fundamental power of redemption and by doing so makes us wonder about this God's need to believe in the reach of his own goodness.

It was, Ohly suggests, in reaction to the dangerous story of Judas's radical refusal that the story of St Gregorius was promoted as a counter-story. Judas, and Oedipus his precursor (rediscovered in the West, according to Ohly, sometime before 1150), like Gregorius, are incestuous parricides. Unlike Judas, however, Gregorius did penance in a way that never ultimately despaired of God's grace. But it was a delicate business, because to presume on God's grace was itself a sin; as one of the medieval German poems that Ohly quotes says, 'God will not suffer someone to dream his own way into a place in heaven.' Because he believed that God would look kindly upon him, Gregorius in some versions of the story becomes Pope, and in all versions became a saint. 'The real question,' Ohly says blithely, 'is not how one gets into guilt, but how one gets out of it.' Judas and Gregorius are the exemplary options. Judas, who through his despair repudiated the whole theocracy, was, he says, 'the man the middle ages most loved to hate'. He has never been thanked for taking this on.

In Ohly's account Faust – who is a transitional figure because in some versions he is elect and in others damned – and his precursor Judas stand, as he puts it a bit portentously, 'on the threshold of modernity'. Both refuse to abide by the limits their respective cultures set for experience. They are the ambiguous Six Six. Six hundred, the over-reachers and the under-reachers punished and secretly envied for their ambition. It is part of the value of Ohly's book to make convincing the possible connections between these historically disparate characters.

For these stories to retain their archetypal status, however, they have to find ways of setting limits to interpretation; they have to come out in a way that validates the suffering they have entailed for the hero. Their peculiar art is to give extreme suffering an inspiring purpose, and to do that it has to be made to seem inevitable, and necessary. So it is of interest that turning pain into meaning – which is the project both of psychoanalysis and of most religions – is usually itself construed as a painful and often ascetic process. Like crime and punishment, that is to say, the cure can seem a mirror-image of the disease. So, for example, the trauma of going to see the silent, orthodox psychoanalyst is that it re-creates the trauma of the child with an inaccessible parent who refuses real contact. The two remarkable case-histories in Coltart's book have obvious parallels with Ohly's more archetypal stories – like all such case-histories they are (ideally) progress narratives describing something coming out of darkness (the unconscious) into the light – but they breathe a fresher air thanks to the quality of her participation in the process: her own enjoyment of psychoanalytic sessions, and her conviction that it is the 'essence' of psychoanalysis 'that in a very singular way we do not know what we are doing'. It is the will to competence, as opposed to what she calls 'the continued action of bare attention', that can destroy the pleasure and the efficacy of the process. And it is the (conscious) intention not to produce an examplary story that frees the conversation: the stories that psychoanalyses produce have multiple beginnings and middles, and no known ends.

It is this liberating refusal of traditional forms of closure that distinguish psychoanalysis from moral pedagogy. So psychoanalysts cannot afford to speak of sins – analysts who use the word 'good' very rarely use 'evil' – but they can use the more scientifically legitimate, and so reassuring, notion of symptoms. From the point of view of the sufferer, psychosomatic symptoms are probably the closest secular equivalent to sins. And Coltart – who, as she says in a superb essay on the subject, prefers the 'silent' patient – is also, perhaps by the same token, fascinated by, and illuminating about, the very real 'mystery' of the construction and cure of these particular symptoms ('they often get better almost in passing,' she says in passing). These silent symptoms which, as it were, do the talking for the patient, when what is unthinkable turns to the body for expression, produce an often unintelligible and intractable 'dumb-show' which the patient brings to the analysis for the processing that is called redescription. Of course, since most children suffer from an excess of attributed meaning by parents and other adults, an unreachable psychosomatic symptom can be a paradoxical area of freedom; something that defies the intrusion of translation.

'The special interest of psychosomatic symptoms,' Coltart writes in the extraordinary title paper of her book, 'is that the rough beast whose hour is not yet come is holed up in the body . . . the beast has crossed that mysterious barrier whose location eludes us (between mind and body), and moved over into a stronghold from which it is only on rare occasions to be delivered.' It is a peculiarly ironic use of the image in Yeats's demonic poem; but 'holed up' seems exactly right for the location of something that absents itself from meaning. This is the poetry, without the sentimental preciosity, of the best kind of psychoanalytic writing; it preserves, as Freud did, the drama of the encounter without all the usual psychoanalytic earnestness. And because Coltart writes rather than pretending merely to record, she can be suggestive in the most apparently straightforward of ways. 'We could say that a psychosomatic symptom,' she writes, 'represents that which is determined to remain unconscious or unknowable, but which at the same time has actually made itself conscious in a very heavy disguise; it is speakable about only in a dense and enigmatic code.' If this is a lucid description of the anonymous authority of such symptoms, it is also a coded description and critique of a certain kind of analyst, the kind Coltart elsewhere in her book is rightly suspicious of: the one who, like a symptom, won't speak his mind.

Nina Coltart, who speaks her mind without advertising that this is what she is doing, refers on several occasions in these papers to her 'outburst' of anger with a patient. She mentions that this has given a 'regrettable' notoriety to what is actually a very interesting and, by psychoanalytic (that is, chronically inhibited) standards, unusually revealing, insight into the inevitably sometimes fraught analytic process. Wary of the 'austere and benevolently neutral manner which we hold as our working ideal', which can easily become a refusal to acknowledge the presence of the other person, Coltart promotes a notion of 'truth in our emotional being with a patient': 'we can do no harm to a patient by showing authentic affect'.

But what kind of profession is psychoanalysis if it prompts its most inspired practitioners into these kinds of confession of faith? For anyone outside the profession, the amount of time Coltart gives to the question of whether the analyst is allowed to laugh in a psychoanalytic session will seem bemusing – or some kind of unconscious parody. From her quibbles and quite reticent self-assertion – one of the intermittent sub-plots in her essays is a critique of the post-war, upper-middle-class English character – we get a vivid picture of an absolutely unendearing psychoanalytic ortho-doxy. The establishment and its 'rebels' always do each other's bidding, but Coltart has managed to find a third position: it is the art of her position to seem undefiant. 'Unless there is a growing openness,' she writes, 'on the part of both patient and therapist, each to the other, and a willingness by both to make efforts in an atmosphere of trust, no treatment occurs.' If this 'atmosphere' does not exist in the training institutions, it is more difficult for it to exist between 'patient' and analyst; and these are things prospective patients can never know about.

By being Freud, of course, Freud was very 'present' in the analytic treatment; despite the reticence of his technique his patients were being treated in a space he had invented. Not surprisingly, it very soon became a bone of contention among the early analysts how much they should make their particular presences felt. Beginning with the work of Freud's greatest follower, Sandor Ferenczi, the issue of the analyst's self-disclosure in the treatment, the possible 'mutuality' of the psychoanalytic process, became the focus of intense and fraught psychoanalytic debate. The Independent Group in Britain, and certain 'intersubsectivist' American analysts, have sustained the legacy of Ferenczi's pioneering work, which sees the supposed authority of the analyst as part of the problem, and what the analyst wants in the treatment as integral to the process, and so something that has to be made available for discussion. It is Coltart's unique contribution to this innovative tradition to link this tradition of psychoanalytic theory with the question of religious belief. Psychoanalysis has always been a religion in which you are not allowed to believe in God.

It is one of the many pleasures of Coltart's book that it is written about a group of related preoccupations that are continually circled round, and re-approached in different contexts, without the essays ever seeming repetitive. But two main issues seem to gather together the range of her interests, and her eloquence. First, the sense in which psychoanalysis is a vocation: that is, how useful a religious vocabulary – which for Coltart means mostly, but not entirely, a language derived from Buddhism – can be in the description of psychoanalytic practice. And secondly, the extent to which it is useful and interesting, rather than sentimental and mystificatory, to talk about psychoanalysis as an encounter between two people as opposed to one person treating another.

People are rightly suspicious of psychoanalysis because the people who do it rarely put the people who don't in a position to evaluate it from their own point of view. By making her particular point of view accessible, Nina Coltart makes psychoanalysis available for consideration, for both the curious and the converted. Psychoanalysis is only for the people who like it (and can afford it). It is pernicious, as Coltart's essays make abundantly clear, only in so far as it is something to submit to. And, one can say, in so far as it is only for those who can afford it.

14
Freud's Circle

Auden once suggested that a literary critic should declare his 'dream of Eden' because 'honesty demands that he describe it to his readers, so that they may be in a position to judge his judgements'. Even though psychoanalysis ironizes dreams of Eden – in psychoanalytic theory paradise is only for the losers – it would be useful for psychoanalysts to say something about these things, about the kind of world they would prefer to live in, and why they think psychoanalysis is a good way of both spending one's time and contributing to this Eden. It will, after all, matter a great deal to their patients what stories they tend to tell themselves and their colleagues about, say, promiscuity, or socialism, or ambition. And, of course, about psychoanalysis and the significance of its history.

Given that ambivalence, and therefore self-doubt, are integral to the theory, it is remarkable how unwilling psychoanalysts have been to write anything about their hatred, or their love, of psychoanalysis. It would be particularly interesting for those who love psychoanalysis to tell us their misgivings about it all, partly because there is no shortage of people who do not like it and are keen to tell us more than their misgivings. And these are the only people who do it with any gusto; though not all of them, fortunately, are as crassly enthusiastic as Phyllis Grosskurth is in her book *The Secret Ring: Freud's Inner Circle and the Politics of Psychoanalysis* (1991). In this history of Freud's first group of colleagues – the Committee who, under Freud's aegis, invented what we now think of as psychoanalysis – Grosskurth 'ponders the question: why, at a crucial point in the history of psychoanalysis, did the Committee mean so much [to Freud]'? 'Ponders' is about right, though it marginally exaggerates the intellectual acuity of her story.

The days must now be over when people who are critical of

psychoanalysis can merely be described as resisting it (of course, in the old days one was always free to ask someone what they were resisting by defending it). And people who disparage psychoanalysis – and psychoanalysts as a tribe – are responding to something in which Freud and his early followers are more than implicated. The contempt or suspicion – the environment that a person or a group creates around itself – is always a kind of alter ego, an essential and revealing part of the production. Psychoanalysis as a profession has become a victim of its most useful and distinctive technique: by not saying much, by not answering the questions, it encourages people outside the profession to invest analysts with power and then punish them for being smug and bossy. That is to say, it turns outsiders too easily into patients, just as the infamous psychoanalytic 'technique', when it is not answerable or intelligible to the patient, is anti-democratic. It disempowers in the name of knowing what's best.

Powerful theories are only powerful because they seem to prescribe the terms in which they can be judged. If a lot of the most interesting psychoanalytic theory and history is now being written by people outside the profession, it is partly because the people inside the profession are more prone to the kinds of fundamentalism that stifle imagination in the name of something often called professional integrity (by 'fundamentalism' I mean here the assumption that something can only be legitimately criticized from within). It is part of the institutional hypocrisy of psychoanalysis to suggest that everything the psychoanalytic institution rejects is valueless, and everything the patient rejects he must be encouraged to reintegrate. But in its documented account – from outside, as it were – of the sometimes very real fundamentalism of the first psychoanalytic group, *The Secret Ring* disparages Freud's character as a way of casting aspersions on the whole psychoanalytic enterprise. Freudbashing, like any kind of bashing, frees one to have contact with something by creating the illusion that one is destroying it. And Grosskurth is certainly devoted and diligent in her dismay about the first psychoanalysts, and particularly the very first one. Indeed, what is most striking about *The Secret Ring* – and links it to her last foray into psychoanalytic history, the biography of Melanie Klein – is how little she seems to like or admire the people she has chosen to write about. So the book invites the kind of collusion that it insistently deplores in the group that provides her with her subject. It is written, in other words, with the kind of snide zeal with which one preaches to the converted.

Why, for example, so early in the book (page 20) does Grosskurth footnote the fact that in 1934 Hitler visited Hildesheim, the town where in 1921 Freud's Secret Committee held their meeting? Perhaps we are to infer, along crude psychoanalytic lines of interpretation, that one kind of similarity is being used to reveal another? Certainly, at first sight, the differences between Freud and Hitler seem more compelling than the similarities. But in this Prologue, as she calls it – the book is organized 'theatrically', beginning with Dramatis Personae and Supporting Cast and finishing with a Last Act and an Epilogue – Grosskurth gives us lots of hints that Freud may not have been a very nice person, and that a professional master-race was in the offing. 'Their main task,' she writes, 'was to preserve the purity of psychoanalytic theory.' We glimpse the Committee members, 'despite the fact' that they were all suffering from colds, maintaining 'a strenuous schedule of hiking and sightseeing'. And then we are told, by way of a conclusion, that 'the circumstances in which Freud felt it necessary to gather about him a small group of henchmen in order to maintain the faith and search out deviance is the subject of this book'. Henchmen?

In the Epilogue Grosskurth confesses that she is 'still not altogether sure of my opinion of Freud'. This seems uncharacteristically tentative in a book studded with the brashest assertions about Freud and the other emotionally inadequate people who were unfortunate enough to come in contact with him. 'Anyone whose ideas differed from his own,' she writes, 'Freud described as an "enemy".' 'For Jones, as for Ferenczi', we are told, 'Freud was the all-wise father to whom his troubled son came for help and advice.' 'There they were,'she writes of the Committee in 1913 – Jones, Ferenczi, Abraham, Rank and Hans Sachs – as though the joke is on all of them, 'bound together by their secrecy against the world, faith in

Freud's theory, and their personal devotion to their leader.' It's as if Enid Blyton were writing about the early days of a Fascist youth movement. So when the Freud Youth become vulnerable Grosskurth gets impatient with their Leader. When Jones's seven-and-a-half-year-old daughter dies in 1928, Freud, she says, could 'only reply: "As an unbelieving fatalist I can only let my arms sink before the terrors of death." Once again, Freud seemed to find it impossible to empathise with the sufferings of another person.' It seems to me that with his usual astringent eloquence he didn't do too badly, but then Freud's Insensitivity to Other People is an important theme in Grosskurth's book. Jones, she also lets us know, was 'pathetically grateful' to receive a telegram of condolence from Freud. She constructs psychoanalytic history as though it were a series of encounters between the emotionally retarded, who come out of every exchange – a meeting, a correspondence, an analysis – looking as though no morally intelligent person could possibly take them seriously.

Psychoanalysis itself, of course, provides a whole new vocabulary for personal disparagement. But writing about the history of psychoanalysis seems to encourage people to assume a morally superordinate position, one in which it is assumed that because *we* already know what a Good person is we can easily recognize a Bad one. Psychoanalysis starts from the position that we don't already know, and it is precisely the conviction that they do that people suffer from. In the inevitably troubled and troubling story that Grosskurth tells it is worth considering what sort of group pastoral we are being offered by way of implicit comparison, and what this labyrinth of betrayal and rivalry, of dependence and idealization, is supposed to be telling us about psychoanalysis as a story and a form of therapy. With her insinuating perhapses – 'Perhaps Ferenczi provided [Freud] with a frisson and a turbulence from which he shrank in his own rather arid emotional life'; 'It is perhaps an indication of Freud's loneliness that he urged Ferenczi to resume the analysis' – she implies that we may be slightly ridiculous to be impressed by these people. Psychoanalytic history often gets trapped in the morally stupefying world of blaming. Instead of trying to discover facts about Freud's life that will finally validate or invalidate psychoanaly-sis, we should figure out what he was trying to do, how he came to do it – and what he didn't realize he was doing – in order to work out whether we think psychoanalysis is worth having; whether it produces the kind of life stories we go for. Proving that Freud did not always behave well is not the best way of doing this.

Freud 'believed', Grosskurth writes, 'that he had discovered the ultimate truth', but there is no evidence to suggest that this is true, or the ultimate truth about Freud. 'Fascinated by the fact that thousands of people continue to idealize and defend him without really knowing anything about him as a person', she seems to believe that some truth may be gained by unmasking him. But most people aren't well-behaved – they just look as though they are. Righteous indignation is always a sign that we are in need of a new description.

15
Futures

For the patient in psychoanalysis the most disabling insights are the ones he cannot forget; and for the psychoanalyst, by the same token, the most misleading theories are the ones he cannot do without. Mental addictions, that is to say, are supposed to be the problem not the solution. People come for psychoanalysis when there is something they cannot forget, something they cannot stop telling themselves, often by their actions, about their lives. And these dismaying repetitions – this unconscious limiting or coercion of the repertoire of life-stories – create the illusion of time having stopped (or rather, people believe – behave as if – they have stopped time). In our repetitions we seem to be staying away from the future, keeping it at bay. What are called symptoms are these (failed) attempts at closure, at calling a halt to something. Like provisional deaths, they are spurious forms of mastery.

The paradox of living in passing time and craving durable truths (or symptoms) as the best equipment for this predicament has, of course, traditionally been the province of Western Metaphysics. But the practice of psychoanalysis, like the practice of ordinary life, raises 'philosophical' questions in rather immediate form. How long is something true for, and why should duration over time be any kind of criteria for the validity of a so-called insight in psychoanalysis, or anywhere else? After all, the repetitions from which the patient is suffering, and which define the realm of pathology for psychoanalysis, are extremely durable, unlike the truths used to explain them. For Freud these repetitions are the consequences of a failure to remember. Psychoanalysis, as Malcolm Bowie writes, 'is overwhelmingly concerned with the production and transformation of meaning'. Whatever cannot be transformed, psychically processed, reiterates itself. A trauma is whatever there is in a person's experience that resists useful redescription. Traumas, like beliefs, are ways of stopping time.

But if, as Freud says, we repeat only what we cannot remember, what is the psychoanalyst or literary theorist doing when he learns a method of analysis that itself involves a repetition of certain skills? A method is only a method because it bears repeating; and yet from a psychoanalytic point of view it is repetition itself that is the problem, that signifies trauma. This is one of the paradoxes that Christopher Bollas and Malcolm Bowie examine implicitly in their differently eloquent and intriguing books (*Being a Character: Psychoanalysis and Self-Experience*, 1993, and *Psychoanalysis and the Future of Theory*, 1993). Embarrassed alike by the subtlety and complexity of the work of art and of the patient can the theorist and the analyst do more than repeat what they already know? Is theory always more of the same, just Where The Tame Things Are? If theory is, by definition, what we already know, what are its prospects? The future, after all, is the place where our prejudices might not work. The aim of a psychoanalytic session is not to prove that psychoanalytic theory is true.

Though there is by now a recognizable psychoanalytic sensibility, for the most interesting (least slavish) theorists Freud simply punctuates traditions that predate him. He gives certain preoccupations a new kind of future. Psychoanalysis may begin with Freud but what it is about does not. Malcolm Bowie and Christopher Bollas have been writing some of the most innovatory psychoanalytic theory of the last few years but out of significantly different traditions. There is an unusual stylishness in their writing and an exhilarating ambition. Bollas's prose, immersed in the poetry of romanticism and the nineteenth-century American novel, allows him to be eloquently grandiloquent on occasions while being at the same time quite at ease with the tentativeness of his project. His prose often has the evocative resonance that his theory attempts to account for. And as his theory describes psychic life as a kind of haunting, we have to be alert to the echoes in his writing (and sometimes in his overwriting). When, for example, he describes the process of observing the self as an object – 'Emerging from self-experience proper, the subject considers where he has been' – it is integral to the process being described that we can hear the cadence of Coleridge's glosses on *The Ancient Mariner*. And echoes work both ways. Bowie also has the virtue of his quite different intellectual affinities, something that is particularly rare in mainstream psychoanalysis, as anyone who has read the specialist journals will know. Though his writing is far too idiosyncratic for pastiche, it is Proust and Mallarmé that we can hear most often in Bowie's work. There is, that is to say, a kind of refined extravagance about the bigger themes – Love, Time, Death, etc. – tempered by a fastidious pointedness about the more ineffable reaches of theoretical ambition. For Bowie, for whom 'the language of psychoanalysis offers clues not solutions, calls to action for the interpreter but not interpretations', prudence is the unlikely virtue that he keeps promoting in his increasingly subtle readings of Freud and Lacan.

For both Bowie and Bollas it is one of the difficult ironies of psychoanalysis that as a theory it seems to preempt the future it is attempting to elicit. Freud's 'account of human temporality', Bowie writes, 'serves . . . to place the future under suspicion, and to keep it there throughout a long theoretical career'. Like Bollas's definition of a trauma – 'the effect of trauma is to sponsor symbolic repetition, not symbolic elaboration' – it is as though, from a psychoanalytic point of view, the future can only be described as, at best, a sophisticated replication of the past; the past in long trousers. Theory itself becomes the symptom it is trying to explain. If in psychoanalytic theory the past, the undigested past, is that which always returns – both as symptom *and* interpretation – how can we return to the future, or get beyond the interminable shock of the old that theory and therapy too easily promote? Our theoretical habits, like our erotic habits, are the revenge of the past on the future.

In *Being a Character* Bollas suggests that the future – future selves and states of mind – arise through a process of evocation. Starting with the mother we unwittingly use the world and its objects to bring parts of ourselves to life. A combination of chance and unconscious intention, even our most concerted projects are forms of sleep-walking. 'Without giving it much thought at all,' Bollas writes, 'we consecrate the world with our own subjectivity, investing people,

places, things and events with a kind of idiomatic significance . . .
the objects of our world are potential forms of transformation'. Our
chosen objects of interest – and this can be anything from the books
we read to the way we furnish our rooms or organize our days – are
like a personal vocabulary (or even alphabet); we are continually, at
our best, 'meeting idiom needs by securing evocatively nourishing
objects'. It is as though we are always trying to live our own
language, hoping to find 'keys to the releasing of our idiom' – what
Bollas calls in one of many felicitous phrases, 'potential dream
furniture' – as we go about setting the scene for the future. Objects –
like different artistic media – have very different 'processional
potential'; what Bollas calls the object's 'integrity' – whatever it
happens to be, what it invites and what it makes impossible – sets
limits to its use. The world in Bollas's view is a kind of aesthetic tool-
kit; and unlike most psychoanalytic theorists he doesn't use a
hammer to crack a nut.

It should be clear by now that Bollas has to draw on a repertoire
of vocabularies to describe his new psychoanalytic landscape.
Orthodox psychoanalysts are not in a hurry to use words like
'consecrate' or phrases like 'idiom needs' or, indeed, to take the
outside world on its own terms. In Bollas's work the language of
Winnicott and of American pragmatism – of 'use-value' – meets up
with Wordsworthian romanticism; the world is sown with, and so
made up by, bits of self, and yet retains its separateness, its
sacrality, its resistance to absolute invention. In Bollas the Self is at
once disseminated – all over the place – and intent, in relentless
pursuit of what he calls 'props for the dreaming of lived experience'. The articulation of the self, as psychoanalysis has always
insisted, is the transformation of the self; to speak is to become
different. For Bollas the Self is like a rather meditative picaresque
hero, the unwitting artist of his own life. Bollas is extraordinarily
adept at describing the moment, or as he prefers to call it, the 'place
where subject meets thing, to confer significance in the very
moment that being is transformed by the object': and it is whatever
baffles this moment that is pathology. The enigma of these meetings, these reciprocal appraisals – their sheer unconsciousness – is

Bollas's overriding preoccupation in this book. And his paradigm for these processes is dreaming. Since 'a day is a space for the potential articulation of my idiom', then perhaps, he suggests, living a day is more like dreaming a dream than waking up from one.

In any day, Freud showed, quite unbeknown to our conscious selves we are picking things out to use as dream material in the night ahead. So in what Freud calls the 'dream-day' we are living out a kind of unconscious aesthetic; something or someone inside us is selecting what it needs for the night's work. Things in the day have a significance for us, are meaningful, in ways we know nothing about until we work them back up in the quite different context of the dream. A perception, a thought, something overheard is noticed and then transformed by an exceptionally furtive artist. 'In a very particular sense,' Bollas writes, 'we live our life in our own private dreaming'. Bollas manages to convey, without simulating mysteries, an ordinary day as a dream landscape full of unexpectedly intense significance. In its account of living a day as a form of dreaming *Being A Character* becomes a truly startling book. It is as though without being spooky or vague, Bollas gets us close to the ordinary but absolutely elusive experience of making a dream; of how, quite unwittingly, in the most ordinary way, we are choosing objects to speak our secretive languages of self.

Psychoanalytic theory has always had a problem keeping the unconscious unconscious; it usually becomes a nastier, or more ingenious consciousness, a wished-for or a dreaded one. What is distinctive about Bollas's work is his commitment to the unconscious – the unconsciousness of everyday life – without becoming speechless or too mystical in the process (the best and the worst of psychoanalytic theory always verges on the mystical). But how much real unconsciousness can one allow in to the picture and still go on practicing and believing in psychoanalysis? If psychoanalysis is really a sleep-walking *à deux*, what is the analyst, and for that matter the patient supposed to be doing? Taking Freud seriously – which doesn't mean taking him all or taking him earnestly – involves acknowledging, as Bollas writes that, 'most of what transpires in psychoanalysis – as in life itself – is unconscious'. Since for Bollas dreaming is the model, patient and analyst use each other as part, though an intense part, of each other's dream day. The official emphasis is on the patient using the analyst as a transformational object, but in Bollas's model the reciprocity of the analytic process cannot be concealed. And the aim is not so much understanding – finding out which character you are – but a freeing of the potentially endless process of mutual invention and reinvention. For Bollas pathology is whatever it is in the environment and/or the self that sabotages or stifles both a person's inventiveness and their belief in this inventiveness as an open-ended process. It is a psychoanalysis committed to the pleasures and the freedoms of misunderstanding, and that Freud called dream-work; distortion in the service of desire: not truth, except in its most provisional sense, but possibility. The core catastrophe in many of Bollas's powerful clinical vignettes is of being trapped in someone else's (usually the parents') dream or view of the world; psychically paralysed for self-protection in a place without the freedom of perspectives. Here what Bollas calls 'that instinct to elaborate oneself' is thwarted: one is fixed in someone else's preconception. Bollas's use of the word instinct here joins the language of psychoanalysis with the languages of romanticism.

In four remarkable linked essays in the book – 'Cruising in the Homosexual Arena', 'Violent Innocence', 'The Fascist State of Mind' and 'Why Oedipus?' – Bollas explores the causes and consequences of stifling a person's internal repertoire of states of mind. For Bollas so-called mental health (or rather, his version of a good life) entails the tolerance and enjoyment of inner complexity; the ability to use and believe in what he refers to as a kind of internal 'parliament', full of conflicting, dissenting and coercive views. There is no final resolution here but rather a genuinely political and psychic vigilance in the face of the insidious violence of over-simplification. In what he calls the Fascist state of mind – a state of mind readily available to all of us – 'whatever the anxiety or need that sponsors the drive to certainty, which becomes the dynamic in the fascist construction, the outcome is to empty the mind of all opposition (on the actual stage of world politics, to kill the opposition)'. This essay makes one wonder which parts of the self need to be expelled to sustain *any* kind of political allegiance; what happens to greed in left-wing sympathies or empathy in certain versions of Toryism? Unusually activist for a psychoanalyst, Bollas offers us in this book both ways of recognizing the seductions of apparent political and psychic innocence – being on the side of Goodness, Truth and Logic – and actual strategies for managing them. One of the bemusing things about this remarkable book is that it is at once a genuinely radical psychoanalytic book, and also a curiously comforting one.

Bollas's lucid commitment to complexity – which never degenerates into a stultifying relativism – has, as it were, its own complication built into it. For Bollas the 'achievement' of the Oedipus complex is that the 'child comes to understand something about the oddity of possessing one's own mind'; and this means being a mind among others. The child inherits, or wakes up to, the notion of point of view: I'm not only my mother's son and possible lover, but also my father's, and my mother looks different from my father's point of view, and my desire for my father looks different from my mother's point of view, and so on. The super-ego – the internalized paternal prohibition – 'announces' Bollas writes, 'the presence of perspective . . . the child discovers the multiplicity of points of view'. And this ever-proliferating multiplicity, informed by desire, will become the 'it' he will call his mind. It is easy to see, as Bollas intimates, how this can begin to feel overwhelming and persecutory; too much music on at the same time. In one of the best speculative moments in the book Bollas suggests the possibility that many people cannot bear the complexity of their own minds and so take flight into the collusive solace of coupledom, or family life, or group allegiance. The 'madness' of being insistently with others is preferable to the 'madness' of one's mind. 'Given the ordinary unbearableness of this complexity,' Bollas writes, 'I think that the human individual partly regresses in order to survive, but this retreat has been so essential to human life that it has become an unanalysed convention, part of the religion of everyday life. We call this regression "marriage" or "partnership", in which the person becomes part of a mutually interdependent couple that evokes and sustains the bodies of the mother and the father, the warmth of the pre-Oedipal vision of life, before the solitary recognition of subjectivity grips the child.' In Bollas's terms this proposal itself might function as an 'object with evocative integrity'. What would it be like to live in a world in which people welcomed their own, and therefore other people's, complication; in which people did not allow their children to be simplified by conventional education, or coercive belief systems? Traditionally the numinous thing has been to simplify the moral life.

For Bollas trauma is that which oversimplifies the self; it is that which, because of the suffering entailed, leaves people with an aversion to their own complexity. Some people, Bollas writes, for good reasons of their own, 'insist that the invitational feature of the object be declined . . . they may narrow the choice of objects, eliminating those with high evocative potential'. Curiosity is a threat to the self as idol; each new person we meet may call up in us something unfamiliar. So from Bollas's point of view psychoanalysis, as a form of therapy, has two implicit aims: to release – to analyse the obstacles to – a person's internal radar for finding the objects he needs for self-transformation; and to elicit, and enable a person to use, their essential complexity. It is part of the subtlety of this book to make these projects seem compatible.

Like *Being a Character*, *Psychoanalysis and the Future of Theory* is about metamorphosis, the pull of the future against the drag of the past. For Bowie works of art are 'transformational devices' – for Bollas anything might be, though art is always a promising candidate; and the Freudian unconscious by definition for Bowie 'prevents meaning from reaching fullness, completion, closure, consummation'. This does, indeed, exempt meaning from a lot of different things, and leaves it with an unenviable fate. It is, of course, very difficult now to write interestingly about an aversion to closure, a world in which because nothing stops nothing starts either. All modern theory is written in the shade of Heraclitus. But however inclined we are to the idea of process, our language seems to need punctuation. A provisional stop makes a difference. Bowie managed to find, in his shrewd prose, interesting ways to describe this relationship between the fluent and the fixed that all theory cannot avoid confronting. It was Bowie's regard for this tension in

Lacan between, as it were, the will to mathematical formulation and the compulsion to pun that made Bowie's book on Lacan so exhilarating and intelligible. By not taking sides he avoided being evasive. In *Psychoanalysis and the Future of Theory*, elaborating these same dilemmas, Bowie concentrates on what he calls the 'world of unstoppable transformational process' that 'Freud's new psychology brought into view'. Unstoppability, of course, is only visible if we know what a stop looks like. We never step into the same river twice because we can see the difference. For Bowie the future of theory, not unlike the future of the psychoanalytic patient, depends on this 'irreducibility, the uncontainability, the unstoppability of the signifying process'. Words do stop somewhere, but psychoanalysis, like literary theory, should not be the art of having the last word. Last words are a different thing entirely.

But having said that about 'the signifying process', what is there left to say? In the first essay in the book, and the one that gives the book its title, Bowie shows how Freud by prioritizing the past made the future a virtually redundant category in psychoanalytic theory. It is one of the important paradoxes of psychoanalysis that wishes for Freud also lead one into the past as well as the future. 'Human beings,' Bowie writes, 'are devoted to the optative mood. This is the time dimension that all desiring creatures inhabit, and "if only such and such were the case" is its characteristic syntactic structure.' But as 'such and such' is in the past the future comes out as more of the same (though this more is always becoming less). In Bowie's view it took Lacan's brilliant enquiries into human temporality (inspired by Heidegger) to reveal how 'past, present and future will always stand outside each other, unsettle each other, and refuse to cohere'. Bowie's unusual image of these quasi-allegorical figures Past, Present and Future 'standing outside each other', squabbling like an unhappy family, is easy to miss in a writer who, unlike Lacan, keeps his artfulness under wraps.

Though Lacan, as Bowie says, was committed to the 'rediscovery of a futurity intrinsic to the structure of the human passions', and, therefore, to the unknowable in human experience, he also had the fatal weakness of all those who are fanatically against all forms of totalization (the complete picture) in the so-called human sciences: a love of system. On the one hand, as Bowie says, Lacan is 'fascinated by the sciences of exact measurement' and in his theory 'dreams of a perfectly calculable human subject'; and on the other he is committed, as a form of virtual revelation, to 'astonishing time-teasing syntactic and semantic display'. When Blake proposed that he should build his own system else be enslaved by another man's he was, of course, acknowledging the powerful fascination of systems, not paying tribute to the individual's freedom.

So what can the system-building theorist do with this dilemma, and with Lacan himself? Either stick to the scheme and make it more rigorous, copy the exhilarating rhetoric (become a Lacanian ventriloquist's dummy) or, as Bowie rightly prefers, 'learn to unlearn the Lacanian idiom in the way Lacan unlearns the Freudian idiom'. This is a salutary suggestion in so far as it might help some people avoid the humiliation – the awful prose style – of the disciple. To be a follower in psychoanalysis, as Bollas and Bowie both make clear, is to miss the point. Disciples are the people who haven't got the joke. And historically, in psychoanalysis, disciples enact the catastrophe their leaders were trying to avert; Freudians become ascetic prigs, Winnicottians become rigorously spontaneous, Kleinians become enviously narrow-minded, Lacanians mirror the master, and so on.

Bowie proposes that the future of psychoanalytic theory depends on an inter-animating relationship with other disciplines and a new fashion of old-fashioned values; 'perhaps the best hope for the psychoanalyst,' he writes, 'lies not in "theory" at all, but in the old-fashioned arts of speaking opportunely and knowing when to stop'. And a tactful psychoanalysis sufficiently alert to futures could teach literary theorists to perform 'flexed, tensed, desirous and prospective critical performances'. The critical question might be: what do I and this text/patient want to be next? What are we going to use each other to become (of course, the only way you know the future is the future is if it's surprising)? Most literary and psychoanalytic theory spends its time establishing its ground and finding positions. Bowie proposes that they find what they did not know they were looking for. As a critic he is interested in the moment – in a sense, the psychoanalytic moment – when a person seems 'suddenly to be speaking or behaving from an alien region'.

Bowie wants the complexity of art to replace, or become the paradigm for, what have become the stultifications of theory. No theory, not even the addictive theory of psychoanalysis, can 'still the rage of a literary text'. Sounding for once more like Carlyle – or perhaps Arnold – he wishfully prophesies that 'by the year 2000 "theory" will have rediscovered art and the threatened but glorious futures that art contains'. For some people, of course, this begs all the questions – whose art? and whose futures? – but it also confronts the absurd omniscience and righteous indignation that goes on passing for much critical theory. There is no reason, as Bollas's book illustrates, that a plea for the value of complexity, should be in itself reactionary or complacently knowing.

Bowie's second essay in this book, 'Freud and Art, or What will Michelangelo's Moses do next?', will, I think, modify the suspicions aroused by Bowie's prediction about the forthcoming death of the theorist. This brilliant chapter functions as the critical consciousness of the book as it teases out Freud's perplexed and contradictory relationship to art and artists. If, in Bowie's view, Freud idealized the past, and Bowie himself seems to idealize art, in this chapter these acts of psychic denial are themselves analysed. For Freud, Bowie writes, art works represented 'the psychical life lived in a triumphant mode': 'by way of art the human being could remove himself for a time from his wretchedness'. It is Freud's 'strangeness' about art that exercises Bowie, his 'impatient' and 'appropriative' and particularly competitive dealings with the art of the past. Once again it is this war between excess and conclusiveness that Bowie is quick to notice. Freud's relationship to literature in *The Interpretation of Dreams* – a 'thinning out' Bowie calls it – is mirrored in his relationship to his dreams. The dreams themselves, Bowie observes, have this 'constant air of semantic overflow and dispersal', while Freud insists 'upon parsimony in his interpretative procedures'. Theory or interpretation are all we are left with after the art-work or the dream have been made habitable. Literature is what gets lost in interpretation. 'From an extremely parsimonious set of causes,'

Bowie writes, 'springs a glittering array of effects'. Bowie is on the side of the effects. To satisfy Freud's scientific super-ego, in Bowie's view, 'the grammar of interpretation had to be purged of merely wish-bearing constructions'. For Bowie a good interpretation is one that re-enacts or discerns the temporal complexity of the object, its mobility of wish and retrospection. It is the bizarre meshing of the future with the past that Bowie wants to recuperate for the act of interpretation. Otherwise 'analysis explains the work of art, and immobilises it in the process'. Art merely becomes an integral part of the larger self-fulfilling prophecy called psychoanalysis, that by explaining everything finds nothing new under the sun. Art is then, in Bowie's tempered words, 'granted no higher privilege . . . than that of accrediting psychoanalysis all over again by adding an aura of cultural value and prophetic grandeur to its scientific claims'. It is the Freud of interminable and digressive meanings, not the Freud in search of causes, that both Bollas and Bowie in their separate ways promote. Psychoanalytic theory should only ever be given free-floating attention.

The 'new' Freud Bowie recommends here is 'a dramatist, a novelist, a fabulist and, above all, perhaps, a rhetorician'. Bollas's Freud is the exemplary and inspiring human subject who 'becomes the dream-work of his own life'; who found a way of describing this banal and enigmatic experience. But both these books, committed as they are to a more 'literary' psychoanalysis, make continual reference, by analogy or allusion, to music, the art-form Freud is known to have disliked. It may also be useful, Bowie and Bollas intimate, to think of the unconscious as structured like a piece of music. If we were to think like that what would psychoanalytic interpretation have to become? Perhaps the function of psychoanalysis in the future will not be to inform but to evoke.

III
WRITING OUTSIDE

16
Philip Roth's Patrimony

'And where did all these sages get the idea that man needs some normal, some virtuous wanting.'

Fyodor Dostoevsky, *Notes from Underground*

A crucial incident in Philip Roth's *Patrimony: A True Story* (1991) comes when Roth's aged and ill father Herman 'beshats himself', as he puts it:

'Don't tell the children,' he said, looking up at me from the bed with his one sighted eye.
'I won't tell anyone,' I said. 'I'll say you're taking a rest.'
'Don't tell Claire.'
'Nobody,' I said. 'Don't worry about it. It could have happened to anyone. Just forget about it and get a good rest.'

Where there is shame there is always the possibility of the direst indiscretion (and between fathers and sons, of the most bemusing kind of triumph). But it is the novelist-son, not the father, who demands, by promising, the larger reticence. 'Fate,' Roth writes towards the end of *Patrimony*, 'had given me a fiercely loyal and devoted father who had never found a thing in my books to criticise.' As the story of his father's death, *Patrimony* is the first of Roth's books that his father would never read.

Roth is the least sentimental and therefore the least cynical of writers, and *Patrimony* is remarkable, among other things, for the complexity of the affection he feels for his father. He is at pains at this moment of the book to show his father, and not only his father now, that it is not the fact of his incontinence alone that is humiliating: it is trying to live in such a continent world. We are not humiliated by our acts but by our ideals. In this incident, Herman Roth – not by choice, it should perhaps be said – joins his son's fictional pantheon, so to speak. The heroes of Roth's novels usually have the defiant but slightly embarrassed wish to be celebrated for what they have been educated or encouraged to deprecate. They have the courage of their brashness. 'Going wild in public,' he has written, 'is the last thing in the world a Jew is expected to do.' Roth has been inventing, that is to say, a new kind of heroism, the heroism of incontinence. 'Portnoy,' he remarked in an interview, 'wasn't a character for me, he was an explosion.' As most of his fictional heroes and some of his heroines know, there's no good performance – no performance, indeed – without indiscretion, or its possibility.

Deception, Roth's previous book and the novel he was finishing while his father was dying, is full of people accusing the Roth-Person of exploiting relationships, and even other people's suffering, for his writing. A 'friend' informs him at one point: 'He didn't fuck her the way you fucked her, for her stories. He fucked her for fucking . . . Life before the narrative takes over is life.' But the Roth-Person has a few things to tell the Truth-Tellers, all those people who are eager to tell him, by way of accusation, what Life is. After all, who decides what we are allowed to use relationships for? And what is our sense of betrayal, or deception, telling us about our ideas of privacy, or honesty, or the sacredness of coupledom? 'Discretion,' he writes in *Deception*, 'is, unfortunately, not for novelists', and because Roth, at least since *Zuckerman Bound*, has been his own most ferocious critic in these matters within the novels, 'unfortunate' seems the fortunate word. Roth has always written interestingly about the uneasy relationship between confidence and confiding in someone, about the sense in which every story is an act of betrayal. The writing usually sharpens, or gets hilarious, at the moment of conspiracy in a conversation, the moment that often only one person in a Roth conversation is pushing for. The moment, that is, in which someone invites the possibility of a betrayal, or just tells someone a good story. Conspiring is inspiring.

Roth has certainly been suggesting in his recent books that what people think they can say that will betray their partner – or their family, or friends – reveals something about the imaginary crime they are committing together (or wish they were committing).

Deception, I think, was greatly underrated, partly because of its minimalism, at least by Roth's standards, but also because he was on to something so discomforting: that one way we get to know people is by betraying them, and that we can suffer most as adults from not being able to let people down. And one lets people down – or 'deceives' them – when one refuses to be only one version of oneself. Consistency is compliance. So when people are alone in Roth's novels – or with people who don't know them – they come to a certain kind of life: as though fidelity, particularly to oneself, constrains the repertoire. 'Being by myself,' Roth writes in *Patrimony*, having to deal with the news of his father's brain tumour, 'allowed me to be as emotional as I felt, without having to put up a manly or mature or philosophical front' – the fronts that all Roth's heroes are cramped by and suspicious of in others, the fronts that define a certain version of adulthood (the Jewish heroes of Roth's novels sometimes experience the Gentiles as people who pretend they were never children). We may regularly be asked to protect people's favourite versions of themselves, but we don't always have to agree. Roth's novels have shown us what it looks like when we don't, and how relieved we are when we do.

Children are compelled, at least at first, to take their parents on their own terms – until they find terms of their own, which usually begins with a vengeance in adolescence. In fact, children are the only people who know what adults are, because adults are people who don't know what it is to be an adult. Roth has always used adolescence – that twilight of the idols – as a state of mind, which it is, and not as some putative stage to be outgrown (the real problem of adolescence is that most people can't sustain it). 'Adolescent', like 'immigrant', is mostly used, and often for comparable reasons, as a pejorative. Roth has implicitly exploited the connection between these two kinds of *arriviste* who threaten the composure of the locals by not subscribing to composure. 'It's the tirade', as he once said, 'that's taboo.' And it is usually in adolescence that the Roth hero famously starts to confront his fictional immigrant father. In *Patrimony*, which is not a novel, the son is freer to realize, once the father is old and dying, how compatible they have always been,

169

even through their differences – that patrimony is what they have always had in common.

'I listen,' says the Roth-Person in *Deception*, a combination of an analyst and a sit-down comedian: 'I'm an écouteur – an audio-philiac. I'm a talk fetishist.' He talks 'openly' only about his father, the man with whom the middle-aged novelist says he has to 'suppress being a 14-year-old'. Accused of being over-sensitive about anti-semitism in England, he is then accused by his lover of something else:

'God, you are your father's son, aren't you?'
'Whose should I be instead?'
'Well, it's just all a bit of a surprise, after reading your books.'
'Is it? Read 'em again.'

If, in Roth's novels, the sons can never take the fathers on their own terms, in *Patrimony* the son begins to see the survival value, the sense, of those terms. *Patrimony* is an extraordinary book about what it is to know a father, because Roth manages to find a language for an unidealized celebration, and this involves realizing the virtue of the father's vices for both the son and the father. 'He understood,' he writes of his father, 'like the rest of us, only what he understood, though that he understood fiercely.'

As a true story – the kind of story that Roth's father would think of himself as telling – *Patrimony* describes in often gruelling detail Herman Roth's final illnesses and death from a brain tumour at the age of eighty-six. The candid resilience of the man amid so much humiliation – a version, as Roth acknowledges, of the 'stubborn prick' that infuriated him as a younger man – is indeed inspiring. The description of what the body can do to itself makes ageing seem far more terrifying than the conventional drama of sons killing fathers. In fact, the Oedipus story, which Roth doesn't allow to ghost-write his book, seems rather comforting in compari-son. It is at least intelligible. Herman Roth's question 'Why should a man die?', stripped of its portentousness because he was clearly a man who didn't need to be grand, becomes a good question, again. Roth refers to his father here as a 'pitiless realist', confirming, as he does throughout this wonderful book, that the antagonist of his adolescence turns out to have been his Muse, his double and his child.

If the 'Bard of Newark', as Roth calls him – 'he taught me the vernacular. He *was* the vernacular, unpoetic and expressive and point-blank' – was his Muse, he was also the source of much of his amusement. The hilarity of *Patrimony*, the double act of father and son and the father's false teeth, for example, or the concentration-camp-survivor pornographer, is Roth unbound at his best. When someone compliments Herman Roth on his son's sense of humour Roth immediately points something out, and the chosen word doesn't make a modesty of it all: ' "The jokes," I told her, "originate with him." ' The jokes and the continual telling of family stories. It is the inheritance that they are both possessed by, and obsessed with. The difference is that for the father, at least in *Patrimony*, the telling of family history is a way of consolidating the family, while for the son it is, and always has been, potentially a betrayal. Because another difference, of course, is that only the son is a writer. In other words, only the son went to college.

In Roth's earlier novels, culture is what Jewish boys try and kill their fathers with (could one take seriously a father who didn't read *Partisan Review*?). Their worldly, immigrant fathers struggled to provide, and idealized, the kind of education that would secure the continuity of the family through the success of the sons; and it was this very education, especially when it was literary, that armed the sons with the weapons for a daunting critique of the family. They went to college and learned mandarin table-manners. They found a world of words their parents could never enter into. Invidious comparisons were available that could be used to ironize the struggle of their parents' lives. Compared with the novels of Jane Austen, Jewish family life does look a bit fraught. With the comfort and protection worked hard for by the parents, the children could entertain ideas. The irony of their disparate experiences, the new kind of conflict between the generations, was never lost on Roth, and was the subject, or one of the subjects, of *My Life as a Man*. 'Suffering and failure,' he wrote there, 'the theme of so many of the novels that moved him, were "human conditions" about which he could speak with an astonishing lucidity and even gravity by the time he was a senior honours student – astonishing in that he was, after all, someone whose own sufferings had by and large been confined up till then to the dentist's chair.'

Traditionally, education and learning had signified continuity for Jews. They now began, in post-war America, to threaten the rupture of tradition and the repudiation of family ties. In an increasingly secularized world 'suffering and failure' became a 'theme'. The catastrophe of the Second World War made the disowning of history, or the appropriation of other traditions, or even the invention of that most improbable figure, a Jewish Emersonian, particularly tempting for the children of immigrants. But the study of literature as an education in high-minded composure, combined with the traditional image of the Jew as ethical standard-bearer, had serious consequences for the literature written by Jews after the war. 'The sympathetic Jewish hero,' Roth wrote in his 1974 essay 'Imagining Jews', was associated with 'ethical jewhood as it opposes sexual niggerhood, with victimisation as opposed to vengeful aggression, with dignified survival rather than euphoric or gloating triumph, with sanity and renunciation as opposed to excessive desire – except the excessive desire to be good and to do good.'

Oppositions like these too easily promote the stereotypes they are trying to avoid ('You know something,' the Roth-Person's lover tells him in *Deception*, 'you're hypnotised by bad behaviour. You think it's stylish'). But Roth has always had a strong and exhilarating sense that character – especially perhaps for the children of his parents' generation of immigrants – is not so much the acquisition of virtue as its defiance. Virtue can merely mean compliance, a fear of the repertoire of private and public parts. Defiance of virtue requires impersonation; the excessive desire to be not too good is suited to the ventriloquence of fiction. 'In my imagination,' the Roth-Person says in *Deception*, 'I am unfaithful to everybody.' But there is a kind of survivor-guilt in the children who are free to invent themselves. The guilt that writing entails, and that Roth has been increasingly explicit about in his books, has something to do with this. The freedom to proliferate selves is subsidized by lives that have been severely circumscribed.

One thing, of course, that novels can do is make new kinds of people available to us. Literature may not be, as Roth remarked in an interview, 'a moral beauty contest', but it can at least show us new styles. Once he had, in *Portnoy*, rejected the traditionally good Jew – and so, by implication, his father and the world his father carried on his back – he had denied himself, as he does several significant times in *Patrimony*, something of his inheritance. But patrimony – unlike matrimony, Roth implies – is an offer one can't refuse. Getting away from his father was usually a way of rejoining him: at school, he had the 'impassioned, if crazy, conviction that I was somehow inhabited by him and quickening his intellect right along with mine'. At college, his father was 'the intellectual homunculus for whose development I felt as responsible as I did for my own'. Education might make one believe that what one needs to know one learns in school; and that not only does one's father need an education, but one needs other fathers. The fathers one finds in books are quite different from the father one finds at home. They are made only with words. What Roth suggests in *Patrimony* is that one may need these other fathers to help one find one's father. That this is what other fathers are for.

Patrimony is deadpan about Hamlet – 'I find that while visiting a grave one has thoughts that are more or less anybody's thoughts and, leaving aside the matter of eloquence, don't differ much from Hamlet's contemplating the skull of Yorick' – because Roth's affiliations are elsewhere. *Patrimony* begins with a diagnosis and ends with an interpreted dream about the death of a father. And in between, so to speak, in a kind of benign rewrite of Kafka's 'Letter to his Father', Roth celebrates what an indulgent and zealously devoted father can do for his son's well-being. Kafka and Freud, the two great Jewish parodists of patriarchy, who showed in their writing that there is no authority, only authority figures, have always been Roth's chosen patrimony. In this context, when he realizes, in the extraordinary scene in which he clears up his father's shit, that '*that* was the patrimony. And not because cleaning it up was symbolic of something else but because it wasn't, because it was nothing less or more than the lived reality that it was', he is saying something that cannot be simple. For Kafka and Freud, survival depended upon interpretation, and interpretation represented the refusal to be dominated by one truth. On the one hand, Roth's refusal of symbolism – the dream of the literal, of the body or the world exempt from interpretation – is the acceptance, or protection, of his father at the cost of the world of his chosen fathers, a world relentless with meaning. On the other hand, Roth is suggesting that what you inherit is what you have to get rid of. But what seems so unacceptable, all the shit, may not be so bad after all, just another front: 'once you sidestep disgust and ignore nausea and plunge past those phobias that are fortified like taboos, there's an awful lot of life to cherish'. This, admittedly, is not a pastoral for the squeamish, but then, unlike most versions of pastoral, it affirms something without making callous exclusions. It allows the possibility of embarrassment, and terror.

Roth is quite explicit that to acquire his patrimony, to see it for what it is, a son may have to become a mother to his own father. Children first become moralists when they realize their parents are children. In *Patrimony* the son writes about the father with astonishing lucidity and tenderness, as though they were similar kinds of people. One of the continual revelations – or rather, one of the running gags – of *Patrimony* is that the antagonism between them was always a form of affinity.

17
Isaac Rosenberg's English

I

It's the man with impudence who has more experience than anybody. He not only varies his own, but makes other people's his own.

Rosenberg, *Collected Works*

In 1911, at the age of twenty-one, Isaac Rosenberg decided, despite the poverty of his working-class immigrant family, to become an artist and so to leave his demoralizing job working for a firm of engravers. 'Free', as he wrote, 'to do anything, hang myself or anything except work', he spent a lot of time copying the Great Masters in the National Gallery. One morning he was copying Velázquez's *Philip IV* when King George was due to come to the gallery to open some new rooms. When it was known that the King had arrived, the other students left their easels and lined the corridors to see him. 'Whether out of shyness, disdain, absorption or ignorance of protocol,' his biographer Joseph Cohen writes, 'Rosenberg did not stop painting to acknowledge his presence, even though the king paused for a moment to watch him paint.' Cohen, quite understandably, wants to give Rosenberg several options. But nevertheless, here was a young Jewish man – whether to be defiant or to gain his regard – ignoring the King of England, and painting a Catholic king under his very eye.

Five years later, having enlisted for the war effort and joined the Bantam Brigade because of his height, Rosenberg wrote 'jokingly' to his friend the publisher Edward Marsh from his barracks: 'The King inspected us Thurday. I believe its the first Bantam Brigade been inspected. He must have waited for us to stand up a good while. At a distance we look like soldiers sitting down, you know, legs so short.' Once again, but for a different reason, Rosenberg considers the possibility of not standing up for the King of England; of doing, at least in his mind, the impudent thing. For a son of Russian immigrants who had to teach themselves English, the war – like the struggle to accommodate himself to a culture so alien to his family – complicated, as we shall see, the always problematic question of his allegiances: who he chose to identify with, whose language he was going to write in, who or what he was prepared to stand up for. 'I never joined the army,' he would write, 'for patriotic reasons'; nor, of course, did his family come to Britain, or learn English for what could be described as patriotic reasons. Having escaped from Eastern Europe – and it is not incidental that Rosenberg's father may have come to Britain to escape conscription in the Russian army – learning English was a contingent necessity. Rosenberg's uneasy relationship with the English language as a poet, was to mark him, for the owners of English poetry, as an unassimilable presence; at once deferential and an eager parricide. 'This is not the first time,' he writes in 1910 to the writer Israel Zangwill, 'I have wearied you with my specimens of desperate attempts to murder and mutilate King's English beyond all shape of recognition.'

Rosenberg's earliest-known poem, 'Ode to David's Harp', written when he was fifteen, does not involve much dramatic disfiguring of the King's English. But he chooses both an interesting subject – a Jewish king, the 'monarch minstrel' David, a warrior and a poet – and an interesting model to imitate, the aspiring warrior and great poet Byron, a most unrighteous and eloquent champion of the oppressed. 'You mustn't forget the circumstances I have been brought up in,' Rosenberg wrote to a friend in 1911,

the little education I have had. Nobody ever told me what to read, or ever put poetry in my way. I don't think I knew what real poetry was till I read Keats a couple of years ago. True, I galloped through Byron when I was about fourteen, but I fancy I read him more for the story than for the poetry. I used to try to imitate him.

Byron, famously, was the poet one read for the story – both the narrative adventures of the poems and the scandalous story of his life which the poems were assumed to reflect. It is not amazing that an impoverished and culturally disaffected Jewish boy of Rosenberg's generation might find Byron an object of emulation. Byron's life as an inspired aristocrat, socially mobile and irreverent, was the vivid antithesis of Rosenberg's life – 'deadened', as he then wrote of it with a lugubrious adolescent allusion to Hamlet, 'by the fiendish persistence of the coil of circumstance'.

In the 'Ode to David's Harp' – based on Byron's *Hebrew Melodies* – Rosenberg promotes a revival of the Jewish spirit through the inspiration of poetry. The poem, it should be noted, is to the harp and not to David, just as Rosenberg's first and apparently whimsical prose piece was about a door-knocker. He was preoccupied, from the beginning of his poetic life, with instruments of transition – what you need to get from one state of mind to another, from outside to inside the door. The poem begins with a prophetic invocation, reminiscent of Blake, that in the poet's view is of more than historical significance:

> Awake! ye joyful strains, awake!
> In silence sleep no more;
> Disperse the gloom that ever lies
> O'er Judah's barren shore.

Rosenberg, even at fifteen, is announcing a big programme. The gloom that 'ever' lies over the Jews – 'ever' meaning 'always', not just 'then' – may be, as the pun suggests, a lie: the lie, he will come to believe, born of a certain kind of submission to a certain kind of God – a God, he will come to believe, that one needs to rid oneself of. It was David's harp that lifted Saul's gloom, and David, the great Jewish folk-hero – 'the sweet singer of Israel' – who would displace Saul. In Rosenberg's poem David's potency lies in his music, his 'melody'; and the man he begins by serving is the man whose position he will take. The guest became the host. 'Fate is weaving / Other bonds than slavery's chains,' he wrote in lines he eventually cut from the poem.

Rosenberg was to be preoccupied in his writing by the complicity – the repertoire of complicities – between hosts and guests. And a host could be, for example, a God, a family, a country or a language. And there could also be a sense in which the past – or ideas about the past – could be seen as the host of the future. Like all great self-inventors and visionaries, he wanted to create his own genealogy, to make his own connections; reinventing the past to make possible a new kind of future. Redoing the past in this way means, among other things, being able to tell the hosts from the guests. And there is an early and ingenuously revealing story on this theme, called 'Rudolph', that Rosenberg wrote when he was twenty-one.

Rudolph is a young artist, 'God's castaway', merely 'his ancestors' remains'. 'I am the first', he announces grandly, 'to scandalise the family with a difference . . . They consider it perfectly immoral to talk and think unlike them.' One day, yearningly despondent about himself as a failing artist, he 'strays' into the National Gallery and suddenly finds himself being asked by an unknown person to remain seated: 'He was awakened from his reverie by hearing a feminine voice saying, "O! please don't rise, oblige me." ' The sexual innuendo – the double-message, so to speak – turns out to be prophetic. Quite unwittingly Rudolph has become part of this woman's painting; he finds himself in somebody else's picture – being painted into her frame. And it is this very involuntary inclusion that gets him, as it were, further into the picture; into the larger picture of this woman's social world, the High Bohemian society that has always excluded him.

Discovering that Rudolph is an artist with remarkable views about painting, she asks him to what he calls 'a wealthy supper' with her brother the famous poet Leonard Harris, whom Rudolph has always admired, and other important and cultured people. But Rudolph soon realizes that he doesn't know the form, that he is not equipped for the occasion; he doesn't have the right clothes. But, as luck would have it, his friend Dave is having an affair with a landlady whose husband – 'a man with mysterious connections with 'igh Society' – has a proper suit, which is secretly borrowed by Dave for the occasion. Virtually everything going on in the story is illegitimate; everyone is an impostor of one kind or another. 'The suit was laid out,' the author writes, 'and Rudolph proceeded to make his entrance into the uniform of a gentleman, into which he completely disappeared.' 'I feel somehow I am lost in it,' he says to Dave; 'but don't you think it will make me look bigger?' He feels 'transformed, transfigured', goes to the grand dinner and performs rather well, expounding some remarkable views on aesthetics that we will come back to. But when the butler serves the coffee he drops the tray in shock, recognizing his suit on Rudolph. His host, the distinguished poet, resolves the problem by telling Henry the butler that Rudolph had thought he was going to a 'fancy-dress ball' and so borrowed the suit from Henry's wife. Everyone is therefore implicitly insulted by the gracious host, but as usual in High Society nobody appears to be ruffled or even to notice. Certainly, High Society might look like a fancy-dress ball to an outsider like Rudolph. Having already begun 'to curse inwardly the artificialities of convention, the forms that bound each man to be a mechanical demonstration of its monotony', Rudolph leaves with a sense both of dismay and of possibility. But he has experienced his performance at the dinner as some kind of betrayal of his heritage. 'His mind was in a whirl. His past – what a horrible waste of God's faculties – unused.'

Rudolph is presented in the story not so much as a Jew in particular but as an *arriviste* – the word 'rude' is barely concealed in the name Rudolph. With the lightest and shrewdest of touches this story condenses a number of Rosenberg's pressing concerns. But for the purposes of this lecture I just want to emphasize the fact that Rudolph is wearing the butler's clothes. Rosenberg uses this familiar device to formulate Rudolph's dilemma as an *arriviste* and an artist; is he a guest or a servant of the host? Or, to put it another way: in a fancy-dress ball, who is the joke on? A fancy-dress ball is as good a picture as any of an alien or unmanageable culture.

In a commentary on Sartre's account of another unplaceable, displaced artist, Jean Genet, Arthur Danto wrote:

Calling the young Genet a thief, for instance, not merely identified him as having stolen, but gave him, according to Sartre's treatment in *Saint Genet*, an identity and a project; it caused him to be a thief, since it was through the network of associations with this term that he henceforth saw himself; and as he believed himself to be, so did he act, and the power of the name consisted in causing the fact it did not neutrally merely designate.

Genet, like an extreme version of Rudolph and Rosenberg himself, is the artist as disreputable outsider. By calling himself an artist – painter and more gradually poet – Rosenberg conferred upon himself a destiny/project. Calling himself a poet – which he did against much internal and external resistance – was like promising himself the life of a poet. It was as though he made himself an invitation, one that was rarely forthcoming from anyone else (in his letters there are many pieces of fervent gratitude for any recognition or praise of his talent). But the network of associations to the notion of a Jewish English poet – as opposed to a Jewish English painter, of which there were several among his friends – was not available as a web he could catch himself in. That is to say, the pressures of self-invention on Rosenberg were considerable. And it is not surprising, then, that he should be so drawn to the American writer Ralph Waldo Emerson – the great self- and country-inventor – and that he should write of Emerson's poems: 'We have here no tradition – no tricks of the trade.' It is a revealing definition of what constitutes a tradition; or rather, of what a tradition can feel like to an outsider.

'In literature,' Rosenberg wrote to Edward Marsh in 1914, 'I have no judgement – at least for style. If in reading a thought has expressed itself to me, in beautiful words; my ignorance of grammar etc. makes me accept that.' Confronted by an established culture, or in the absence of a sustaining group, different judgement might begin to feel like no judgement; 'grammar etc.' becomes another country. For Rosenberg there were Jewish poets who did not write in English, and English poets who were not Jews. And he had no formal education in the tradition to which he aspired, primarily the Romantics, Blake, Keats, Shelley and Byron, and through them to Rossetti, Swinburne and Francis Thompson. Like Rosenberg himself, the English Romantic poets thought of themselves as reviving a tradition, the true English tradition of poetry, lost after Milton. Rosenberg was in the paradoxical position of reviving a tradition that did not exist, a tradition of Jewish English poetry; he wanted to 'wake the zeal in Israel's breast', but in a language foreign to the origins he wanted to redeem.

By all accounts, including his own, always an outsider, Rosenberg also felt estranged within his own family. Isolated and unconnected, he could, a contemporary of his wrote, 'sit from morning to evening without uttering a word'. 'He never had anything in common with any of the family,' his youngest sister Ray said of him, 'we were not sufficiently artistic for him.' He was known, as a young man, for his 'ungainly appearance, inarticulateness and self-effacing shyness'. In fact his biographers, Cohen and Jean Moorcroft-Wilson, the sources of this information, convey a curious impression of Rosenberg, as though he coupled a kind of slapstick inattention – absentmindedly dropping all his paintings into Cape Town harbour, forgetting to address envelopes – with an intense visionary, poetic vocation. A schoolfriend, Joseph Leftwich, wrote of him in his diary: 'His people are very unsympathetic to him. They insist on treating him as a little out of his mind. They consider him as an invalid . . . he says his taste is very poor and he enjoys boys' magazines and his sisters' novelettes. It is only in poetry that he fills himself with something.' Rosenberg began to think of poetry, and not the orthodox Judaism of his parents and their contempories, as redemptive, as really filling; and of the artist as the true provider. In the attempt to realize his vision he had to reject much that he had been given and much that was expected of him, both by his family and by the arbiters of taste in contemporary British poetry.

'My circumstances have not been very favourable,' he wrote in 1910, 'for artistic production.' So what did Rosenberg have to reject, or relinquish, to create the circumstances he needed? There are, of course, many ways to describe the project of a life; but one useful way of talking about a life – and Rosenberg's life in particular, I think – is to ask the question: what does a person believe he has to get rid of to have the life he wants? Because in these disposals a person can be, often unconsciously, creating a space in which something else can happen (so Rosenberg could have been at risk if he had gone for a certain kind of psychoanalysis in which he would have been encouraged to reappropriate what he needed to get rid of). By deciding to be an artist, I think, and then by enlisting, he was creating the circumstances, however unpleasant, in which he could become the man he wanted to be. 'I think the safest place is at the front,' he wrote in 1914, '– we'll starve or die of suspense anywhere else.'

II

A poet's words and rhythms are not his utterance so much as his resistance.

Geoffrey Hill, *The Enemy's Country*

Drawing a curious parallel, in 1911 Rosenberg writes facetiously to another Jewish writer, Ruth Löwy, of 'the wickedness of the times (with suffragettes throwing hatchets at kings – and poets compelling people to read their poems)'. If poets are like suffragettes and poems are like hatchets thrown at kings, then poetry, despite the odd joke, is a serious, indeed a violent, threat to the established order. The suffragettes, like the poets, refuse to comply with the order of things.

The woman in the National Gallery who painted Rudolph confessed to him that she thought 'Van Eyck the greatest artist who ever lived. I adore him because he makes the commonplace so delightfully precious.' 'I think a picture should be something more,' protested Rudolph. 'Van Eyck is interesting to me just as a pool reflecting the clouds is interesting, or a landscape seen through a mirror. But it is only a faithful transcript of what we see. My ideal of a picture is to paint what we cannot see. To create, to imagine.' To paint the world as you see it may be to comply with the commonplace. Simple mimesis is the antithesis, for an outsider like Rudolph, of the visionary transfiguration of reality that he aspires to. Mimesis has to be rejected because it signifies – or might represent – assimilation; it is an implicit form of consent to the way things are supposed to look. But if straightforward imitation – however skilled – compromises vision, if Rosenberg was critical of Velázquez, in a striking sentence, because 'His truth was more the practical truth of the mirror', then what kind of aesthetic was Rosenberg, or rather Rudolph, prepared to promote?

Showing his portfolio of drawings to the dinner party,

[Rudolph] stood by to explain and elucidate where elucidation was necessary, which was not seldom; for he painted on the principle that the art of painting was the art of leaving out, and the pleasure in beholding a picture was the pleasure of finding out. Where he had not left out the whole picture, sometimes it was successful.

What the painter leaves out – what he disposes of – becomes the invitation that constitutes his art; an invitation to curiosity, to the pleasure of finding out. And by implication strictly mimetic art might create the illusion that everything is already there, that what you see is what there is. It is not unusual – despite Rosenberg's disavowal of any polemical or ideological allegiances (he never joined a group or signed a manifesto) – that he should, as the child of immigrants, be suspicious of, or dismayed by, the available versions of reality. And often, I think, and sometimes unwittingly, his poetry was a form of resistance; a way of joining a culture by not joining in.

Rosenberg was always keen in his writing to emphasize the differences between the arts. But this art of leaving out that he ascribes here to painting was remarkably prescient both of the way he would come – not programmatically, but by inclination – to write poetry and of the way his poetry would be judged, even by some of his most sympathetic critics. From the judgement of the first poetry competition that he entered at the age of sixteen – 'original but rather vague in parts' – to Frank Kermode's and John Hollander's comment in the 1973 *Oxford Anthology of English Literature* about 'Rosenberg's visionary fragments', there is a striking consensus: that his poetry is patchy and obscure – intermittently vivid – but leaving out too many connections.

In his opening speech for the Memorial Exhibition of Rosenberg's Paintings and Drawings in 1937 Edward Marsh described Rosenberg inappositely as 'an Aladdin whose lamp was a strong but slender searchlight which lit up now and then, but only for a moment, some jewel in the cave of darkness in which he groped'. More visceral, but no less critical of the apparent absence of structure in his poems, Laurence Binyon wrote to tell Rosenberg that his poetry came out in 'clotted gushes and spasms'. Clearly, the art of leaving out does not always lead to the pleasure of finding out; abortions and momentary illuminations can spell the failure of the artist to those who supposedly know what they are talking about. As the reviewer of Rosenberg's posthumously published *Poems* of 1922 wrote in the *Times Literary Supplement* with supercilious condescension: 'he had a genius for the vivid phrase, for illumination in flashes; if he could have learned coordination, and calmness, the broad handling of the texture of his art, he must surely have won a lasting place in the annals of our literature'.

Rosenberg's correspondence provides a gloomy record of his bemused accommodation – his bowing to *and* resisting – to what felt like the alien aesthetic standards offered to him by the guardians of what the *TLS* reviewer called *'our literature'*. 'People are always telling me my work is promising', he wrote to the poet Gordon Bottomley from France in 1916, 'incomprehensible but promising, and all that sort of thing, and my meekness subsides before the patronising knowingness.' Such patronizing knowingness can only come from those who recognize 'our literature' when they see it. 'Most people find them difficult,' Rosenberg wrote of his poems in 1915, 'and won't be bothered to read into them.'

But Rosenberg as a kind of double agent between cultures – in a no-man's-land of aspiration and resistance – felt that there was something inside him that he couldn't define, and that seemed to sabotage the versions of intelligibility – of poetic form – that he was constantly being judged by. 'There is always behind or through my object,' he wrote from the army in 1915, 'some pressing sense of foreign matter, immediate and not personal, which hinders and disjoints what would otherwise have coherence and perhaps weight.' There is, of course, on the one hand the foreign matter of the war, doubly foreign for Rosenberg because he was fighting for and against countries he did not belong to. But there is also the perhaps inevitable equivocation here of the resident alien, the difficulty of valuing the 'foreign matter'; of articulating what was foreign about him without making it seem disabling. If one rejects allegiances, is one thereby compelled to experience oneself as either a saboteur or a parasite? What other positions can one take, apart from the always ambiguous position of self-promoted failure?

Modesty Rosenberg referred to, when he was twenty-two, as 'that most heinous crime'. Though one finds genuine abjection in his letters, in his poetry one finds an inquiry into the tactic of abjection.

Criticizing his poems consistently for the lack of connections in them – for their fragmentariness – none of his critics realized the sense in which his poetry was always about – intensely preoccupied by – the very question of connections; the question of what might link people or things without destroying their integrity. Drawn to explicitly define the kind of poetry that he valued and aspired to produce, he wrote to Gordon Bottomley: 'Simple poetry – that is where an interesting complexity of thought is kept in tone and right value to the dominating idea so that it is understandable and still ungraspable.' If something is understandable but ungraspable it eludes possession; you can have access to it but you cannot take it. To grasp a poem might be to assume a comprehension of it that makes it redundant. The poem is subsumed by one's apparent knowledge of, or competence in, what Rosenberg called 'grammar etc.'. The art of leaving out leads to the pleasure of finding out; but the pleasure of finding out depends upon there always being something ungraspable; or what Moses will call in Rosenberg's verse-play *Moses*, 'ineffable and usable'. His poems, not incidentally, are full of images of hands unable, or unwilling, to grasp. His formulation is suggestive of the sense in which language is understandable and ungraspable; the sense in which – and this may be particularly obvious to an immigrant – a language can be used but not mastered or owned. The poet – and the immigrant – can be the people who release a language from its proprietors.

The Scottish poet Edwin Muir touched on something very important about Rosenberg, not least because it reflects some affinity with Rosenberg's own expressed intentions. 'He used language,' Muir wrote, 'as only the great poets have used it; as if he were not merely making it serve his own ends; but ends of its own as well, of which it had not known.' This acknowledges both the possibility of creating something new and the sense in which language might use the poet if, as a virtual émigré in Rosenberg's case, he has not already been converted to the culture by assimilation – if he has not, that is to say, over-internalized the proprieties as a kind of second nature. Relatively uneducated, and so without the official grammar of association, Rosenberg did not always make the obvious connections. But the impudent man, as he once wrote, has more experience; he brings some foreign matter to the occasion.

'[C]ould a miracle destroy the dawn,' Moses says in the play, 'night would be mixed with light/ No night or light would be, but a new thing.' If you refuse the obvious connections, leave out the transitions – 'destroy the dawn' – you may create a new thing. The art of leaving out is the pleasure of finding out. Or alternatively, you might be so promiscuous in the making of connections – like the lice and the bullets, the worms and the bees, the rats and the death that haunt his poems – as to be without any discernible allegiances at all. Or to put it another way: as a Jewish English poet, was he merely a go-between, an anonymous opportunist, or potentially a new kind of man, a visionary poet? Or were they different versions of the same thing?

III

. . . who knows what we miss through not having spoken.
Rosenberg, *Collected Works*

In Rosenberg's poetry, as I have said, there is a refusal of the kinds of competence that would have successfully assimilated him by compromising what he had to say. And this is because what he had to say was sometimes so strange – so close to the limits of language – that it involved him in what was often a covert critique of available forms. Even on a cursory reading, the poems are strikingly variable in both metre and rhythm. But it is clear, from what Rosenberg was himself compelled – often under pressure from others – to describe as a 'clumsiness' of technique, that he found it difficult to fit himself into the poetic forms and languages he was familiar with. One of his earliest 'war poems', 'The Troop Ship', alludes, at one level, to precisely this problem:

Grotesque and queerly huddled
Contortionists to twist
The sleepy soul to a sleep,
We lie all sorts of ways
And cannot sleep.
The wet wind is so cold,
And the lurching men so careless,
That, should you drop to a doze,
Winds' fumble or men's feet
Are on your face.

I don't want to do the kind of reading of this poem that in any way obviates the sense in which it is about a terrible and physically immediate predicament. But I think in addition to this fact it can be read as a parable of Rosenberg's poetic struggle. It is a lurid description of people trying to fit themselves in; people being turned into contortionists, into grotesque shapes because there is no room to do what they most want. And what they most want – and have to 'lie all sorts of ways' to do – is in this case that most natural thing, to sleep. But if they succeed in doing what they most desire, dozing off in this cramped space, they are damaged: 'should you drop to a doze/ Winds' fumble or men's feet/ Are on your face'. If you succeed – which in my reading means, express your deepest desire in this imposed form – then you are subject to violation, 'feet are on your face'.

For Rosenberg – the most unpromising-sounding soldier, losing his socks, failing to oil his boots, falling over on parade – to enlist was to make vivid in a peculiarly literal way the dilemmas that constituted the struggle of his life. Because in the British army, his life as a working-class Jew and an artist consisted of having alien forms imposed upon him against which he could struggle and with which he could cooperate. 'Believe me,' he wrote to the writer Lascelles Abercrombie in 1916, in a partial allusion to his *Moses*, 'the army is the most detestable invention on this earth, and nobody but a private in the army knows what it is to be a slave.'

Anti-semitism in the army, as Rosenberg's letters testify, was rife; and his notorious inattention was continually getting him into trouble. 'I have the morning to sleep in,' he writes in his deadpan way from the front, 'unless I happen to be doing some punishment for my forgetfulness.' But in this terrifying war – 'we spend most of our time,' he reports in 1917, 'pulling each other out of the mud' – in which he is at least nominally on the British side, he begins to write some of his most extraordinary and ungraspable poems. And in these inexhaustible, visionary works he seems to be drawn to those creatures I have mentioned – the lice and the rats, for example, that by being on neither side are everywhere, resilient in their opportunism – 'The Immortals', as he entitles a poem about the lice (the Immortals, of course, being both the pagan gods, and the great poets). And alongside these inspiring and dispiriting figures there are his more elusive but characteristic images of absence, of non-differentiation, of blendings – like the famous description of the war dead, 'joined to the great sunk silences', in 'Dead Man's Dump'. As we shall see, it is these images of paradoxical connection that take Rosenberg to the limits of description.

In 'Dead Man's Dump' he refers to the young soldiers being shot as the moment when 'the swift iron burning bee/ Drained the wild honey of their youth'. In this inversion of the spring the bullets are like bees, passing freely between the warring sides, and when they connect they don't pollinate, they kill; they don't suck honey, they drain blood. Like the 'mixed hoofs of the mules' later in the poem that pull the carts for the dead, they are, as it were, the product of two different sides. The most resilient creatures in the war seem, from Rosenberg's point of view, the most indiscriminate, like the lice in 'The Immortals'. It is a terrible and pertinent irony for him that the enemy is potentially everywhere. Even the titles of the two famous poems about the lice that infected their clothes ironize the predicament. In the first, calling such parasites 'the Immortals' is itself suggestive (and it is perhaps worth remembering that Rosenberg wrote an early poem entitled 'Tess', and that the last paragraph of Hardy's novel ends with the famous sentence: ' "Justice" was done, and the President of the Immortals, in Aeschylean phrase, had ended his sport with Tess'). 'I killed them but they would not die,' Rosenberg writes, likening the lice to devils, Satan, Beelzebub; and in the second stanza: 'for faster than I slew/ They rose more cruel than before'. In a characteristic paradox just like Satan's party in *Paradise Lost* (Rosenberg reports reading Milton in 1912), the more you try and kill them the more you inspire them with life. And calling the second poem 'Louse Hunting' is to suggest that it is not clear who is hunting whom. The 'wizard vermin', as he calls them, have magical powers, creating an anarchic rage in the soldiers; and once again everything is inverted, the tiny creatures making a mockery of the men's power:

> See gargantuan hooked fingers
> Pluck in supreme flesh
> To smutch supreme littleness.

The question of supremacy arises again in 'Break of Day in the Trenches' when a rat – who knows no treachery because he has no allegiances – jumps out in front of the poet. And the poet is struck by the rat's curious privilege, that by being on neither side in the war he can be on both.

> Droll rat, they would shoot you if they
>   knew
> Your cosmopolitan sympathies.
> Now you have touched this English hand
> You will do the same to a German –
> Soon, no doubt, if it be your pleasure
> To cross the sleeping green between.
> It seems you inwardly grin as you pass
> Strong eyes, fine limbs, haughty athletes
> Less chanced than you for life,
> Bonds to the whims of murder,
> Sprawled in the bowels of the earth,
> The torn fields of France.
> What do you see in our eyes
> At the shrieking iron and flame
> Hurled through still heavens?
> What quaver – what heart aghast?

It is the rat's 'cosmopolitan sympathies', his grand promiscuous pleasure, that free him possibly – 'perhaps', Rosenberg writes – to mock the soldiers on both sides, 'haughty athletes/ Less chanced than you for life'. The rat has no kind of Olympian view, but sees things on the ground, so to speak. It was, of course, current anti-semitic jargon to refer disparagingly to Jews as 'cosmopolitan' and of course, as vermin and parasites; but it is the very opportunism of the rat's mobility – his ability, if it is his pleasure, 'To cross the sleeping green between' – that Rosenberg promotes here as a strength. But 'touching' both sides, the rat belongs to neither, and Rosenberg, I think, is genuinely perplexed about such a point of view. The questions he addresses to the 'queer sardonic rat' (and there is an implication that the rat might be a kind of dandy) are ambiguous in their implications: 'What do you see in our eyes/ At the shrieking iron and flame/ Hurled through still heavens?/ What quaver – what heart aghast?' Perhaps the rat is so free because he sees and feels nothing, identifies with no one; is simply a figure for Death, or the kind of supreme nonchalance that Rosenberg, given his circumstances, may have aspired to.

The worm in one of his finest poems, 'A Worm Fed on the Heart of Corinth', is also, like the droll rat – and like Moses, as we shall see – a go-between of sorts, and an opportunist. But unlike Moses, he is not a visionary, though he is a paradoxical source of inspiration.

> A worm fed on the heart of
>   Corinth,
> Babylon and Rome:
> Not Paris raped tall Helen,
> But this incestuous worm,
> Who lured her vivid beauty
> To his amorphous sleep.
> England! famous as Helen
> Is thy betrothal sung
> To him the shadowless,
> More amorous than Solomon.

Here we have, as it were, the parasite of Western culture; eating hearts, it inspires to act. Incestuous, shadowless and amorous, it knows neither boundary nor taboo, connecting and collecting disparate powerful cultures, cosmopolitan in its appetite, and reducing their extraordinary forms – Helen's 'vivid beauty' – to formlessness, to 'amorphous sleep' (and in 'amorphous' one can hear the buried pun of being a-Morpheus, without Morpheus the god of sleep and dreams, and so in a sleepless sleep). The worm is the triumphant hero, seducer, bridegroom and lover, the figure of desire as desire for death. But the final four lines of the poem are particularly revealing of Rosenberg's confused and ironized patriotism during the war in which he died. England is described as 'famous as Helen', and Helen is famous for being desirable and divisive; and for being forced to move from one side to another. Rosenberg connects England to the great imperial cultures of the past; and yet England's betrothal – sung perhaps wishfully in this poem – is to death. All these imperial pretensions are as nothing against the worm (Jewish imperialism was, of course, only ever the fantasy of anti-semites). And, as we saw in the 'droll' rat, there is a grandeur and a mockery in the worm, and in the poem.

And there is also, in this extraordinarily impacted poem, a juxtaposing of the great structures of empire – Corinth, Babylon, Rome, Greece, Troy – and the great heroic figures – Helen, Paris, Solomon – against images of formlessness, of dissipation, 'amorphous sleep' and the 'shadowless' worm. It is a poem about the precariousness of structures (it's worth noting that phrases crop up in Rosenberg's poetry suggestive of a kind of eroticization of disorder, like 'gorgeous disarray' and 'promiscuous bewilderment'). But in trying to describe death – that which, by definition, eludes representation – he has to use the structure of language to evoke its imagined dissolution. If something is shadowless it does not cast a shadow; but worms are shadowless because they are mostly underground, because they do not sufficiently differentiate themselves from their environment (in one sense they are images of compliant assimilation, close to the earth). There is no space between themselves and their world. Something, one could say, that happens in sleep – another of Rosenberg's recurrent poetic preoccupations – except that in sleep the shadows cast are dreams, and they are shadows inside. Indeed, in his poem 'Returning We Hear the Larks' he describes the doubly effaced image of 'a blind man's dreams on the sand/ By dangerous tides'.

Rosenberg returns again and again in his poetry to images of things joined or connected invisibly, like a dream and its dreamer. It is, of course, profoundly difficult to imagine the connection between things assumed to be identical, something one cannot represent in painting or music. In the line, 'Joined to the great sunk silences' ('Dead Man's Dump'), for example, where is the join and what is being joined? Where does one silence end and another begin? For there to be a discernible connection, there has to be a difference. In his poetry Rosenberg entertains the idea of people being joined in, or by, their absence. 'Untuned air shall lap the stillness/ In the old space for your voice,' he writes of a dead soldier in a poem called 'In War'. Air lapping the stillness is a relationship between two invisible 'things'; the phrase 'the old space for your voice' formulates something more terrifying for its lack of limit. The space of a person's voice is an extraordinary thing to imagine, and points to the infinity of loss. 'Invisibly – branches break/ From invisible trees', Rosenberg begins the final stanza of his poem 'Chagrin', confronting us again with the illogicality – the affront to logic – of absence. Whether they be family trees or the trees of tradition, words are being used to evoke what we cannot otherwise imagine, something invisible happening to – breaking a connection with – the invisible. And yet, as in the penultimate line of 'August 1914', 'A burnt space through ripe fields', absence can make of something a revelation.

Rudolph, we may remember, expounding ironically on the 'art of leaving out', had explained how 'Where he had not left out the whole picture, sometimes it was successful.' Rosenberg was experimenting in language with the possibility of leaving out the whole picture, something he couldn't do in the same way with painting; a white page is very different from a white canvas. 'Snow is a strange white word,' he begins his poem 'On Receiving News of the War'.

This preoccupation with connections and absences, and so with forms and structures – the virtual obsession of his poetry – was the product in Rosenberg of an overlap of apparently disparate phenomena: a whole spectrum, from the death of his twin brother at birth to his ambiguous position both as the rejector of his family ethos and tradition, and as a first-generation working-class Jew aspiring to be an artist in the language of his host country, but not of his parents (it is striking indeed how many of his best poems sound like translations). The war, in the very confusion of loyalties it revealed, in the midst of so much death, offered terrifying images of assimilation: what he referred to from the trenches as 'The huge and terrible sensations of sinking in the mud'. But it also produced in Rosenberg's mind, in anticipation, the great visionary figure of Moses: Moses before the exodus and before the covenant, and subject to Rosenberg's dramatic and heretical transfiguration; the arch-liberator of his vision.

IV

I am rough now, and new, and will have no tailor.
                                        Moses

He has something in him, horribly rough, but then 'Stepney East' . . .

                    Ezra Pound to Harriet Munro, 1915

As a kind of coda to this lecture I want to make a few brief remarks about Rosenberg's finest poem, the verse-drama *Moses* – mindful of the fact that it was also the Romantic poets who had tried, unsuccessfully, to revive the verse-drama in the first two decades of the previous century. 'Moses,' he wrote to the poet R. C. Trevelyan, 'symbolises the fierce desire for virility and original action in contrast to slavery of the most abject kind.' This is clearly a dramatic redescription of the Moses of the Old Testament, carrying with it as it does an emphasis on sexual as opposed to ethical potency, and the suggestion that Moses might have forfeited 'original action' by becoming the abject slave of God. The God whom Moses – disguised as a minstrel, reminding us of the 'Ode to David's Harp' – sings of in the poem, as a kind of anti-visionary poet; 'God's unthinkable imagination,' he sings in disguise, 'invents new tortures for nature. 'The idea in Moses's brain,' Jon Silkin has written in the best essay on Rosenberg (quoted in Cohen's biography), 'is the creative impulse which tears up the old dead idea that the Jews must bear perpetual slavery.' But Rosenberg's Moses claims, like Marlowe's Tamburlaine, that he will 'ride the dizzy beast of the world/ My road – my way'. His voice is one of megalomaniac rupture and release: 'Voices thunder,' he says, 'voices of deeds undone . . . Virgin silences waiting a breaking voice.' 'Who has made of the forest a park?' he asks; 'Who has changed the wolf to a dog?/ and put the horse in harness?/ And man's mind in a groove?' In Moses' language there is an insistent idealization of masculine energy, a pagan identification with the energies of a potentially Dionysiac nature. That is to say, Rosenberg is not presenting us with a man who will be freed, so to speak, by the Ten Commandments. This is a visionary poet in whom, as he says, 'Startled to life starved hopes slink out/ Cowering incredulous.' The play ends with Moses being arrested for killing his slave Abinoah, whom he ironically refers to as his 'father'.

In a review of an exhibition of Jewish painters published in the *Jewish Chronicle* in 1912 Rosenberg wrote: 'The travail and sorrow of centuries have given life a more poignant and intense interpretation, while the strength of the desire of ages has fashioned an ideal which colours all our expression of existence.' He wanted, I think, to reject not everything that interfered with achieving the ideal itself, but anything that interfered with the fashioning of it, with its articulation. And *Moses* is, among other things, a statement of this rejection, because for the Jews God had, through the covenant with Moses, fashioned the ideal already; and it was fashioned as something to submit to, or comply with, in a way that from Rosenberg's point of view pre-empted any further articulation of alternative ideals. The paradox he used *Moses* to fashion was that to be a great visionary Jewish poet who could 'wake the zeal in Israel's breast' was to challenge God; and to succeed, to win, would be to break the convenant and cease to be a Jew.

The only extended quotation from Shakespeare, the 'father of English poets', to be found in Rosenberg's writing is, appropriately, in his piece on Emerson. It is from *The Tempest*, and it is about the death of fathers:

> Full fathom five thy father lies;
>   Of his bones are coral made:
> Those are pearls that were his eyes:
>   Nothing of him that doth fade,
> But doth suffer a sea-change
> Into something rich and strange.

18

Karl Kraus's Complaint

*Leopards break into the temple and drink to the dregs what is in
the sacrificial pitchers; this is repeated over and over again;
finally it can be calculated in advance, and it becomes a part of
the ceremony.*

Franz Kafka, 'Leopards in the Temple'

In *fin de siècle* Vienna politics had become the least convincing of the
performing arts. Life, Karl Kraus wrote, had become an effort that
deserved a better cause. By the turn of the century it was not
politicians but actors, painters, writers and musicians who had
captured the imagination of the upper middle classes. As the
Hapsburg Empire disintegrated, it seemed to Kraus that life in
Vienna was no longer imitating art: it was parodying it. And for
Kraus it was the 'mental self-mutilation of mankind through its press'
that had done most to trivialize and misrepresent what was becoming
a terrifying political situation. Kraus exposed, often by imitation, the
new decadent facetiousness. Journalists, he wrote, were now capable of 'launching a première one day and a war the next'. They 'write
because they have nothing to say, and have something to say because
they write'. Editing and writing most of his own newspaper *Die Fackel*
(the *Torch*) in Vienna from 1899 to 1936, he believed that the collapse
of the Empire and the drift to world war could only be accurately
documented as satire. Only the satirist was honestly suspicious. All
forms of representation, advertisements, the wearing of beards, the
way people strolled in the streets, had to be understood in terms of
what it was they were being used to misrepresent. Events, and the
reporting of events, had to be interpreted now as artistic genres
concealing vested interests. In May 1916, in the middle of the war, it
was still not clear to Kraus what play of Shakespeare's was actually
being performed. By October 1918 he was clear that it was *Hamlet*.

A certain vigilance was required, Kraus began to realize, to deal with the 'masquerade' of modern life. The unprecedented number of competing ideological claims, the sheer volume of other people's words, that the new mass media made available, was turning character into a kind of cultural ventriloquism. People suffered from other people's ideas and never recovered themselves. The individual was becoming merely a repertoire of identifiable voices, a collage of new vocabularies. 'In these times,' Kraus wrote, 'you should not expect from me any words of my own.' It was an age of unavoidable quotation, and the newspapers, in his view, were playing on the prevailing air of unreality. The gradual breakdown of political consensus had estranged people from the old sense of a shared world, and in its place a new one was being fabricated by a press committed only to the business interests it served. Language had to be redeemed from its new status as a commodity depreciated, but for Kraus never inspired, by mass consumption. 'Contemporaries,' he wrote, 'live from second-hand to mouth.' His passionate denunciation of social injustice was accompanied by a pious fantasy of purity, of a language being violated.

It was Walter Benjamin, in 1931, who wrote what is in many ways still the most revealing essay on Kraus and his 'struggle against the empty phrase, which is the linguistic expression of the despotism with which, in journalism, topicality sets up its dominion over things'. The muted violence of the empty phrase could only be countered by the shrewdest form of ridicule, a contempt close to the heart. His aphorisms turned empty phrases inside out. The goat-like satyr on the front cover of *Die Fackel* suggests, as Edward Timms says in his book *Karl Kraus: Apocalytic Satirist* (1986), 'that for the Kraus of the 1890s satire was a vaguely defined primitive force disrupting the civilities of a philistine society'. But as the political situation worsened, Kraus embarked on the graver, more apocalyptic project of seeing the signs of the end of the world.

'The satirist,' Benjamin suggested in his essay, 'is the figure in whom the cannibal was received into civilisation.' Because satire is so overtly reactive to circumstance, and because of the satirist's complicity with his victims, academic research can be useful, as

Timms's book is, in explaining the occasion for what Benjamin calls the 'devouring of the object'. Kraus was not, as both Benjamin and Timms make clear, an indiscriminate consumer, but his work was seriously compromised by the confusion of divided loyalties. Despite the fact that, as Timms writes, 'the greatest enterprise of his career' was 'his satirical campaign against the inhumanity of war', there was 'an unresolved tension between Kraus's growing opposition to the war and his continuing respect for the army'. All satirists run the risk of being paralysed by their own self-contempt. Admirers of Kraus have had to accommodate a number of these 'unresolved tensions': a loathing of racism alongside an occasionally virulent (Jewish) anti-semitism; a commitment to women's political rights which was not incompatible with embittered misogynistic attitudes. These things, one might say, merely make Kraus a representative figure; but there is something elusive about him which has to do with the fact that while the targets of his contempt have always been clear, the nature of his allegiances has not – except in the case of his often acclaimed allegiance to language itself. 'My language,' he wrote as the ironic proprietor, 'is the common prostitute that I turn into a virgin' (for Kraus the question was always: what kind of woman is the German language, and what kind of relationship will she allow him to have with her?). 'I only master the language of others, my own does with me as it pleases,' he wrote, describing his favourite version of the romantic triangle.

But the romance too easily lent itself to what Benjamin described as 'the strange interplay between reactionary theory and revolutionary practice that is found everywhere in Kraus', and which has become a familiar contradiction in cultural criticism. The few commentators in English on Kraus have tended to simplify him by a curious sort of idealization, suggesting either that he was a man of consistent positions, many of which were astonishingly prophetic of events – 'Progress makes purses out of human skin' – or that his self-elected role as guardian of the German language, the mother tongue, exempted him in some mysterious way, as he himself sometimes claimed, from taking sides. What they don't see is that his particular brand of satire was to show how the use of a language was always a form of investment. In what amounts to a series of linked essays in his immensely informative book, Edward Timms restores Kraus's contradictions, though not always with the gusto of his subject. From the different intellectual and biographical perspectives that Timms provides, Kraus becomes a more puzzling kind of prophet.

Kraus was born in 1874 in northern Bohemia, the youngest son of a Jewish paper manufacturer who would eventually finance his son's newspaper. The family moved when he was three to Vienna, the city which he despised and to which he was deeply attached, and which was to become within twenty years the most spectacular setting for what Timms calls Kraus's 'passionate parochialism'. 'The streets of Vienna,' he would write, 'are paved with culture, the streets of other cities with asphalt.' In the work of his contemporaries – the poetry of Hofmannsthal, the plays of Schnitzler, the paintings of Klimt, the writings of Freud and Wittgenstein – the links between new, recondite kinds of private experience and the public world were being radically redescribed. In a period of political disintegration and extraordinary cultural production Kraus served his apprenticeship as a journalist in the thriving literary coffee-houses of the 1890s. Timms gives a compelling account of the way *Die Fackel* was made possible by an audience, at least in retrospect, unwittingly prepared for it. So enthusiastic was this audience that the first number sold thirty thousand copies. By 1900, Vienna was one of the great artistic capitals of the world, and the sophisticated city culture created by the emergence of a prosperous bourgeoisie was unusually receptive to Kraus's ridicule. 'I and my public understand each other very well,' he noted: 'it does not hear what I say, and I don't say what it wants to hear.' This was the kind of profitable misunderstanding that for Kraus characterized the beglamoured crisis of everyday life in Vienna, in which people learned from the theatre 'how to be Viennese'.

The city itself was like a stage set, the façade, Timms writes, 'moulded and embellished, according to the principle that opulent appearance was more important than functional design'. The architecture of the city, like much else, revealed 'the triumph of façade over function'. In an interesting chapter on Kraus's relationship with the architect Adolf Loos, Timms shows how Kraus began to incorporate 'the motifs of ornament and façade into his satire'. 'In Austria,' Kraus wrote, 'the painters are being overshadowed by the decorators, just as the writers are being swallowed by the journalists.' Cultural pastiche was being used to mask social contradictions. As the dynastic centralism of the old Empire gave way to various multinational claims, political instability was being concealed by ostentatious display. What Timms refers to as 'the ideological saturation of everyday life' Kraus saw as a 'masquerade' brash with contradictions. The cover of the most influential Viennese newspaper, *Die Neue Freie Presse*, published earnestly instructive articles about the sanctity of family life, while the back cover ran advertisements for 'Miss Birch, Box No. 69'. There were so many prostitutes on the streets that it was more difficult to avoid them than to find them, the novelist Stefan Zweig recalled.

Kraus's newspaper was revolutionary because Austria had no tradition of independent critical journalism. Austrian newspapers represented government policies and the vested interests of their owners, most of whom had links with the large banks and finance corporations. It was routine practice, for example, to disguise advertisements as news articles. August Zang, the founder of *Die Presse*, was quoted as saying that ideally he would like 'a newspaper that did not contain a single line that had not been paid for'. Maximilien Harden, the editor of *Die Zukunft* in Berlin, had managed to maintain his independence only by owning the newspaper he edited. Inspired by the example of Harden, Kraus got his father to back the first issue of *Die Fackel*. Its extraordinary success made it self-financing, though Kraus's independence was in any case to be guaranteed by the private income he inherited after his father's death in 1900. But the uniqueness of his position misled him into believing that he had invented himself, that he could be, as he said, 'a writer without preconceptions who observes things without party spectacles'. He thought that to be aligned in any way was to be contaminated. As part of his 'draining of the vast swamp of slogans and clichés' he used *Die Fackel* at first to attack all ideological affiliations: socialism, capitalism, anti-semitism, Zionism, Pan-Germanism, Pan-Slavism, liberalism.

He satirized the idea of militant conviction. 'His reformist campaign,' Timms comments, 'could only be implemented with political support. But his intransigence towards organized factions effectively precluded it.' His reformism was too broadly based to lead to recognizable policies, and this was surely connected with what Timms calls 'the tension between vigorous polemical commitment and self-absorbed verbal artistry' in his writing. 'Let language be the divining rod that finds sources of thought,' he wrote; but he believed he could then exempt himself from ideological commitment through his obligation to language. In this way, his early, and often brilliant, fanatical unmasking of others turned into diffuse self-justification, perhaps in an unconscious attempt to find a position beyond criticism in a language without history. 'It is deeply rooted in Kraus's nature,' Benjamin wrote, 'and it is the stigma of every debate concerning him, that all apologetic arguments miss their mark.' Kraus was only ever fickle by necessity, not by conviction, and this may be bound up with what Timms calls, in one of his chapter titles, 'The Dilemma of the Baptised Jew'. Born a Jew, Kraus finally renounced his Judaism in 1899. In 1911 he converted to Catholicism, which he renounced in 1923. A committed journalist who condemned journalism, he was also, as Timms says, 'a Jew by birth, an Austrian by nationality, a Viennese by residence, a German by language, a journalist by profession, bourgeois by social status and a rentier by economic position. Amid the ideological turmoil of Austria-Hungary, all of these ascribed identities seemed like falsifications.' Or the idea of coherent identity had itself become meaningless for the increasing number of people who had never settled (and the Freudian unconscious that Kraus was so interested in was itself nomadic). It may have been Kraus's nature to assume, often unwittingly, impossibly self-contradictory positions out of fear of being misrecognized, even by himself. 'I don't like to meddle,' he wrote, 'in my private affairs.'

By the same token Kraus was a great critic of psychoanalysis, who saw that it was pernicious only in so far as it seemed to be conclusive and who understood its crucial paradox: that its method was inspired, but its stated aims were not. Kraus realized that the psychoanalyst was also a satirist of sorts; and that unmasking is always a form of hypocrisy. 'One of the most widespread diseases,' he wrote, 'is diagnosis.' In one of the most interesting chapters in his book Timms gives a persuasive account of Freud and Kraus as 'essentially complementary'. It was Freud's followers, rather than Freud himself, that Kraus was wary of. Freud had described an unconscious of ferocious inventiveness, yet psychoanalysts seemed to have an ominous anxiety about loose ends. The discoveries of psychoanalysis, Kraus believed, were being used by Freud's followers in a pre-emptive strike against the imagination. Psychoanalysis seemed merely to have created one more cramping kind of seriousness. Psychoanalysts were full of greedy explanations and peculiarly ironic blind-spots. 'So-called psychoanalysis,' he suggested, 'is the occupation of lustful rationalists who trace everything in the world to sexual causes – with the exception of their own occupation.' The expert on sex is by definition a tyrant. Kraus evolved a style, which could never be turned into a method, to show how ideas could be subtly dogmatized into propaganda.

In what he called 'this pseudonymous civilization' it was literature that had to be 'an independent force, countering the pernicious influence of the press' in particular, and all the other potential forms of propaganda that disarmed criticism. Kraus's first ambition had been to be an actor. His contemporary the playwright Frank Wedekind thought Kraus had missed his vocation by not working in the theatre. Kraus would describe himself instead as 'perhaps the first case of a writer who simultaneously experiences the process of writing as an actor'. Just as the mask was one of the unifying motifs of *Die Fackel*, and featured on the early covers, so the writer as actor was increasingly the role in which Kraus was to cast himself. It was Shakespeare who had shaped what Timms calls Kraus's 'histrionic imagination'. By the age of thirty he had seen twelve productions of *King Lear*; he was himself to do remarkable translations of

Shakespeare into German. Shakespeare, for Kraus, was the exemplary artist. And from about 1905 he came to believe that the artist alone could resist the ideological pressures of the age – any age. Wilde was the contemporary artist who became his model for the artistic identity he was consciously trying to cultivate in his search for a true mask. He conceived of the artist, Timms writes, 'as a self-sufficient figure. His sensitivity sets him apart from the philistinism of the surrounding world. And he tends to stand disdainfully aloof from the nexus of human society. He is essentially an inner-directed figure.'

Although, as Timms shows, genial by inclination, Kraus always struggled to find a way of being sufficiently isolated to give an accurate warning of the catastrophe that he foresaw. 'I hear noises which others don't hear,' he wrote, 'and which disturb for me the music of the spheres, which others don't hear either.' The idea of the artist which Kraus had evolved was only a temporary solution to the general bewilderment of a culture that was disintegrating around him. Under the pressure of events he began to do public performances of his own and other writers' work. Between 1910 and 1936 he gave over seven hundred recitals. Timms explains in convincing detail how in the same period the tone of his work changes to one of foreboding. He becomes, in Timms's phrase, 'a visionary satirist'. Timms quotes, with his own translation, what he calls a 'dream-aphorism' of February 1911:

I dreamed that they refused to believe that what I said was right. I maintained that there were ten of them. No, 12, they said. As many as there are fingers on a pair of hands, I said. Then one of them raised his hand and behold it had six fingers. All right then, 11, I said, appealing to the other hand. And behold it had six fingers. Sobbing, I ran into the forest.

Although *Die Fackel* was the only Austrian newspaper critical of the war effort, the war itself was to reveal what Timms calls the 'glaring deficiency' in Kraus's critique of newspapers as propaganda. In March 1914 he reminded his readers of the Austrian government's bribing of the press, yet by November of the same year he is suggesting that the authorities are not in fact to blame and that the government should curb the freedom of the press. Kraus appeared to be mystifyingly naïve about the actual workings of the press, vilifying individual editors and journalists, several of whom were Jews, who he must have known were not in charge. Timms's detailed account explains Kraus's 'fundamental argument . . . that an apparatus now exists with an almost unlimited capacity for corrupting the public mind . . . and that at moments of crisis it actively participates in a process of self-mystification'. But he also shows that Kraus's eagerness to name names and ride his contradictions undermined some of his shrewdest insights. During the First World War six thousand men were killed every day. The Austrian press spoke of the war as a heroic crusade, but, in Kraus's view, made it sound more like an operetta: they were, he insisted, making it impossible to believe that people really died.

Between 1915 and 1922 Kraus worked on his epic documentary drama of the First World War, *The Last Days of Mankind*. He tried to find a form commensurate with the horrific magnitude of the event. Virtually unperformable with over two hundred scenes and an enormous cast of characters, it was described by Kraus as a 'tragedy' performed by 'figures from an operetta'. Timms defends the play as 'the submerged masterpiece of the twentieth-century theatre', but it is possible that Kraus might have appreciated the irony of its present status as a symptomatic and intriguing failure. There is, of course, no full English translation available, and this raises the question of how Kraus is best represented to non-German readers. Great claims have been made for the importance of his work – in English most notably by George Steiner and Erich Heller – but he is known, if at all in England, as an influential contemporary of Wittgenstein and Freud, and as a writer of aphorisms. Auden, for example, in his Faber anthology has twenty-four entries by Kraus. So Harry Zohn's *Half-Truths and One-and-a-Half-Truths: Selected Aphorisms of Karl Kraus* (1986), from which I have quoted in this review, is welcome, but also, in a sense, misleading. The aphorisms are inevitably taken out of context, which is, of course, in the nature of aphorisms (aphorisms, often like their authors, are socially mobile). But what kind of picture would one get of Bacon, or Johnson, or Hazlitt from a comparable selection of aphorisms translated into German? Timms's book will be indispensable when we have that most unlikely thing, an English Kraus.

19
John Clare's Exposure

I

There is so much to be seen everywhere that it's like not getting used to it . . .

John Ashbery, 'For John Clare'

In one of John Clare's earliest manuscript notebooks there is a four-line poem entitled 'A Simile':

> A Mushroom its Goodness but Shortly Endures
> Decaying as soon as its Peeping
> – Woman much like them – for 'ts known very Well
> That they Seldom Get better by Keeping

A misogynistic poem, it has a modest title. Though the poem contains one overt simile, it smuggles in two others; and it is about the senses in which a simile might describe the relationship – or the impossibility of the relationship – between the sexes (and what kind of a relationship a simile is). A woman may be like a mushroom in the way the poem suggests, but conventionally a mushroom is like a man because it is phallic. So by the tacit logic of the poem – which the ambiguous syntax exploits – a woman is also like a man: neither 'Get better by Keeping'. Peeping – appearing from under ground as both seeing and being seen – leads to destruction, being eaten or going off. Women both like mushrooms and are like them; but too prolonged an exposure to their company makes them infinitely less palatable. Peeping – at once shy and illicit – is preferable to keeping because more than a peep is not worth keeping. Desire is a glimpse; too long a look spoils.

'The dominance of the visual image,' the psychoanalyst Wilfred Bion writes, 'is related to inaccessibility – peculiar to objects of memory and desire . . . The sense of sight seems to bring objects

206

into reach when not within scope of other senses.' I want to suggest in this paper that there is a conflict enacted in Clare's often intensely visual writing about accessibility; both his own accessibility, and the kind of access he is allowed and allows himself to others. Unpublished, 'A Simile' like much of Clare's poetry was not to be seen.

II

Kind of empty in the way it sees everything . . .
John Ashbery, 'For John Clare'

Writing in 1836 to his longstanding correspondent and patron Eliza Louisa Emmerson, a woman who had perhaps kept his poems too long without responding, Clare excuses them both of suspicion with polite tact:

My Dear Eliza
   Did you get the vol of poems I sent a long time ago I wished you to write directly & as you did not write we think you did not get them I still keep ill & am no better.

At the time of writing this Clare was in a disturbed state, but even here the continuity of preoccupation that sustained him throughout his life is discernible. The longer things are kept – poems, mushrooms, women – the more their goodness is in question, or threatened. Having a good look, for both the seer and the seen, is always a risk ('as I meet with [a book],' Clare writes of his reading habits, 'I dip into it here and there'). Does Eliza Emmerson's silence mean she has received the poems or not 'got' them? Is she keeping the poems and keeping quiet about them? If he is keeping ill, what can he make of her keeping?
   Clare was uncertain in his life, as in his poetry, whether keeping things to himself was the only way of keeping things for himself, and of protecting them; whether exposure – the exposure of writing poems and the different exposure of being known as a poet – was a dangerous invitation. Making himself known, he was there to be

stolen from. Despite the insistent eagerness in his letters for 'poetical fame', Clare's ambivalent unease about recognition itself should not be read as exclusively reactive to his defeating circumstances. The very vice of obscurity could be its virtue. 'Ah what a paradise begins with the ignorance of life & what a wilderness the knowledge of the world discloses,' he wrote as the 'world' began to want knowledge of him. Certain kinds of knowledge – or ways of knowing – turn the world for Clare into a wilderness.

He certainly found that his brief celebrity as a 'peasant poet' robbed him of something more than his place in his own community. When an admirer came to visit him from London he found that he had 'little or nothing to say for I always had a natural depression of spirits in the presence of strangers that took from me all power of freedom or familiarity & made me dull & silent'. It was the bitterest and most telling irony that his fame as a poet could take from him his words – as his editors did, in a different sense, by manicuring his diction – and his sense of mobility. Publishing poems is an invitation to strangers; and especially if by doing so one enters a literate culture from a largely oral culture. For Clare, wider circulation meant less room for himself.

As his autobiographical writings show, Clare more often felt his 'power of freedom or familiarity' in the protections of solitude; and eventually in 'that lonely and solitary musing that ended in rhyme'. He often represents himself as a person cramped simply by the presence of other people, though marginally (and significantly) less cramped by the people from his own community. But solitude secured him. 'The rich man,' he wrote – the two parts of himself and the two economic classes doubling for each other – 'is invisible', but the poor man is 'caught in the fact of an overt act'. John Clare has been celebrated as a poet who celebrates the pleasures of observation, but his poetry is equally alert to the terrors of being seen. His poems often expose different forms of solitude – nests, love affairs, madness, hiding places, private walks, furtive creatures, poems – but to make plain the perils and ambitions of exposure.

Keats remarked to Clare's editor John Taylor that in his poem 'Solitude' 'the Description too much prevailed over the Sentiment'. But seeing, and being seen to see in a particular way – the visionary documentary of rural life that seemed to characterize his poetry – presented Clare with a dilemma about description that was integral to the project, and the sentiment, of his poetry. His unwitting self-definition as a particular kind of poet – a 'country poet', in Raymond Williams's more apposite term – made him available for appropriation and exploitation; for circulation in a world that he was unfamiliar with, and in which he was a curiosity. It made him quickly prone to what Tom Paulin has called 'the spiked trap Clare fell into – his success set him apart from his own community, while the system of patronage and publishing could offer nothing but a fitfully marketable public image'. But through the startling illusion of visual clarity, the 'love of seeing' he proclaimed in so many of his poems, he opened himself and his familiar world to certain forms of scrutiny. He was drawn into a system of patronage and publishing that commodified his 'character', his place and his dialect (in so far as his editors would permit its usage).

Clare began to realize that description – defining and evoking through vivid representation – could be complicit with, and even analogous to, certain forms of ownership. He had to struggle, in other words, to find a language – which involved holding on to his own 'native' language without merely marketing it – that would differentiate his way of feeling proprietorial about his world from the ways, the new ways, of the people who employed and oppressed him, the owners of land and the owners of poetry (Clare could never have owned or had a stake in the countryside he wrote about). There is a conflict about description itself, enacted in his poetry; that description may be redemptive – provide a voice for otherwise marginalized people and experiences – but it may also be predatory and encourage other predators. Once nests are located they are there (asking?) to be stolen from. So Clare's distinctive clarity is always accompanied by a more paradoxical and protective celebration of obscurity, and silence and mist: the affirmation that

> . . . full many a sight
> Seems sweeter in its indistinct array
> Than when it glows in morning's stronger light.

Many of Clare's finest poems – 'To the Snipe', 'The Fox', 'The Badger', 'The Wild Duck's Nest', 'Obscurity', 'Don Juan, A Poem', and others from all periods of his writing – record the violation of privacies as second nature. And this is clearly, among other things, an account and disturbing transcription of the historical trauma that he and his community were living and dying through; what Raymond Williams has called, in assessing the significance of enclosure for Clare's work, 'the cry of his class and generation against their fundamental subordination'. As a poet from his particular labouring community, Clare was in a bind that his poetry could not avoid: if he succeeded (through plentiful description of 'rural life', and 'poetical fame') he failed (to protect the world that he loved, and himself); to find and to see, he began to realize very early in his work, was to use and exploit. 'A second thought tells me I am a fool,' he wrote to John Taylor in 1821; 'was People all to feel & think as I do the world could not be carried on – a green woud not be ploughed a tree or bush woud not be cut for firing or furniture & every thing they found when boys would remain in that state till they dyd'. Clare's idyll here is of a world seen but unused; a world accessible but left to itself.

If visibility was such a mixed blessing because to be found was to be appropriated (or at least to be changed) then the visible invisibilities of madness – of being anonymously, as Clare at one time or another thought himself to be, Byron, a prisoner of the Bastille, a slave, a Babylonian captive, a prize-fighter, John Clare himself – must have been a compelling option. In his daunting last letter, to James Hipkins from the Northampton Asylum, it is as though he has no privacy left to violate. There is nothing to hide and nothing to show for anything, but something to be said: 'I have nothing to say so I conclude.'

III

. . . the terrible journey towards feeling somebody should act,
that ends in utter confusion and hopelessness . . .
John Ashbery, 'For John Clare'

Clare referred to his poems in an early prose piece as 'my stolen fugitives'. The language of hiding and stealing and secrets that runs through his poetry is also the language he uses in his autobiographical writings to describe the actual writing of poems. To begin with, he writes, 'my poems had been kept with the greatest industry under wishd concealment, having no choice to gratify by their disclosure'. Here 'keeping', which is a form of 'wishd concealment', suggests the hoarding of stolen property. Working as a gardener, Clare writes, 'when I fancyd I had hit upon a good image or natural description I usd to steal into a corner of the garden & clap it down'. Writing poetry was time stolen from his employer: 'I always felt anxiety to control my scribbling & would as leave have confessd to be a robber as a rhymer when I workd in the fields.' If poetry is theft – the claiming of time – and the poet writes some of his most compelling poems about the act of thieving, who is to be gratified by the 'disclosure'? The poet may never know whether he is the witness, the accomplice, or the criminal. 'Clapping' something down is a celebration and a confinement.

For Clare it was as though the countryside played a harsh kind of hide and seek with the people who lived in it; and that, for some creatures with whom he identified, to be seen, to be found out, was a risk. But the risk was always one of mutual exposure, especially for the poet. The birds that 'from mans dreaded sight will ever steal', in 'To the Snipe', are disclosed by the poet's sight to be found in 'the most dreary spot'; but by telling us where they are, he is, as he knows, complicit with the killers. Just as Coleridge's dejection is cured in the process of writing his poem, Clare's poetic sight is, in part, condemned in the writing of his. Coleridge writes himself out of the thing he fears, Clare writes himself into it.

In 'Don Juan, A Poem', written while he was in High Beach

Asylum, Epping, Clare presents the misogynistic version of this fear of unconcealment, of disclosure, as catastrophe:

> The flower in bud hides from the fading sun
> And keeps the hue of beauty on its cheek
> But when full blown they into riot run
> The hue turns pale and lost each ruddy streak
> So 't'is with woman who pretends to shun
> Immodest actions which they inly seek.

In 'A Simile' it was the moment of appearance, of 'peeping', that was also the moment of 'decay': in this image everyone is safe as long as the flower hides in the bud. Once out in the open the flower, like a woman (and perhaps like Clare as the 'mad poet'), is free to run riot, 'to be man's ruin', to be 'nasty'. Exposure corrupts. In Clare's pastoral of the covert – of the moment before disclosure, the poem before its publication – 'Goodness but Shortly endures' its description and 'turns pale and lost'. He is always trying to figure out in his poetry in what sense, if at all, recognition – the recognition that leads to circulation and exchange – can be redemptive. If, as John Lucas suggests in his book *England and Englishness*, 'Trespasser, fugitive, outlaw . . . are the kinds of condition, the forms of experience, which Clare addresses in his many poems about birds and animals', then the question for Clare is: what is the cost of claiming that status in a poetic tradition and an exploitative economy in which the owners of land and the owners of poetry, from his point of view, are also trespassers and outlaws? Who owns the language in which one can be described as an outsider, in a world in which to be recognized can be to submit? Clare becomes unavoidably a trespasser in the poetic tradition.

In his 'Address to an Insignificant Flower Obscurely Blooming in a Lonely Wild', the ironically obtrusive title already begs (and parodies) the questions that the poem will address. Why address the flower as a way of addressing your readers? For whom is this poem being written, with its famous allusion that already makes the flower's insignificance significant ('I know Gray, I know him well,' Clare said to a visitor in the asylum). Is the poem for the poet, for the flower or for the reader? Is the flower or the poet to be rescued by this address, and if so from what – and, more to the point, for what? The poet sees himself in the flower, but sees himself as decidedly mixed about being seen. Because in the act of being addressed, spoken to and located, something is being done to the flower that can make a mockery of it, or of the genre of poetry that idealizes such Wordsworthian recognition scenes. The flower begins, as does the poem, as perhaps just what it seems:

> And tho thou seemst a weedling wild
>   Wild and neglected like to me
> Thou still art dear to natures child
>   & I will stoop to notice thee

At first this might seem like an ingenuous imitation, or unconscious parody, of Gray and Wordsworth, legitimating the marginalized with the (admittedly obscure) grandeurs of obscurity. But its artfulness is in its stooping; if the poet stoops to notice the flower is he submitting or condescending? Perhaps recognition is lowering. Certainly 'improvement', Clare suggests, is in the eye of the beholder, or the gardener:

> For oft like thee, in wild retreat
>   Array'd in humble garb like thee
> Theres many a seeming weed proves sweet
>   As sweet as garden flowers can be
>
> & like to thee, each seeming weed
>   Flowers unregarded like to thee
> Without improvement runs to seed
>   Wild and neglected like to me

The stanza break that both completes and then complicates the meaning by stopping and running over goes on to suggest that being wild can also be the privilege of the neglected. To run away from something – in 'wild retreat', a phrase that would define much of the movement of his life – is to run towards something else. Running to seed in this cartoon-like poem suggests both going to waste and being keen to disseminate oneself. Weeds can be as sweet as garden flowers or wild and degenerate, depending on one's point of view. One man's neglect is another man's protection. 'The continual sameness of a garden,' Clare once noted, 'cloyed me.'

The paradox that he addresses in this poem – and that is integral to his radical uncertainty about being a poet, one who notices such things – is that recognition can be theft. That to notice something privileges the observer over the observed – the describer over the described – and can bring with it assumptions of ownership. The poet knows, as the poem goes on to say, that his Emma, the woman he desires and who is, like him, 'a lowly flower',

> If fancied by a polish'd eye
> It soon would bloom beyond my power
> The finest flower beneath the sky.

A more cultivated, 'polish'd' recognition would steal her from him with all the prerogative of privilege (but she would still be 'beneath' the sky in the hierarchies that Clare plays off against each other throughout the poem). He had, he wrote, 'always that feeling of ambition about me, that wishes to do something to gain notice or to rise above its fellows'. It was the complicity of noticing and being noticed with rising above others – 'and' would have been less disingenuous than 'or' – that confronted Clare in his poetic vocation.

In the 'Address' all the positions in the recognition game are untenable. And this leaves the poet, he suggests, with two unpromising options that are virtually synonymous: either to live as one of the 'unknown' ('their sweets are sweet to them alone'), or to hope that friends will 'find out my lowly grave/ & heave a sigh to notice me'. They will indeed have to heave it because the only 'me' that will be there will be absent. Poetry, he implies, is all epitaph and elegy. The only recognition worth having, or the only recognition available, is the recognition of having been unknown (his much anthologized poem 'I Am' is an elegy not only for the poet, but for recognition itself). This was the 'identity' that Clare was tempted – and coerced – to settle for, and sometimes, more paradoxically, to make a case for in poetry. Some of his finest poems are delighted and distraught epitaphs to the possibility of being known.

Throughout his life as a poet he flirted – the opposite of compromise in its unwillingness to settle for things – with the idea of recognition. For him to be, or to think of himself as, a poet involved him in a complex and contradictory set of identifications. If poets are people who are noticed and celebrated for their powers of 'disclosure' and recognition – and recognition is always from above, from a position of literacy, or wealth, or both; from a higher position in the social hierarchy – then how could Clare be a poet and a man who could protect his affinity for, and allegiance to, his origins? This dilemma forced him to continually vacillate in his life, as narrated in the autobiographical writings, between the wish to be seen and be genial and be published and the wish to hide or withdraw or flee. The conflict between participation and isolation found a parodic resolution in the terrible madness of his later years.

IV

Waiting for something to be over before you are forced to notice it.

John Ashbery, 'For John Clare'

Despite the fact that Clare, as he wrote, 'did not much relish the confinement of apprenticeship', he had 'a restless hope of being something better than a plough man . . . to make a better figure in the world'. If he wasn't to be a farm labourer, then apprenticeship, in one form or another, was the only way to any larger kind of recognition. But in his autobiographical writings he represents himself as someone made acutely vulnerable by this wish for recognition:

A bragging fellow named Manton from Market Deeping usd to frequent the public house when I livd there. He was a stone cutter and sign painter he usd to pretend to discover somthing in me as deserving encouragment and wanted to take me apprentice to learn the misterys of his art but then he wanted to trifle with me that had dissappointed my former prosperitys he usd to talk of his abilitys in sculpture and painting over his beer till I was almost mad with anxiety to be a sign painter and stone cutter but it was usless.

This is, for Clare, like a paradigmatic recognition scene. The sign painter, an artist himself of sorts and a keeper of the 'mistery', is inevitably an object of interest and emulation for the young poet, but he only 'pretends' to discover something in him. In fact, he only wants to trifle with Clare (who would often refer to his poems in his letters as 'trifles', as though only his correspondents were in a position to decide if they were the real thing). The man who appears to be encouraging, 'a bragging fellow', is in fact promoting himself: 'he usd to talk of his abilitys in sculpture and painting over his beer till I was almost mad with anxiety . . .'. From being a stone cutter and a sign painter the man becomes, in Clare's artful narrative, a painter and a sculptor. The recognition scene is a seduction – he makes Clare 'mad with anxiety' – and the seduction has all the disappointments and prosperities of tantalization. The man who makes signs for other people is representing himself. This was to be Clare's experience with many of the sign painters – patrons, employers, publishers, doctors – that the circumstances of his ambition were to bring him into contact with. There were many senses, as he discovered, in which promise is false.

What gives Clare's poetry, and the life that contained it – and eventually could no longer contain it – its distinctive complexity is his growing sense that the poetic vocation, with all the 'misterys' of the art (and the mist in mystery), could be complicit with those forms of life it appeared to repudiate, or to provide a refuge from, that the sign painter could be a figure for the poet (so in this reading, his famous sonnet 'Poets love nature and themselves are love', contrary to Harold Bloom's pressing claims for it in his book *The Visionary Company*, is a mock-heroic because it protests too much). It is his discomfort with the business of poetry – sometimes expressed through his distrust of other poets – that makes Clare such an unusual figure among the poets of the period. For him the idea of poetry, despite the extraordinary resilience of his commitment to his own poetic project, was fraught with contradictions. High claims for poetry brought high anxieties, especially for a 'low'-born writer. And it is this profound suspicion about the virtue of poetry that makes Clare, among many other things, an anti-poet of Romanticism.

Clare, who described himself in an early letter, when he was indeed unknown beyond the confines of his village, as 'a Clown who as yet slumbers in Obscurity', made in the name of Obscurity one of his finest poems, or anti-poems:

> Old tree, oblivion doth thy life condemn
> Blank and recordless as that summer wind
> That fanned the first few leaves on thy young stem
> Then thou wert one year's shoot – and who can find
> Their homes of rest or paths of wandering now?
> So seems thy history to a thinking mind
> As now I gaze upon thy sheltering bough
> Thou grew unnoticed up to flourish now
> And leave thy past as nothing all behind
> Where many years and doubtless centurys lie
> That ewe beneath thy shadow – nay that flie
> Just settled on a leaf – can know with time
> Almost as much of thy blank past as I
> Thus blank oblivion reigns as earths sublime

Knowing with time is not the same as the knowing in time that is poetry. It is possible to grow 'unnoticed' and still to flourish. There is a history and a growth process, Clare is saying, that exists without the record of the poem. One of Clare's most powerful wishes was that a life need not be constituted by its witnesses. His poetry counters and confirms, or rather, affirms, the 'blank oblivion'. Only the greatest of visionary anti-poets can celebrate without irony that 'blank oblivion reigns as earths sublime', but do it, of course, in a poem, on record. 'Hopes unrealized,' Clare wrote, 'are hopes in reality.'

Bibliography

David Aberbach, *Surviving Trauma: Loss, Literature and Psychoanalysis* (New Haven, Yale University Press, 1990).

Isaiah Berlin, *Four Essays on Liberty* (Oxford, Oxford University Press, 1969).

W. R. Bion, *Cogitations* (London, Karnac Books, 1992).

Harold Bloom, *The Visionary Company* (Ithaca, Cornell University Press, 1971).

Christopher Bollas, *Being a Character: Psychoanalysis and Self-Experience* (London, Routledge, 1993).

Malcolm Bowie, *Psychoanalysis and the Future of Theory* (Oxford, Blackwell, 1993).

Daniel Burston, *The Legacy of Erich Fromm* (Cambridge, Mass., Harvard University Press, 1991).

John Clare: *John Clare's Autobiographical Writings*, ed. Eric Robinson (Oxford, Oxford University Press, 1983).

John Clare: *The Early Poems of John Clare: 1804–1822*, ed. Eric Robinson and David Powell (Oxford, Oxford University Press, 1989).

John Clare: *The Parish*, ed. Eric Robinson and David Powell (Harmondsworth, Penguin Books, 1986).

John Clare: *Clare: The Critical Heritage*, ed. Mark Storey (London, Routledge & Kegan Paul, 1973).

John Clare: *The Letters of John Clare*, ed. Mark Storey (Oxford, Oxford University Press, 1985).

John Clare: *Selected Poetry*, ed. Geoffrey Summerfield (Harmondsworth, Penguin Books, 1990).

John Clare: *Selected Poetry and Prose*, ed. Merryn Williams and Raymond Williams (London, Methuen, 1986).

J. M. Coetzee, *Foe* (London, Secker & Warburg, 1986).

Joseph Cohen, *Journey to the Trenches: The Life of Isaac Rosenberg 1890–1918* (New York, Basic Books, 1975).

Nina Coltart, *Slouching Towards Bethlehem . . . And other Psychoanalytic Explorations* (London, Free Association Books, 1992).

Arthur C. Danto, *Sartre* (London, Fontana, 1975).

Donald Davidson, interviewed in *The American Philosopher*, ed. Giovanna Burradori (Chicago, University of Chicago Press, 1994).

Leslie H. Farber, *Lying, Despair, Jealousy, Envy, Sex, Suicide, Drugs, and the Good Life* (New York, Basic Books, 1976).

Sandor Ferenczi, *Final Contributions to the Problems and Methods of Psychoanalysis* (London, Hogarth Press and the Institute of Psychoanalysis, 1955).

Sigmund Freud: *Letters of Sigmund Freud, 1873–1939*, ed. Ernst L. Freud (London, Hogarth Press, 1960).

Sigmund Freud and Ernest Jones, *The Complete Correspondence of Sigmund Freud and Ernest Jones 1908–1939*, ed. *Andrew Paskauskas (Cambridge, Mass., Harvard University Press, 1993).*

Sigmund Freud: *The Standard Edition of the Complete Psychological Works of Sigmund Freud*, ed. and trans. James Strachey (London, Hogarth Press and the Institute of Psychoanalysis, 1953–74).

Marjorie Garber, *Vested Interests: Cross-Dressing and Cultural Anxiety* (London, Routledge, 1992).

Phyllis Grosskurth, *The Secret Ring: Freud's Inner Circle and the Politics of Psychoanalysis* (London, Jonathan Cape, 1991).

Ernest Jones, *Papers on Psychoanalysis* (London, Hogarth Press, 1948).

Ernest Jones, *Free Associations: Memories of a Psychoanalyst* (London, Hogarth Press, 1959).

M. Masud R. Khan, *Hidden Selves* (London, Hogarth Press, 1983).

Sarah Kofman, *The Childhood of Art*, trans. Winifred Woodhull (New York, Columbia University Press, 1988).

Julia Kristeva, *Black Sun: Depression and Melancholia*, trans. Leon S. Roudiez (New York, Columbia University Press, 1989).

J. Lacan, *Écrits* (London, Tavistock, 1977).

J. Laplanche and J.-B. Pontalis, *The Language of Psychoanalysis*, trans. Donald Nicholson-Smith (London, Hogarth Press, 1973).

John Lucas, *England and Englishness* (London, Hogarth Press, 1990).

James Merrill, *Nights and Days* (New York, Atheneum, 1966).

James Merrill: 'An interview with James Merrill', Ashley Brown, *Shenandoah*, 19 (Summer 1968).

J. S. Mill, *Autobiography*, ed. John Robson (Harmondsworth, Penguin Books, 1989).

Jean Moorcroft-Wilson, *Isaac Rosenberg, Poet and Painter* (London, Cecil Woolf, 1975).

Friedrich Ohly, *The Damned and the Elect: Guilt in Western Culture*, trans. Linda Archibald (Cambridge, Cambridge University Press, 1992).

Tom Paulin, *Minotaur* (London, Faber, 1992).

Isaac Rosenberg: *The Collected Works of Isaac Rosenberg*, ed. Ian Parsons (London, Chatto & Windus, 1979).

Bob Perelman, *The First World* (Great Barrington, Mass., The Figures, 1986).

J.-B. Pontalis, *Love of Beginnings*, trans. James Greene and Marie-Christine Reguis (London, Free Association Books, 1993).

Marcel Proust, *Swann's Way*, trans. Terence Kilmartin (London, Hogarth Press, 1981).

Philip Roth, *My Life as a Man* (London, Jonathan Cape, 1974).

Philip Roth, *Reading Myself and Others* (Harmondsworth, Penguin Books, 1985).

Philip Roth, *Deception* (New York, Simon & Schuster, 1990).

Philip Roth, *Patrimony: A True Story* (New York, Simon & Schuster, 1991).

Charles Rycroft, *A Critical Dictionary of Psychoanalysis* (Harmondsworth, Penguin Books, 1972).

Georg Simmel, *On Women, Sexuality and Love*, ed. and trans. Guy Oakes (New Haven, Yale University Press, 1984).

Joseph H. Smith, *Arguing with Lacan* (New Haven, Yale University Press, 1991).

Edward Timms, *Karl Kraus: Apocalyptic Satirist*, (New Haven, Yale University Press, 1986).

Frances Tustin, *Autistic Barriers in Neurotic Patients* (London, Karnac Books, 1986).

Estela Welldon, *Mother, Madonna, Whore: The Idealization and Denigration of Motherhood* (London, Free Association Books, 1988).

Bernard Williams, *Moral Luck* (Cambridge, Cambridge University Press, 1981).

D. W. Winnicott, *The Child, the Family and the Outside World* (Harmondsworth, Penguin Books, 1964).

D. W. Winnicott, *The Maturational Processes and the Facilitating Environment* (London, Hogarth Press, 1965).

D. W. Winnicott, *Playing and Reality* (Harmondsworth, Penguin Books, 1972).

D. W. Winnicott, *Through Paediatrics to Psychoanalysis* (London, Hogarth Press, 1975).

Richard Wollheim, *Freud* (London, Fontana, 1971).

Michael Wood, review of *Genet* by Edmund White, *London Review of Books*, 10 June, 1993.

Elisabeth Young-Bruehl, *Anna Freud: A Biography* (London, Macmillan, 1989).

Harry Zohn, ed. and trans., *Half-Truths and One-and-a-Half-Truths: Selected Aphorisms of Karl Krauss* (Manchester, Carcanet Press, 1986).

Index

Aberbach, David: *Surviving Trauma: Loss, Literature and Psychoanalysis*, 80, 84–5, 86
Abercrombie, Lascelles, 187
Abraham, Karl, 88, 115, 150
accidents, 8–9, 11–13; and coincidence, 17, 20; Proustian, 13–16
Adler, Alfred, 120
Adorno, Theodor, 133
Aeschylus: *The Oresteia*, 79
Aichorn, August, 90
ambition, 48–51; of J.S. Mill, 43–8; and success, 49, 52–8
America, flirtation in, xx–xxii
Ammons, A.R., 48
Andreas-Salomé, Lou, 91, 97
Aphinisis, 25
Arrowsmith, William, 52
art, 29, 32, 79–81, 84–6, 154, 160, 162–4; 'Mona Lisa', 35–6; and mourning, 81, 84–5, 86
Ashbery, John, 59, 206, 207, 211, 215
Auden, W.H., 148, 204
autobiography, 66, 68, 69–75

Barrie, J.M.: *Peter Pan*, 125
Beckett, Samuel, 29
Benjamin, Walter, 133, 135, 197, 198, 201
Bentham, Jeremy, 43
bereavement, 27
Berlin, Isaiah, 43
Berlin Psychoanalytic Institute, 133
betrayal, 168–9
Bettelheim, Bruno, 86
binarism, 125–6, 129–30
Binyon, Laurence, 183
biography, 95
Bion, Wilfred, 30, 136, 206–7
Blake, William, 162
Bloom, Harold, 216

Bohemian Club, 127–8
Bollas, Christopher: *Being a Character: Psychoanalysis and Self-Experience*, 154–60, 164
Bonaparte, Marie, 118
Boobenheim, Bubbles, 128
Borges, Jorge Luis, x
Bottomley, Gordon, 184, 185
Bowie, Malcolm: *Psychoanalysis and the Future of Theory*, 153, 154, 155, 160–64
Bowlby, John, 80, 84, 86, 102
Buddhism, 134, 136–7, 139, 147
Burlingham, Dorothy, 98
Burston, Daniel: *The Legacy of Erich Fromm*, 131–7
Byron, Lord, 176–7

Cage, John, 17
children, xviii, xxiii–xxiv; Anna Freud on, 98–9; and coincidence, 17–19; and deferred action, 34; and goodness/evil, 62–4; and incest, xxiii, 100–101; and loss, 82–3, 86; and memory, 65–6; and perversion, 100–108; and success, 46, 51, 53–7; *see also* Oedipus complex
Christianity, 140, 141; and goodness/evil, 61, 62–4
Clare, John, 206–17; 'Address to an Insignificant Flower Obscurely Blooming in a Lonely Wild', 212–14; 'Don Juan, A Poem', 210, 211–12; 'I Am', 214; 'Obscurity', 210, 217; 'Poets love nature and themselves are love', 216; 'A Simile', 206, 207, 212; 'Solitude', 208; 'To the Snipe', 210, 211
Coetzee, J.M.: *Foe*, 8
Cohen, Joseph, 175, 181
coincidence, 17–21
Coleridge, S.T., 62, 155, 211